The Truth is the Way

The Truth is the Way

Kierkegaard's *Theologia Viatorum*

Christopher Ben Simpson

CASCADE *Books* · Eugene, Oregon

THE TRUTH IS THE WAY
Kierkegaard's *Theologia Viatorum*

First published in Great Britain in the Veritas series, by SCM Press, 13–17 Long Lane, London EC1A 9PN, England.

First U.S. edition published by Cascade Books under license from SCM Press.

Cascade Books
An imprint of Wipf and Stock Publishers
199 W. 8th Ave., Suite 3
Eugene, OR 97401
www.wipfandstock.com

ISBN 13: 978-1-61097-149-2

Cataloging-in-Publication data:

Simpson, Christopher Ben, 1973–.

The truth is the way / Christopher Ben Simpson.

xii + 214 p. ; 23cm. —Includes bibliographical references and index.

ISBN 13: 978-1-61097-149-2

1. Kierkegaard, Søren, 1813–1855. 2. Truth. 3. Faith. I. Title.

B4378 .S4 S56 2011

Manufactured in the U.S.A.
Typeset by Regent Typesetting, London, UK.

Contents

Preface

In this brief work, I have endeavoured to give an interpretation and perhaps a kind of interpretative introduction to Kierkegaard's published writings. I have tried to let Kierkegaard 'speak for himself' in his own singular idiom by integrating his own words into my presentation and exposition. Because of the integral nature of the subject matter, I have found the writing of this book to be like ironing a shirt – covering the same *topoi*, places, differently in order to move, to expand, toward other *topoi* – a circling back on itself as it moves on, a repetition that is the same and yet different, progressing.

The image on the cover of this book intimates several of the themes within. It is a photograph taken on Mount Sinai of the Steps of Repentance leading up the mountain under Saint Stephen's Gate, a doorway filled with the sky.

I would like to thank Lincoln Christian University for making the research and writing of this book possible, Gordon Marino and Cynthia Lund at the Hong Kierkegaard Library for their hospitality at various points in the course of this project, Steven Cone, Eric Austin Lee and Seth Thomas for reading earlier drafts and making helpful suggestions, and Michael Robinson for his help in compiling the index. What is lacking in what follows is my own responsibility.

Having mentioned responsibility, this may be the proper place to include, if not a revocation, a certain suspension of what follows. It is, perhaps of its very nature, incomplete and calls for a prefatory recognition of the lack of the necessary postscript for such a book – that, in attempting to be true to Kierkegaard's works, the book's end is not in itself, is not fulfilled in itself. It is my hope that this exposition – these carried 'reckonings, shredded like a bundle of hay' – might serve for upbuilding and awakening (SLW 363; SUD 1–6).

Christopher Ben Simpson
Lincoln Christian University

Hong Kierkegaard Library
Holy Week, 2010

List of Abbreviations

These abbreviations are used to refer to Søren Kierkegaard's works:

BoA   *The Book on Adler.* Eds and trans. Howard V. Hong and Edna H. Hong. Princeton: Princeton University Press, 1998.

CA   *The Concept of Anxiety.* Eds and trans. Reidar Thomte and Albert B. Anderson. Princeton: Princeton University Press, 1998.

CD   *Christian Discourses* (published with *The Crisis and a Crisis in the Life of an Actress*). Eds and trans. Howard V. Hong and Edna H. Hong. Princeton: Princeton University Press, 1997.

CUP   *Concluding Unscientific Postscript to* Philosophical Fragments. Eds and trans. Howard V. Hong and Edna H. Hong. Princeton: Princeton University Press, 1992.

EO   *Either/Or: A Fragment of Life.* Trans. Alistair Hannay. New York: Penguin, 1992.

EUD   *Eighteen Upbuilding Discourses.* Eds and trans. Howard V. Hong and Edna H. Hong. Princeton: Princeton University Press, 1990.

FSE   *For Self-Examination* (published with *Judge for Yourself!*). Eds and trans. Howard V. Hong and Edna H. Hong. Princeton: Princeton University Press, 1990.

FT   *Fear and Trembling* (published with *Repetition*). Eds and trans. Howard V. Hong and Edna H. Hong. Princeton: Princeton University Press, 1983.

JC   *Johannes Climacus* (published with *Philosophical Fragments*). Eds and trans. Howard V. Hong and Edna H. Hong. Princeton: Princeton University Press, 1985.

JFY   *Judge for Yourself!* (published with *For Self-Examination*). Eds and trans. Howard V. Hong and Edna H. Hong. Princeton: Princeton University Press, 1990.

JP   *Søren Kierkegaard's Journals and Papers.* Eds and trans. Howard V. Hong and Edna H. Hong, assisted by Gregor Malantschuk. Bloomington: Indiana University Press, 1967–78. (In these references, the number designates the entry number.)

LFBA   *The Lily in the Field and the Bird of the Air: Three Devotional Discourses,* published in the volume entitled *Without Authority.* Eds and trans. Howard V. Hong and Edna H. Hong. Princeton: Princeton University Press, 1997.

MLW   *The Moment and Late Writings.* Eds and trans. Howard V. Hong and Edna H. Hong. Princeton: Princeton University Press, 1998.

PF   *Philosophical Fragments* (published with *Johannes Climacus*). Eds and trans. Howard V. Hong and Edna H. Hong. Princeton: Princeton University Press, 1985.

PIC   *Practice in Christianity.* Eds and trans. Howard V. Hong and Edna H. Hong. Princeton: Princeton University Press, 1991.

PoV   *The Point of View.* Eds and trans. Howard V. Hong and Edna H. Hong. Princeton: Princeton University Press, 1998.

R   *Repetition* (published with *Fear and Trembling*). Eds and trans. Howard V. Hong and Edna H. Hong. Princeton: Princeton University Press, 1983.

SLW   *Stages on Life's Way.* Eds and trans. Howard V. Hong and Edna H. Hong. Princeton: Princeton University Press, 1988.

SUD   *The Sickness Unto Death: A Christian Psychological Exposition For Upbuilding And Awakening.* Eds and trans. Howard V. Hong and Edna H. Hong. Princeton: Princeton University Press, 1983.

TA   *Two Ages: The Age of Revolution and the Present Age. A Literary Review.* Eds and trans. Howard V. Hong and Edna H. Hong. Princeton: Princeton University Press, 1978.

List of Abbreviations

TDIO   *Three Discourses on Imagined Occasions*. Eds and trans. Howard V. Hong and Edna H. Hong. Princeton: Princeton University Press, 1993.

TERE   *Two Ethical Religious Essays*, published in the volume entitled *Without Authority*. Eds and trans. Howard V. Hong and Edna H. Hong. Princeton: Princeton University Press, 1997.

ThDCF *Three Discourses at the Communion on Fridays*, published in the volume entitled *Without Authority*. Eds and trans. Howard V. Hong and Edna H. Hong. Princeton: Princeton University Press, 1997.

TwDCF *Two Discourses at the Communion on Fridays*, published in the volume entitled *Without Authority*. Eds and trans. Howard V. Hong and Edna H. Hong. Princeton: Princeton University Press, 1997.

UD   *An Upbuilding Discourse*, published in the volume entitled *Without Authority*. Eds and trans. Howard V. Hong and Edna H. Hong. Princeton: Princeton University Press, 1997.

UDVS   *Upbuilding Discourses in Various Spirits*. Eds and trans. Howard V. Hong and Edna H. Hong. Princeton: Princeton University Press, 2005.

WL   *Works of Love*. Eds and trans. Howard V. Hong and Edna H. Hong. Princeton: Princeton University Press, 1995.

The designation 'sup' after a page number refers to the supplementary material at the end of the Hong Princeton editions.

Introduction

Theologia Viatorum

In a footnote in *Fear and Trembling*, Kierkegaard's pseudonym Johannes de Silentio mentions without further explanation, set off in parenthesis '(*Theologia viatorum*.)' (FT 88). This term – this crumb dropped at the bottom of a pseudonymous page, the only time it is used in the entirety of Kierkegaard's authorship – provides, nonetheless, a concise, accurate and comprehensive description of Kierkegaard's work as a whole.

What is implied in this footnote is that the theology best suited for existing human beings is a *theologia viatorum*: a wayfarer's theology, a theology for one on the way, for a traveller. For on a journey, one's vision, one's grasp of the whole yet to be completed, of the goal yet to be achieved, will not measure up to the most expansive impulse of reason – it is a theology that is systematically incomplete, not grasped comprehensively, not so complete on earth as it is in heaven.[1] It is a theology for those who see incompletely and grasp with faith; it is not the theology of the blessed (*theologia beatorum*), for whom 'faith is abolished in eternity' (CUP 30).

There is a second meaning for a *theologia viatorum*. It is not just a theology *of* and in some sense *by* those in the midst of things; it is also a theology *for* wayfarers. No mere doctrine, its primary purpose is that of guidance and direction on life's way, on the way to the end. Yet, this is no mere pragmatism either. A *theologia viatorum* is, indeed, a kind of theology. It guides from a perspective beyond that of the traveller. Such a theology is also *about* the traveller, the way, its origin and end, its author and perfector, the one that comes

---

1 It is with this meaning in mind that Barth writes: 'All theology is *theologia viatorum*' (*Church Dogmatics* III, *The Doctrine of Creation* 3, tr. G. W. Bromiley and R. J. Ehrlich, Edinburgh: T. & T. Clark, 1960, p. 293).

I

alongside the traveller to help. And it is this, the substance of the *theologia viatorum*, which serves to illumine the proper end and manner of such a theology, its purpose and humility.

Kierkegaard's works are filled with travel metaphors. 'There is', he writes, 'in authorized language a universal, generally accepted metaphor that compares life to a road' (UDVS 289). This road of life – the 'path to the good . . . which is just as long as life' – permits no 'shortcuts' (CUP 428). This road is a path through a spiritual geography: 'the place and the road are within a person, since the place is the blessed state of the striving spirit, the road the continual transformation of the striving spirit' (UDVS 49). Though many may walk the same road physically, say the road from Jericho to Jerusalem, 'yet each one walked his own road' (UDVS 290) – for 'the road is: how it is walked' (UDVS 291).

On this journey, one finds oneself where one is – in a given 'location' along life's way (PIC 67; PoV 46; CD 215–16). From this location, the journey of life is a progression, a procession, a 'repetition', a movement through and over time towards an end. It is a becoming in the middle, in the midst of a story, a narrative with a beginning and an end and is so (or so can be) held together as a meaningful unity over time. Though along this road there are 'biding places' – places of rest (TDIO 12; CD 12) – the road is a hard one and the journey perilous. 'Life', we are told, 'is perfidious and has many charms and spells with which it tries to capture the adventurer' (SLW 444); its way is 'narrow and solitary . . . always disturbed by aberrations, exposed to predatory attacks by sin, and pursued by the arrow of the past' (CA 117) such that 'wherever a person goes, he walks in danger' (EUD 331). And on this difficult progress through life, 'the contender' is one who walked with resolution and firm steps, for life is 'a life-and-death struggle' in which 'danger followed him constantly' (EUD 351–2, 401).

A *theologia viatorum*, as Kierkegaard presents in his work, is intended to give orientation, direction and guidance for travellers on life's perilous way. A theological vision of the world provides orientation towards and on the way life is to be travelled, and the Christian walks strangely in the world for she is ordered to that beyond it (CD 21). For such a wayfarer in the ever-shifting world, theology moves the eyes, diverts the mind with such 'godly diversion' that directs, continually redirects, into the right direction

(UDVS 184). One's gaze – the goal, the end, the 'kingdom', which one seeks – determines the way one walks, the course one travels (LFBA 10).[2] Thus does the good news of Christian faith (though it may seem but philosophical crumbs) serve to guide – directing and urging one forward on one's way (as a trail of crumbs to be followed) (LFBA 20; CUP 277).

So guided, the Christian traveller – though a stranger and an alien, though at times threatened and insecure (MLW 257; EUD 343–5) – is no mere nomad. Guided by a *theologia viatorum* – as ever between a *theologia nomadicum* and a *theologia beatorum* – the Christian is a pilgrim. As such, he does not merely wander but follows after – drawn by the good desired – seeking an end seen if but through a glass darkly, and so needing the help of the 'prototype' – the one that has gone before – that would 'stand very clearly before the eyes of the soul in order to dispel the mists' (UDVS 217; CD 30–4). As such an ordered journey, 'Christianity is the direction forward' with 'salvation ahead of it, perdition behind' (CUP 602) – a continual turning from the winding way and being drawn 'from the way of perdition to the way of truth' (PIC 261).

Christianity as the Essential Human Truth

Christianity, for Kierkegaard, is this true way – the one way upon which there are two ways, the one path upon which the traveller may turn towards blessing or perdition (CD 19–20, 47).[3] Christianity does not deny worldly existence in favour of pious devotion to ghostly forms. It claims to be the truth of human existence. As such, the Christian truth is universal. It is not the universal but inhuman truth of Enlightenment and modern rationality – an 'objectivity' at home with matter in motion but utterly foreign to what gives our lives meaning. Nor is it a purely local 'truth' – a 'subjectively' held belief that is 'true' for Christians because it is believed by them – the truth of Christians for Christians . . . true for me, if not for

---

2 So Kierkegaard writes: 'What I am seeking is not here, and for that very reason I believe it. Faith expressly signifies the deep, strong, blessed restlessness that drives the believer so that he cannot settle down at rest in this world' (UDVS 218).

3 'From the point of view of the eternal, there are never two ways; although there are the crossroads, there is only one Way' (CD 20).

you. Christianity stakes the more radical claim that it reveals 'what it means to exist' (CUP 274) – that the only fully human existence is to be found in the Christian religion, the one way (CUP 249). 'Christianity', Kierkegaard's pseudonym Johannes Climacus writes, 'has itself proclaimed itself to be the eternal, essential truth that has come into existence in time' (CUP 213). This 'essential truth' is essential for human life. It is in light of this that Kierkegaard saw his task as that of 'the clarification of Christian concepts' (MLW 10) – 'to bring out the orthodox forms ... to want Christianity to be given its due' (PF 220; JP 5827) – that 'the issue κατ' ἐξοχήν [in the eminent sense] of the whole authorship [being that of] becoming a Christian' (PoV 8).

More precisely, the one way *is* Jesus Christ. Christ is the Way – through life, to God (WL 248; PIC 20) – the Truth – of life, in life – the Life (PIC 78, 207).[4] The central question of Kierkegaard's authorship – of what it means to become and to be a Christian – is nothing less than the question of what it means to enter upon and to walk in the way of Christ. Christ's teaching, foremost the Sermon on the Mount (Matt. 5—7, especially Matt. 6), has a key role in explaining this way. Christ is the one who from on high, and yet in our midst, with authority, yet humbly, shows and calls us to follow him and so to seek first the higher and to find the lower will be added to it.[5]

Subjectivity and (un)Truth, The Truth is the Way

Christ, however, does not merely mirror our immanent humanity back to us – as a surrogate, a ladder that once climbed becomes redundant, a static circle revealing what was so with us all along. Christ, in Kierkegaard's work, reveals, 'gives' something we lack. This is paradoxical for what we lack is what we are – a right relation to the reality, to the fundamental truth of human existence and so of our own lives. It is we who are, somehow have become,

---

4 'Being the truth is a life – and this is indeed how Christ speaks of himself: I am the Truth and the Way and the Life' (PIC 207).

5 As is intimated here, John 14 and Matthew 6 are the scriptural touchstones for Kierkegaard's intensively Christological *theologia viatorum*, as will be seen throughout this text.

shadowy and distorted, stuck secretly lacking but not seeing ourselves as lacking and so not seeking ourselves in an empty circle.
Kierkegaard's Climacus expresses this privative state provocatively
as one in which our 'subjectivity is untruth' (CUP 207). We are
'outside the truth' (PF 13). And so Kierkegaard acts as a kind of
physician, diagnosing the reality of the self's (true) subjective condition – the state of oneself as an existing human subject – beneath
one's subjective perceptions of oneself.[6] It is because of this priva-
tion that the movement of becoming, the journey of life's way can
have meaning – that we can seek and receive (again paradoxically)
the truth that is the way as a task and a gift, the life that is ours in
Christ.

This is the furthest thing from the common (relativist) understanding of that best-known (and easily misunderstood) 'Kierkegaardian'
maxim: 'Subjectivity is truth' – that the truth for me is my singular, 'subjective' 'way' over any universal, 'objective' state of affairs.
The phrase that is the title of this text, 'the truth is the way' (PIC
207), is not to be taken as implying a strict convertibility between
'truth' and 'way'.[7] To be sure, the way of truth is not a static state
but a way of being, of living, of existing – this is the sense in which
Climacus states the 'the way is the truth'.[8] But this 'way' is not to
be taken as just any way, as flexible and amenable to our present
sensibilities. This almost entirely misses the point in Kierkegaard's
work. It is due, one could say, to a wilful ignorance of the definite
article. For when Kierkegaard writes that 'the truth is the way' and
'the way is the truth', he means that the one and only truth is the
one and only way to (and of) life. This reading is something much
less banal (less bereft of any existential, ethical and religious call
upon us) and much more offensive, difficult, demanding, radical.
The latter voice (though refracted through many) is Kierkegaard's
– from first to last.

---

6 'The physician has a defined and developed conception of what it is to be
healthy and ascertains a man's condition accordingly ... the physician, precisely
because he is a physician (well informed), does not have complete confidence in what
a person says about his condition' (SUD 23).

7 This is the kind of logic (not a good kind) that says God is dead because God is
love, love is blind, Ray Charles is blind and Ray Charles is dead.

8 'Suppose someone wanted to communicate that the truth is not the truth but
that the way is the truth, that is, that the truth is only in becoming, in the process of
appropriation, that consequently there is no result' (CUP 78).

It is this voice and this truth that is the way that challenges 'the present age', Kierkegaard's and our own – where being a Christian has at times come to mean little more than the common human ('a good person') – where Christianity is one of many 'equally valid' ways, universal common human values mixed with, at best, colourful and, at worst, violent particular ('intolerant') mythological, archaic, supernatural supplements. Such is our 'religious confusion' – our enlightened, worldly, (all too) human religion without religion, without God, without the higher and so without the lower, without the human, without the world, without illumination. Such is the 'religious confusion' of our present age, 'an age of disintegration' (BoA 1; PoV 119).

Survey of Chapters, the Title

This work falls roughly into two parts of unequal size. The first part, 'On Truth' (Chapters 1 to 4), deals with Kierkegaard's understanding of truth – what it is, how it is communicated (and, more specifically, how Kierkegaard tries to communicate it) and how one enters into it. In Chapter 1, I explore Kierkegaard's method of communication (his 'rhetoric of engagement'), my understanding of how this is manifest in his own authorship and, consequently, how one should read Kierkegaard's corpus. In Chapter 2, I explore Kierkegaard's understanding of faith as foundational, as founding, as the way into the truth. Chapter 3 examines Kierkegaard's concept(s) of truth. The fourth chapter then concerns the fundamental place of metaphysics and theology in Kierkegaard's understanding of truth. The second part, '*Theologia Viatorum*' (Chapters 5 to 7), deals with the substance, the content of Kierkegaard's understanding of truth and makes up the bulk of the work. Chapters 5 and 6 lay out Kierkegaard's theological understanding of the way things are (his systematic theology of sorts) – of God, the world, humanity and the relations between them (in Chapter 5) and his understanding of the person and work of Jesus Christ as central to this schema (in Chapter 6). In Chapter 7, I endeavour to present Kierkegaard's understanding of the nature and shape of Christian existence in light of his theological understanding of reality – the Christian way. The first part then (Chapters 1 to 4) forms the prolegomena to the second part (Chapters 5 to 7), which constitutes more properly Kierkegaard's *theologia viatorum.*[9]

The title, *The Truth is the Way,* can be taken in three senses – a threefold contention – that each characterize the guiding vision that is Kierkegaard's *theologia viatorum.* As an existential vision (engaged with the actual), the truth is the way in the sense that the highest truth for Kierkegaard is a way of being. As a positively metaphysical vision, the truth is the way in the sense that the way one should go, the path one should follow/seek, is the true one. As a Christian theological vision, the truth is the way in the sense that the one truth, the one way, is Jesus Christ – the gift to us, the pattern for us, and so our way, our truth, our life.

---

9 This book works primarily (if not exclusively) with Kierkegaard's published writings. It attempts the ambitious (if not overly ambitious) task of presenting a coherent vision of Kierkegaard's thought throughout his voluminous authorship. With this end in mind, I for the most part do not interact with the substantial body of Kierkegaard scholarship on the broad array of topics covered. To do so, even minimally, would make this small and hopefully accessible book a much less small and much less accessible tome. Doubtless the Kierkegaard scholar will be aware of the positions and problems and personae in which my interpretations are situated. For they that have such ears, let them hear.

PART I

Prolegomena: On Truth

I

Communication

On Communication

Communication – as a topic for reflection and as cunningly enacted – has a central place in Kierkegaard's thought. He was a communicator concerned with how one is to communicate. At the beginning of Part Two of *Either/Or*, Judge Vilhelm (Kierkegaard's pseudonym) deliberates on how to address 'A' – the pseudonymous author of Part One (EO 384). Vigilius Haufniensis (another pseudonym) writes of preaching, and about communication more generally, that it 'is really the most difficult of all arts and is essentially the art that Socrates praised, the art of being able to converse' (CA 16). Very broadly, Kierkegaard recognizes in communication a dialectic of proximity and distance – that one needs to draw near to what one takes to be the reader's or listener's perspective, to the actual lives of the real persons one would address, so that what one says is meaningful, accessible, plausible to them, despite communicating a perspective that is not their own, or at least a perspective that the reader does not initially recognize as their own. For the distance, the ideality in communication, can allow a reader to reflect on what is often too close to see – their own (or something like their own) perspective on life as a 'theoretically educe[d] life-view' (BoA 16). Kierkegaard writes: 'The art in all communication is to come as close as possible to actuality, to contemporaries in the role of readers, and yet at the same time to have the distance of a point of view, the reassuring, infinite distance of ideality from them' (BoA 15). The end goal here is no cool comprehension of ideas. Kierkegaard is interested foremost in a form of communication that 'seeks and looks for that favourably disposed person who takes an interest in the seeker, gives an opportunity to what is said, brings the cold thoughts into flame again, transforms the discourse into a conversation'. It is thus that 'the recipient accomplishes the great work of letting the perishability of the discourse arise in imperishability' – in the actuality of existence, in the truth as that lived (EUD 231).

Indirect communication

This method of starting where a person is and leading onward is at the heart of Kierkegaard's process of indirect communication. 'The secret in the entire art of helping', he writes in *The Point of View*, is to be 'a willing and attentive listener' – to 'be the astonished listener who sits and listens to what delights that other person' (PoV 45–6). For when 'a teacher is truly to be the learner' (PoV 46), such a teacher is enabled to deal with readers on their own terms. Hence the title of the section in that book: '*If One Is Truly to Succeed in Leading a Person to a Specific Place, One Must First and Foremost Take Care to Find Him Where **He** Is and Begin There*' (PoV 45).

In order to communicate the truth to another where they are, it is assumed that the truth, in whole or in part, is what the other is lacking.[1] But to presume to communicate the truth directly to one who is in untruth, who believes falsehood, will likely be met with resistance, rejection, dismissal – for, from the perspective of the other, one is presuming to give them something they already have, something they do not lack, namely the truth. 'By a direct attack', Kierkegaard writes, one that would communicate 'only strengthens [the other] person in the illusion and also infuriates him' such that this other person then 'love[s] in [his] secret heart that bewitchery even more fanatically with clandestine passion' (PoV 43, 46). Such an antagonistic posture 'also contains the presumptuousness of demanding that another person confess to one or face-to-face with one make the confession that actually is most beneficial when the person concerned makes it to himself secretly' (PoV 43).[2] Communication,

---

1 Thus, 'the true communication of truth is circumspectly aware of the contingency that it was indeed possible that the recipients were in untruth' (BoA 170). Kierkegaard makes the stronger statement earlier on the same page: 'All true communication of truth must always begin with an untruth' (BoA 170). This is probably more technically accurate. One wonders if all communication as mediated over a distance is ultimately indirect . . .

2 Thus: 'The art consists of making oneself, the communicator, into a nobody, purely objective' (PIC 133).

especially communication of that which is most important and so most intimate, is inhibited by the frame of winning and losing.

Kierkegaard's method of indirect communication has to do with communicating to one in the midst of an illusion. As such, it has a certain negative function. The truth has a 'salutary terror' (CD 220). The upbuilding, the healing, to the one who is sick but does not know it, does not recognize it, is not unequivocally welcome – 'for the presumably healthy and strong it is bound to appear at first as the terrifying' (CD 96). Common (fallen human) understanding is dominated by the 'lies and baseness and injustice [that rule] the world' (PoV 63). 'Truly', he writes, 'it is not truth that rules the world but illusions' (PoV 59). While Kierkegaard's dissident, 'polemical' stance as a 'religious author' vis-à-vis the dominant discourse of the world is nothing terribly new (PoV 67), he proposes 'a totally new science of arms' – a 'strategy . . . constituted on the basis of having to contend with a delusion, an illusion' (PoV 52–3).[3]

Because 'an illusion can never be removed directly' (PoV 43), one must use an indirect method – a method 'permeated by reflection' (PoV 52). The reflected form is existentially disengaged. Reflection takes a step back from one's immediate involvement – the reader's view is presented to them as an ideal possibility that they can imaginatively 'try on' as something other than 'their own' view – to see its failings as one would in another person who is too involved in their folly to see it as such – but only then to *recognize* the ideal, reflected possibility so evaluated and judged (by oneself) as being *one's own*.[4] Alternatively, the writer's/speaker's view can be considered and appropriated by the reader/hearer, as their own – not as one cowed into submission – but as one given the freedom to consider the reflected idea as possible, to consider it as an alternative to their own view – to their illusions (PoV 7). This method of helping another to recognize and leave behind their illusions through reflection is presented as loving (PoV 44). One can see one's failings for oneself freely – and not be coerced by or humiliated before the communicator. 'The secret of communication specifically hinges on setting the other free' for the discourse 'wishes to be received as if it had arisen in his own heart' (CUP 74; UDVS 5).

---

3 This is set in contradistinction to the 'old science of arms' which Kierkegaard identifies as 'apologetics' (PoV 52).

4 See Nathan's statement to King David: 'Thou art the man!' (2 Samuel 12.7).

Paradoxically, this loving and 'Christian' manner of communicating the truth entails a certain deception – for to address one in the midst of illusion one must speak the language of illusions (PoV 44).[5] The deception, to be precise, is not directly naming the other's view as it is, as a delusion, but starting 'from another angle' (EO 480). In indirect communication, one 'deceives people' into the truth'[6] – for

> direct communication presupposes that the recipient's ability to receive is entirely in order, but here that is simply not the case – indeed, here a delusion is an obstacle. That means a corrosive must first be used, but this corrosive is the negative, but the negative in connection with communicating is precisely to deceive.

And this 'begins by taking the other's delusion at face value' (PoV 54).

This is a first negative moment in relation to faith's stepping forward, stepping up, stepping into a life-view as a lived actuality. Kierkegaard writes:

> One does not become a Christian through reflection, but in reflection to become a Christian means that there is something else to discard. A person does not reflect himself into being a Christian but out of something else in order to become a Christian. (PoV 93)

The second moment of the double-movement of indirect communication is that of positive appropriation (or faith) (PoV 6). The truth that Kierkegaard is interested in communicating, the deep truths about human life, are 'concerned truths', truth that is to be edifying, that is 'not indifferent to how the individual receives it, whether he wholeheartedly appropriates it or it becomes mere words to him

---

5 It is thus that Kierkegaard, reflecting upon his own writings (in which he 'portray[s] the esthetic with all its bewitching charm' (PoV 45–6)), writes that: 'the religious the crucial, the esthetic the incognito . . . the esthetic writing is a deception' (PoV 53).

6 'The method is neither more nor less than the consistent redoubling of truth in itself. But *Mundus vult decipi* [the world wants to be deceived]. Insofar as the method is slow, it is calculated precisely to hinder the deception; for this very reason it deceives people into the truth instead of the more usual method of helping people into the deception by way of assurances of the truth' (BoA 171).

... not indifferent to whether the truth becomes a blessing or a ruination to him' (EUD 233–4). What Kierkegaard wishes to communicate is not an abstract truth but something that cannot be communicated directly – cannot be simply 'given' to another (EUD 13–14). The appropriation, the decision must be his own.[7]

This indirect communication is an 'artistic communication' in which one is 'required to think of the receiver and to pay attention to the form of communication in relation to the receiver's misunderstanding' (CUP 76). It is a poetic endeavour that uses the 'being-in-between' of an imaginary construction – versus direct confrontation and communication – in order to influence 'by means of the ideals' (CUP 264; FSE 21). By means of indirection and 'deception', it 'drives out devils only by the power of the devil' (FT 61).

The end, the goal of the communication intended in Kierkegaard's work is that of helping the reader to change their viewpoint, their 'life-view' and so the way they live. Its end, it could be said, is the attaining of wisdom (as opposed to mere knowledge) – true living, truth in existence. In this process of communication, Kierkegaard often likens himself to a Socratic midwife, a teacher who does not give the desired result to the learner but helps, enables, provides the space, the possibility for one to bring forth the end on one's own (though not simply on one's own), to appropriate, to change one's mind, one's view, one's life. This is 'the highest relation a human being can have to another' for 'ethically-religiously one cannot essentially benefit another' (PF 10; SLW 344). In relating to one with a false perspective, 'one owes it to a person who has gone astray in this way to shout: "Think of the end!"' – to say to them: 'ask yourself' (EO 585, 608). The truth – what is actual and is to be lived in as actual – is presented in terms of possibility, of an alternative way to be:

> If actuality is to be understood by a third party, it must be understood as possibility, and a communicator who is conscious of this will therefore see to it, precisely in order to be oriented to existence, that his existence-communication is in the form of possibility. (CUP 358)

---

7 'I can compel him to be aware', even 'to judge . . . what he judges is not in my power' (PoV 50).

Rhetoric of engagement, out-narration, the higher and the lower

Kierkegaard's rhetoric of engagement is neither a defensive posture nor one seeking (simply) to accommodate Christianity, the truth to be communicated, to the perspective of the reader – to justify it to the reader on her own terms, within her own perspective. This is precisely backwards (CD 162; SUD 87). For Kierkegaard, it is Christianity that provides the broadest and truest perspective in the midst of which all lesser perspectives are located, relativized, their relative truth and falsehood made evident (teleologically suspended, *aufgehoben*). It is the reader's terms, their perspective, which is lacking. This is a strategy of 'out-narration'.[8] In this vein, the higher, the truer view is the one that presents the broadest and most coherent perspective or narrative – 'a world-view, a life-view' (BoA 8) – which can locate and account for less true perspectives.[9] Thereby the lower perspectives are 'assumed into a higher concentricity' (EO 403) – re-narrated from the perspective of the higher discourse, finding their deeper truth and proper home there.

Kierkegaard writes from a fundamentally theological perspective.[10] The question he attends to is how to speak from the perspective of theology – of theological matters – to one in a sub-theological or non-theological or not-as-explicitly theological perspective. The question is how a higher perspective addresses a lower perspective. The lower perspective on the higher

> can explain only up to the explanation and above all must guard against leaving the impression of explaining that which no science can explain and that which ethics explains further only by presupposing it by way of dogmatics. (CA 39)

The lower cannot understand the higher, cannot 'get a perspective' (FT 33). The higher addresses the lower, however, by addressing concerns of the lower and showing that the lower perspective lacks

---

8 See John Milbank, *Theology and Social Theory*, 2nd edition (Oxford: Blackwell 1990, 2006).

9 For example: The religious can recognize and incorporate the insights of the aesthetic while aesthetic can only provide parodies of the religious, Christianity, Christ. See EO: Don Juan in the third stage of the immediate erotic stages (93ff.), 'the unhappiest one' (209ff.).

10 See Chapter 4.

the ability to address these fundamental concerns. Thi[s]
seen vividly in *Either/Or*, in which Judge Vilhelm (from t[he]
perspective of the ethical) addresses the aesthete, 'A', and argues to
what the aesthete cares about, namely, himself – that the aesthete
harms himself (EO 386–7) – that ultimately the aesthetic view fails
on its own terms, as aesthetic – it ends in boredom, depression,
masochism – that the pinnacle of the aesthetic, the seducer, far from
attaining an ideal of pleasure, is 'demonic', joyless, horrible (EO
32–3).[11] The lower perspective does not even measure up to its own
narration.[12]

Kierkegaard's theological method

Kierkegaard's theological method is one of translating dogmatics,
the claims of Christian theology, into existential (subjective) terms
and then using these translated doctrines to define the structure of
Christian existence. Here the doctrinal language of conceptualized
Christian theology is translated into existentially meaningful language. While this process of translation brings the focus upon the
'subjective' side of Christianity, it must be seen that Christianity is
not thereby reduced to a purely subjective phenomena – an object-
less feeling. Kierkegaard, as a theologian, seeks out and examines the
meanings of Christian doctrines. In doing this, he wants to present
Christianity in such a way as to be heard freshly in the forgetful and
numbed ears of slumbering Christians, reminding them that existence is the proper arena of influence for Christian dogma.

Kierkegaard's theological method serves to define Christian existence. By 'definition' we here mean the setting forth of the virtues,
qualities and activities that define Christian existence. It is this movement that is present in Kierkegaard's intent to introduce Christianity
not as a doctrine but as an 'existence-communication' (CUP 383).
The end goal of the 'existence-communication' is to elicit a certain
kind of existence. Kierkegaard sees that inherent in Christianity is

---

11 So Part Two of *Either/Or* is something like a play within a play – doing what
the work as a whole intends to do at the indirect remove of a fictional pseudonym
– namely, addressing the aesthete and calling him or her to change.

12 Indeed, the two tasks of EO Part Two, showing 'the aesthetic validity of
marriage' and 'how the aesthetic element can be sustained' within marriage and not,
it is implied, within the aesthetic shows just this kind of out-narrating on a large
scale (EO 386).

the goal that persons 'be remodeled according to the requirement' (JFY 158).[13] This is a process of appropriation through which 'objective' doctrine becomes a 'subjective' way of living.

It is in this context that one can best see Kierkegaard's objection to a purely objective (objectivist?) Christianity that never makes this move toward appropriative faith. The 'what' of Christianity comes to bear upon the 'how' of Christianity. The way in which one assimilates the doctrines of Christianity – the 'what' – ends up being a very particular 'how' (CUP 607–11). It is because of the translated doctrines' role in forming Christian existence that there ultimately exists a 'happy relation' between Christian doctrine and Christian existence (PF 65).

This Christian existence defined by theology is 'the second ethics' which, as Kierkegaard's pseudonym Vigilius Haufniensis writes, 'presupposes dogmatics but completes it also in such a way that here, as everywhere, the presupposition is brought out' (CA 24). This 'second ethics' is 'the new science [that] begins with dogmatics. . . . Here ethics finds its place as the science that has as a task for actuality the dogmatic consciousness of actuality' (CA 20).[14] It is thus that 'with dogmatics begins the science that, in contrast to that science called ideal *stricte* [in the strict sense], namely ethics, proceeds from actuality. It begins with the actual in order to raise it up into ideality' (CA 19).

How to Read Kierkegaard

We should read Kierkegaard in light of his own theory of communication, for it was not just about communication generally but about how he intended to go about communicating (or, perhaps, to help his readers, who were being a little slow on the uptake). I will set out my approach to reading Kierkegaard in the context of an explanation of how I will come at his authorship throughout this work.

A more adequate/faithful reading of Kierkegaard is one that happens within the broad context of his entire authorship, seeing the specific contexts of particular pseudonyms and works from this

---

13 This stands in opposition to what is usually the case, that 'the requirement must be remodeled according to the people' (JFY 158).

14 Again: 'The new ethics presupposes dogmatics' (CA 20).

perspective. In the present text I approach Kierkegaard's author-ship from such a 'broad reading'. An initial consequence of such a reading is a turn from a common trajectory in the interpreta-tion of Kierkegaard which tends to focus on certain 'canonical' or 'major' works of Kierkegaard that are mostly from the earlier half of his authorship (from his first or pseudonymous authorship). While there is great value in paying critical attention to particular works, this selectivity can lead to characterizations of Kierkegaard's thought that, from a broad reading, are perplexing. While paying a great deal of attention to these major works (EO, FT, CA, PF, CUP), I will also look to the signed works and specifically his later, more mature writings – which, if somewhat neglected, make up the lion's share of his literary output (approximately 3,100 pages vs 2,500 pages for the earlier pseudonymous works in the Hong edi-tions). Indeed, I take the signed and mature works that comprise the majority of the authorship – and in which Kierkegaard is more straightforward – as taking a certain hermeneutical priority over the pseudonymous works.

Pseudonymity

How is one to read Kierkegaard's pseudonyms? To begin, we should see the pseudonyms as Kierkegaard's. While Kierkegaard wants people to take the pseudonyms seriously and not simply see them as straightforward expressions of his own thoughts, he claims them as his own. In *The Moment*, near the end of his life, he writes: 'See Fear and Trembling [written by one Johannes de Silentio], where for the first time, I took aim at assistant professors' (MLW 290). In fact, in several places we see Kierkegaard winking at his own pseudonymity – hinting to the reader that one should take it with a grain of salt. See the blatant cheekiness of Victor Eremita in the editorial preface to *Either/Or* (EO 33, 36) where he wonders 'if regarded as the work of one man' what kind of person such an author would be; where Victor took it upon himself to 'add a few things under their hands' guidance' (EO 37), in order to leave the reader with the content of the view presented (EO 36). Witness Johannes Climacus's tongue-in-cheek criticism of 'Magister Kierkegaard' and his finding himself (while surveying the other pseudonyms' work in 'A Contemporary Effort in Danish Literature' in the Postscript) 'continually intending to do what the pseudonymous authors are doing' (CUP 261). Consider also such points as the pseudonym Vigilius Haufniensis being added to *The Concept of Anxiety* just before it was submitted to the publisher, as was Anti-Climacus to *The Sickness Unto Death*[15] – or how Kierkegaard changed pseudonyms for a given speech in *Stages on Life's Way* from Victor Eremita to Constantin Constantius (SLW 544). My suggestion is that we should not take the pseudonyms more seriously (as distinct personae with their own perspectives that need not cohere with the broader authorship) than Kierkegaard himself did.[16]

The pseudonyms were intended to present Kierkegaard's life-views or stages or existence-spheres, not merely as intellectual abstractions, but in such a manner that the reader encounters as a character 'one' writing from an idealized perspective – they function 'to depict and make visible psychologically and esthetically' (R 302 sup). The pseudonyms are thus 'ideally limited only by psychological consistency, which no factually actual person dares to allow himself' (CUP 625). The pseudonyms are perspectives or thoughts pushed to their extremes (R 133) – this is what Constantin Constantius (pseudonymous author of *Repetition*) sees 'A' (the pseudonymous author of most of Part One of *Either/Or*) as doing. Each pseudonym is a 'poetized author' who 'has his definite life-view' (CUP 627). When Kierkegaard says that in the pseudonymous works there is 'not a single word by me', that 'I am just as little, precisely just as little, the editor Victor Eremita as I am the Seducer or the Judge' (CUP 626), we should see that Kierkegaard is not presenting himself as the character that is speaking/writing.[17] It is because of this that Kierkegaard requests for himself 'a forgetful remembrance' (CUP 629). One has to suspend the authorial voice

---

15 See Niels Jørgen Cappelørn, Joakim Garff and Johnny Kondrup, *Written Images: Søren Kierkegaard's Journals, Notebooks, Booklets, Sheets, Scraps, and Slips of Paper*, tr. Bruce H. Kirmmse (Princeton: Princeton University Press, 1997).

16 On a certain level, does anyone really question who the author of the pseudonymous works is – does anyone take the pseudonyms (in Kierkegaard's own day or since) as other than pseudonyms? Surely other Kierkegaard scholars have the same rainbow of the Hong Princeton edition as I have on my bookshelf. To whose credit is the depth and breadth of understanding of the aesthetic life-view in *Either/Or* I? To whose credit is Ivan's argument against God in *The Brothers Karamazov*?

17 Dostoevsky is not Ivan Karamazov. Shakespeare is not Hamlet.

of Kierkegaard (as a particular writer with a particular perspective) in order to encounter more fully the perspective of the pseudonym as a character – as a literary conceit (as one would a character in a work of literary fiction). Constantin Constantius describes 'the magic of theater' (R 154) in which the individual (the theatre-goer) projects his many shadow-selves upon the roles represented in the play, has empathy with the characters for they express a part of him, as 'the shadows in which he discovers himself' – 'recognize[s] himself in this reflected image' (R 156). Thus, one can encounter oneself, come to see a flaw that one would normally hide from oneself and perhaps change. It is this kind of encounter that Kierkegaard intends with his pseudonyms.

The unity of Kierkegaard's pseudonyms can be conceived in terms of stages on life's way – as multiple stages (stagings) on a singular way that makes sense of the stages as more than a sheer plurality of incommensurable perspectives. While there are those that would advocate taking the pseudonyms seriously to the point of denying common Kierkegaardian ideas or concepts being developed – thereby following Kierkegaard's pleading that one take the pseudonyms on their own terms (end of CUP) – we ask why we should not take seriously Kierkegaard's claims (such as in *The Point of View*)[18] that his authorship is a singular project? To do both, one can think of plural, distinct voices (the pseudonyms) within a common project (the authorship).[19] The 'definite life-view' of each 'poetized author' can be located in the larger schema of Kierkegaard's understanding of the 'teleologically suspended' hierarchical ordering of such life-views (CUP 627).[20] Kierkegaard's use of 'pseudonymity or polyonymity' (CUP 625) then constitutes his authorship (or, to be more precise, the pseudonymous work within his authorship) in terms of

---

18 See also Climacus's tacit claim in his 'A Glance at a Contemporary Effort in Danish Literature' in the same CUP in which he surveys the pseudonymous authorship as cohering with his own project.

19 I recall hearing C. Stephen Evans suggest seeing the pseudonyms as characters in a huge, multi-volume philosophical novel that would be Kierkegaard's pseudonymous authorship as a whole.

20 Climacus suggests such a common project when, referring to the other pseudonyms, he writes: 'the cause I had resolved to take up is advancing, but not through me' (CUP 251–2). He writes later that 'what they themselves intended, I am unable to decide, since I am only a reader, but that they do have a relation to my thesis is sufficiently clear' (CUP 280).

a 'plurivocity' – community of different voices – or, more properly, a 'communivocity' – a genuine plurality of different perspectives that can yet be seen as unified through an ordering of the perspectives as lower (or less complete) and higher (or more complete).[21]

The unity of Kierkegaard's authorship

Kierkegaard considered publishing in 1849, 'the fruit of the year 1848', a three-volume work (with the title 'The Collected Works of Completion') including (among other minor works) *Sickness Unto Death* and *Practice in Christianity*, his last major works. The last volume in this hypothetical publication was to be entitled: 'On My Work as an Author' (PoV xvi), the main part of it being: 'The Point of View'. Though Kierkegaard would publish a severely abbreviated[22] version of this in 1851 (under the title: *On My Work as an Author*), *The Point of View for My Work as an Author* (the more complete version) was published posthumously in 1859 by his brother, Peter Christian Kierkegaard. *The Point of View* was intended 'for orientation and attestation' (PoV 24) – 'to explain as directly and openly and specifically as possible what is what, what I say I am as an author' (PoV 23).

In this work, Kierkegaard endeavours, 'in the capacity of a third party, as a reader' (PoV 33), to show how his authorship arose from a sense of religious purpose and that the subject matter of the authorship is unified around a central issue.[23] Regarding the intent, he contends 'that I am and was a religious author' (PoV 23), that the author '"has willed only one thing"' – that the authorship then, taken 'in one breath', 'regarded as a totality' is 'religious from first to last, something anyone who can see, if he wants to see, must also see' (PoV 6). As to the unifying idea, 'the fundamental idea in the whole authorship' (PoV 92), 'the total thought in the entire work as an author' (PoV 41, 55) is the issue and the task of *becoming a Christian* – what this means and how one does it (PoV 23, 55). While, Kierkegaard admits, this 'boring' unifying idea might

---

21 These concepts are William Desmond's. See William Desmond, *Philosophy and Its Others* (Albany, NY: SUNY Press, 1990), pp. 60, 212.

22 In the Hong edition, 13 pages vs 76 pages.

23 This present work, can be seen, if in part, as showing forth the unity that Kierkegaard claimed could be found in his authorship.

be difficult to see in the more flamboyant indirect, pseudonymous writings, he contends that this is due to the deceptive nature of these works (as 'taking the other's delusion at face value' (PoV 54), as enacting a negative moment of removing delusion, 'a necessary emptying' (PoV 77)).[24] Nevertheless, in 'the esthetic writing . . . [t]he religious is decisively present already from the first moment, has decisive predominance, but for a little while waits patiently so that the poet is allowed to talk himself out' (PoV 77) – the poetic/ aesthetic is a moment with a specific purpose (disabusing one of delusion) and strategy (indirect) within the broader religious author-ship, whose unity is like 'the crisscrossing threads in a web' (PoV 6). Kierkegaard's account of the 'duplexity of the whole authorship' (PoV 85) – of 'the essential dialectical qualification of the whole authorship' (PoV 29) between the pseudonymous works (from the 'left hand') and the signed religious works (from the 'right hand') (PoV 36) – is that 'the entire esthetic production' was 'continually in the custody of the religious' (PoV 85–6). It is, thus, 'the purely religious writing . . . which specifically provides the point of view' (PoV 55). The two authorships (the first, pseudonymous, 'esthetic' authorship and the second, signed, 'religious' authorship) are two parts of one authorship, unified in content and purpose over time.

The fundamentally religious purpose of Kierkegaard's author-ship is to present Christianity, what it means to become a Christian, what Christianity requires (PoV 16)[25] and so 'to cast Christianity, becoming a Christian, wholly and fully into reflection' (PoV 97). A central characteristic of such a 'work of love' – as with all works of love – is that it is 'upbuilding' (WL 204, 206–7). The authorship's upbuilding work is intended to be modest and patient (not dominat-ing) – seeking to understand the reader and help them where they are (PoV 44–5; UDVS 106). Kierkegaard presents his authorship – as such an upbuilding work – as motivated and sustained by 'Governance'[26] – by the motivating and sustaining work of God in

---

24 This, he writes, is 'why I had to be pseudonymous in connection with the esthetic production, because I had my own life in altogether different categories and from the very beginning understood this writing as something temporary, a decep-tion, a necessary emptying one' (PoV 86).

25 'My strategy was: with the help of God to utilize everything to make clear what in truth Christianity's requirement is' (PoV 16).

26 Kierkegaard writes of 'Governance, who is compassionate love, precisely out of love uses such a person, rescues and brings him up, while he uses all his sagacity,

his own life, his 'God-relationship' (as, Kierkegaard would argue, is the case with all works of love).[27] As participating in some way in God's loving work of redemption, Kierkegaard sees his authorship as a 'gift' to God, as a work of worship and thanksgiving.[28]

An analogy between the substance, the method and the origin of Kierkegaard's authorship[29]

The truth that Kierkegaard seeks to communicate is a transformed existence. There is a mirroring between this 'teleological truth' (PoV 34) as that which is communicated – a changed perspective, a changed form of existence – and the mode of communication – as providing the opportunity for one to change one's perspective, leading one from one form of existence to another – and Kierkegaard's own development in the course of his communicating.[30] Kierkegaard is concerned, not only to teach Christianity, but 'to instruct Christianly' – to show what one teaches in how one teaches, as the bird and the lily (CD 10). The religious is what 'should advance' and

which in this way is sanctified and consecrated. But in need of upbuilding himself, he realizes that he is duty-bound in the most unconditional obedience' (PoV 87).

27 This 'God-relationship' – 'an indescribable bliss for me to think and speak about' – he describes as 'in many ways the happy love of my unhappy and troubled life' (PoV 71). Kierkegaard's relationship to God as 'one and only confidant' (PoV 75) in the midst of the 'torments', the 'anxieties unto death', the 'meaningless of existence' (PoV 75) – he describes this relationship in 'what is repeated every day in my prayer, which gives thanks for the indescribable things he has done for me, so infinitely more than I ever had expected; about what has taught me to marvel, to marvel over God, his love, and over what a human being's weakness is capable of with his help' (PoV 72), wishing 'to do nothing other than to thank him' (PoV 73). Kierkegaard thus wanted to be remembered as one 'who historically died of a mortal disease but poetically died of a longing for eternity in order unceasingly to do nothing else than to thank God' (PoV 97).

28 'In relation to God I offer this my entire work more shamefacedly and bashfully than a child who gives its parents a gift the parents have given the child. Oh, but what parents would be so cruel as to take the gift from the child and say, "Why, this is ours!" instead of smiling at the child and going along with its idea that it is a gift – so also with God; he is not that cruel when someone brings him as a gift – his own' (PoV 89).

29 What is presented in the following is an intimation of what will be seen from further down the road.

30 Something like this is echoed in Climacus's statement: 'The religious discourse is the path to the good, that is, it copies the path, which is just as long as life' (CUP 428).

that 'at which [the authorship] was to arrive', whereas the aesthetic is 'what should be left behind, what should be abandoned' (PoV 8–9). This teleological ordering, as of a journey from the lower to the higher, is the movement, the transformation, to which the authorship invites the reader ('becoming a Christian', the substance of the authorship) that is like the movement of the authorship itself (the method of the authorship) that is like, as well, the movement of life from which the authorship arises – the author's own life (the origin of the authorship).[31]

Kierkegaard writes of a correspondence between the development of his authorship and 'indeed also my own development' (PoV 12) – such that 'my existence-relations turned around in altogether accurate correspondence to the change in my writing' (PoV 70). If there is a real shift in Kierkegaard's authorship, it is not in substance, but in his own development – from merely observing the issue (of becoming a Christian) to there being 'no misunderstanding . . . as to whether it was I who needed Christianity or Christianity that needed me' (PoV 93). This is due to Kierkegaard's own participation in God's work in his life: 'the expression for Governance's part in the authorship is this: that the author is himself the one who in this way has been brought up, but with a consciousness of it from the very beginning' (PoV 90).[32] The Christian life is such a participation; the authorship relates to the reader as such a participation; the author of the authorship so participates with the author's 'Author'. 'It is Governance that has brought me up, and the upbringing is reflected in the writing process. . . . The process is this: a poetic and philosophic nature is set aside in order to become a Christian' (PoV 77). It is such a participatory gift (that is given but must be actively appropriated) that Kierkegaard received (and was perpetually receiving) and that he sought to communicate to his readers in the proper manner – a communication that begets communication – that awakens and builds up a life of communicating communion.

---

31 'This again is the dialectical movement (like that in which the religious author begins with esthetic writing, and like that in which, instead of loving oneself and one's advantage and supporting one's endeavor by illusions, one instead, hating oneself, removes illusions)' (PoV 9).

32 See also how Kierkegaard sees his 'persecution' as an author as mirroring the suffering fate of religious truth in the world: 'The essentially religious person is always polemical' (PoV 67). 'I demonstrate it by this, that I am persecuted; it is truth, and I demonstrate it by this, that I am laughed to scorn' (PoV 67).

2

Faith

The entry into the way that is the truth is faith. Faith is the beginning and the foundation of Christian existence. This chapter progresses through four 'faiths' in Kierkegaard's work: from faith 'in the ordinary sense', to ethical faith, to religious faith, and finally to Christian faith as the foundation for Christian thinking and living. One can envision concentric circles raised into ascending plateaus (like a wedding cake). Moving from the perimeter toward the centre, from the lower to the higher, each 'faith' marks a transition, a 'leap', from one stage to another on the ascent. These progressive crossings into reality (not escapes from it, into another realm) are such that the highest has not left the circle of any of the prior stages, but has raised them, as a series of reverse echoes, toward the truth.

Faith in the Ordinary Sense

Standing against faith, commonly understood – barring the way – is doubt. Doubt brings about an uncertainty, an instability, a disputability to our beliefs (PF 84).[1] Not wanting to be deceived, doubt 'protest[s] against any conclusion that wants to go beyond immediate sensation and immediate knowledge' (PF 84). Doubt is a negative moment – a 'break', 'a polemic against what went before' – that would 'destroy everything in order to build anew' (JC 145; EO 433). It is a choice – such that Kierkegaard can talk about it in terms of insubordination or presumptuousness (UDVS 273; CD 89).[2] Doubt, for Kierkegaard (and against Descartes), cannot conquer itself, cannot provide a foundation upon which one

---

1 'The movement of doubt lay precisely in his being at one moment in the right, at the next in the wrong' (EO 606).

2 This is what Kierkegaard means when he writes that 'it is faith that brought doubt into the world' (JP 891; JC 256 sup).

can go further (FT 5).[3] As beginning with a decision, it cannot be 'thought through' to a demonstration, to an indubitable conclusion (EUD 135; UDVS 274).[4] The best doubt can do in this regard is to doubt itself, to open beyond itself.[5] For as doubt begins as a choice – though this may be forgotten in abstraction – so it terminates, is concluded, is answered with a choice, a decision – with faith (JC 256; PF 84; EUD 134-5).

Kierkegaard's conception of faith in the ordinary sense is best understood in the context of the relationship between immediacy, reflection and resolution. It is, Vigilius Haufniensis writes, 'the fundamental error of recent philosophy . . . to begin with the negative instead of with the positive, which always is the first' (CA 146). 'The passion of philosophy and the passion with which all philosophizing began' is not doubt, the negative, but a positive immediacy, a 'positive principle', namely, wonder (CA 146).[6] Receptive of the contingent (non-necessary, could be otherwise) arrival of what happens, wonder 'stands *in pausa* and waits for the coming into existence' (PF 80) – it is 'the passionate sense for coming into existence' (PF 80). In this immediacy, reality is simply present: 'Immediacy is reality' (JC 168). We, however, do not remain in immediacy. In simple immediacy there is no relation, no consciousness, no linguistic articulation.[7]

The moment of reflection mediates the immediate moment of wonder. Reflection 'steps back' from immediacy – cancels imme-

---

3 Kierkegaard asks: Does doubt conquer doubt? (as strength drives out the strong man) or will it only make doubt stronger? (the demon returning to the empty house with seven others). 'No, therefore one first of all binds the strong man' (EUD 128).

4 'If the demonstration cannot be made, then can doubt not be halted? That is not the case. If the demonstration could be made in the way that doubt demands, then doubt could not be halted anymore than sickness can be halted by the remedy the sickness requests' (EUD 135).

5 'False doubt doubts everything except itself; with the help of faith, the doubt that saves doubts only itself' (EUD 137).

6 'Wonder is plainly an immediate category and involves no reflection upon itself' (JC 145).

7 'In immediacy there is no relation. For as soon as there is relation, immediacy is canceled. Immediately, therefore, everything is true, but this truth is the untruth the very next moment, for in immediacy everything is untrue. If consciousness can remain in immediacy, the question of truth is canceled. . . . Immediacy is reality; language is ideality; consciousness is contradiction. The moment I make a statement about reality, contradiction is present, for what I say is ideality' (JC 167, 168).

diacy (as immediate) – considers it from the perspective of ideas, words – posits an 'ideal' over against, and in relation to, the 'real' of immediacy (JC 168; SLW 157). In the incomplete and tantalizingly brief *Pars Secunda* of Kierkegaard's unpublished work *Johannes Climacus*, he describes the relation between the two opposing poles of reflection as being 'consciousness'. 'Reality', he writes, 'is not consciousness, ideality no more so. Yet consciousness does not exist without both, and this contradiction is the coming into existence of consciousness and is its nature' (JC 168). This relation is presented as an active subjective relation – a relating, not a merely static relation but an *interesse* – an interested being between (JC 170).[8] Conscious reflection asks about truth, about whether the idea, the word corresponds to the real, the actual. Such conscious reflection may attempt to ground or to found reflection on something immediate and thus unquestionable – a secure, self-evident foundation. So, now in order for reflection to get off the ground (to stand) in a properly grounded manner, reflection must find its ground through a kind of 'retrogressive reflection' – this is the path of doubt. However, if immediacy is a product of reflection then reflection is not grounded in the immediate. Climacus states: 'This thought in all its simplicity is capable of deciding that there can be no system of existence and that a logical system must not boast of an absolute beginning.' If immediacy is a product of reflection, then 'the immediate never is but is annulled when it is' (CUP 112). Reflection of itself cannot ground itself in immediacy, for 'reflection is immediacy's death angel' (SLW 157). Reflection 'cannot stop of its own accord' – it is a 'spurious infinity' – a fugue (CUP 112–13). Reflection does not terminate in an immediate and self-evident origin. Instead, the infinity of reflection is only stopped by a resolution.

The final moment (of the conscious relation to that which is other to thought) is that of resolution, 'a breakthrough', which 'breaks forth through the endlessly perpetuated reflection' – 'only in that way', Climacus states, 'can reflection be stopped' (CUP 113). Climacus continues: 'When a beginning with the immediate

---

8 This early formulation of consciousness as the active relation in the second moment of 'reflection' is a trajectory of thought on which Kierkegaard does not follow through – the second moment is usually just described as 'reflection'. It is helpful, though, in fleshing out what is at work in reflection for Kierkegaard.

is achieved by reflection, the immediate must mean something different than it usually does' (CUP 113–14). This 'new immediacy' is a different kind of immediacy – one that is neither anterior to, 'founding', reflection nor passively 'found' by reflection – but is rather based on *resolution* and 'reaches far beyond any reflection' (CUP 347; SLW 163). This decision is a beginning 'made by virtue of a resolution, essentially by faith' (CUP 189); in it 'reflection is discharged into faith' (SLW 162), deliberation is transfigured into action.[9] Faith in the ordinary sense, then, is a second immediacy, 'a later immediacy', one not attained through reflection but acquired 'after reflection' (FT 82; SLW 162). Thus, Kierkegaard calls faith 'immediacy or spontaneity after reflection' (JP 1123, 6135) – an immediacy of affirmation.

Faith (Danish: *Tro*) in the ordinary sense is a transcendent process with its *telos*, its end, outside itself (PF 80). As such, it is not an 'immanent movement' (which Vigilius Haufniensis calls 'no movement at all' (CA 13)), not necessitated by any prior moment, not a conclusion forced upon it by reflection – but a true movement, a transcendence. The object of faith in the ordinary sense is any actuality – 'existence understood as actuality', 'that such and such actually has happened' – be it present or in history (CUP 110, 581; EO 434; PF 87). Such an object – as that which is beyond 'immediate sensation and immediate cognition' – has the 'illusiveness' of having come into existence, for all that has 'come into existence' is not by necessity (it could not have been) but has been brought to be (or to its current state) by a process that could have been otherwise – it cannot be established as an immanent certainty (PF 81).[10] This is how belief or faith in the ordinary sense is the only answer to reflection's doubt:

---

9 'Perhaps', Kierkegaard writes, 'it would happen that what deliberation understood in pieces would suddenly come together reborn in the moment of decision, that what deliberation sowed in corruption would rise up on the day of distress in the incorruptible life of action' (EUD 114).

10 'Existence', Climacus writes, 'can never be demonstrated' (PF 40). This is so because demonstration, as a chain of necessarily valid reasoning yielding certain results, can only operate in the realm of ideal being, of essences. For it to apply to existence, to actuality, to factual being, there must be a 'leap' . . . This, it should be noted, is rooted in Kierkegaard's creation theology, which we will explore in Chapter 5.

Belief is a sense for coming into existence, and doubt [not wanting to be deceived] is a protest against any conclusion that wants to go beyond immediate sensation and immediate knowledge. (PF 84)[11]

This faith 'in the ordinary sense', the 'organ of the historical', is how we relate to anything beyond immediate sensation which is therefore an 'objective uncertainty' (PF 81; CUP 322). 'This', Climacus writes,

> is precisely the nature of belief [*Tro*], for continually present as the nullified in the certitude of belief is the incertitude that in every way corresponds to the uncertainty of coming into existence. Thus, belief believes what it does not see. (PF 81)

It is before and because of such (necessary) uncertainty that belief (faith in the ordinary sense) entails a 'qualitative transition', a movement (κίνησις), which Kierkegaard calls a 'leap' (CUP 12, 113–14, 342).[12] 'The leap', Climacus writes, 'is the category of decision', a venturing, and is thus 'rooted in subjectivity' (CUP 99, 425–7, 129); it is 'an act of freedom, an expression of will' (PF 83). As such a decision, as a resolution, a transcending transition/ movement, faith in the ordinary sense 'runs the risk that it was in error, but nevertheless it wills to believe'. It does so, not out of some irrational 'existential' heroics, but because, for Kierkegaard, 'one never believes in any other way; if one wants to avoid risk, then one wants to know with certainty that one can swim before going into the water' (PF 83).

Kierkegaard's position implies that inasmuch as there is any affirmation about existence/actuality, faith ('leaping' beyond the necessary impossibility of reflection) is itself necessary. This is implicit in Kierkegaard's statements, that 'all cognition requires an expression of will' and that 'knowledge comes after faith' (JP 1094, 1111). Keeping with the metaphor of 'a founding immediacy', Kierkegaard presents faith as a 'new immediacy' (CUP 347n).

---

11 'The conclusion of belief is no conclusion [*Slutning*] but a resolution [*Beslutning*], and thus doubt is excluded' (PF 84).

12 Climacus described this transition as *metabasis eis allo genos*, as a transition from one genus or category to another, for relative to immanent necessity 'even the smallest leap' possesses 'the quality of making the ditch infinitely broad' (CUP 98).

Beyond modernity's phantom unconditional and self-evident first immediacy, beyond the utter conditionality of the fugue of reflection, faith presents a second immediacy that is an affirmation in the face of uncertainty, a commitment and a risk (JP 3715). Faith's founding is the immediacy of affirmation and is fundamentally different than the foundered founding of doubt – whose sought immediacy is never found. Kierkegaard writes: 'The method of beginning with doubt in order to philosophize seems as appropriate as having a soldier slouch in order to get him to stand erect' (JP 775). As fallible as it may be, faith is the only possible road to affirmation – to truth (JP 3315). So, for faith, that which is impossible (immediacy) is possible, and this possible impossibility is necessary. Faith affirms a new immediacy as a 'non-foundational' founding for reflection 'beyond reflection'. Philosophy does not begin with the negative, with doubt, but with an affirmation, a 'yes' – something, Kierkegaard writes, like wonder (JP 3284).

Faith, Actuality and the Ethical

From faith in the ordinary sense, the faith involved in our beliefs about the world, we make the move to faith in an *ethical* sense. Faith, for Kierkegaard, is the path through which one enters into, comes to engage in the actual, the real world. Over and against speculation and mere deliberation – staying in the realm of infinite possibilities (EO 484–7) – faith has to do with decision, with acting, with choosing. To risk acting means not being paralysed by being unable fully to calculate the consequences of an action (EO 389). This choosing to 'venture a decisive act' is to enter into ethical actuality (JFY 191).

'The act of choosing', (the pseudonym) Judge Vilhelm writes, 'is a literal and strict expression of the ethical' (EO 485).[13] He continues: 'The aesthetic choice is either wholly immediate, thus no choice,

---

13 Thus, Judge Vilhelm, as representing the ethical sphere in *Either/Or*, writes that choice is 'my watchword, the nerve of my life-view' (EO 514). For the ethical 'either/or', the options are choosing or not choosing (EO 491). This 'either/or' is a 'stumbling-block' for the aesthete (analogous to the incarnation) – a marker for a choice between the spheres (the aesthetic and the ethical) from below (from the aesthetic) (EO 484).

or it loses itself in multiplicity' (EO 485).[14] The aesthetic 'choice' is either not deliberative (not weighing choices and thinking about which is best) and thus only an unreflective first immediacy, or gets lost and paralysed in reflection, in deliberating over possibilities. Either way it does not make it to the third moment, it does not make a decision, does not choose.[15] It is thus that Judge Vilhelm writes to the aesthete that, in preferring the 'endless detour which may never lead you to your goal', 'what you lack, lack entirely, is faith' (EO 390).

For Kierkegaard, this faithful resolution is the way, not only into the ethical, but into the ethico-religious. One cannot come to the religious save that one choose the ethical engagement with life. Ethical resolution is the beginning of a life in which freedom and responsibility are meaningful – a life with a purpose transcending the pleasurable and the interesting (TDIO 47; SLW 111). Faith in this more generally ethical sense, as resolution, is the entry into the way to relating to actuality.

Religious Faith: The Double-Movement

Religious faith, for Kierkegaard, has the structure of a double-movement. This, as we have seen, is reflected in Kierkegaard's mode of communication (PoV 6–9). The general schema is one of a redoubling (*Fordoblelse*) in which a given position 'is first of all its opposite' (JFY 98). There is first the negative then the positive, first renouncing and then receiving, first emptying and then filling, first death and then life.

The first moment, the first movement of the double-movement of faith, is a negative one – an initial 'wounding' that has, nevertheless, a constructive end (TDIO 9; EUD 130; UDVS 279). Throughout his authorship, Kierkegaard names this first negative moment, the

---

14 The aesthetic gospel is *vanitas vanitatum vanitas* for in it there is no choice (EO 485).

15 Judge Vilhelm, in *Stages on Life's Way*, presents marriage as an example of faith, of resolution, of decision as the necessary foundation of the ethical (SLW 90–1, 106, 118). Ironically, for the aesthete, continually seeking distraction, the only thing that could truly distract, truly grasp one's attention, a fidelity that did not fail is precisely what aesthetic doubt and cynicism keeps one from seeing (EO 53).

'first element' of faith, as 'despair' (CUP 225–6; SUD 78, 116).[16]
Despair, strangely, is a way forward – 'a man's true salvation' –
'a hidden trapdoor – to ascent' (EO 522; CD 114).[17] This first,
negative movement is also described as 'infinite resignation' (FT
36–8, 46), such that one has 'resigned everything infinitely' (FT
40). This infinite resignation is the 'movement of infinity' whereby
one negates, resigns, gives up the finite such that one is left with
the infinite (FT 38) – whereby one 'practic[es] the absolute relation
through renunciation . . . of relative ends' (CUP 431–2). Despair
or infinite resignation is a benefit in that with them one renounces,
abandons, gives up the finite, the lower, in favour of the infinite,
for the higher (FT 18, 48) – one 'renounce[s] the whole temporal
realm in order to gain eternity' (FT 49) – one turns from Mammon
to seek first the kingdom of God.[18] With this, one gives up on all
finite possibility.[19] It is a 'dying to' (*at afdøe*) – a 'middle term' in
which one 'die[s] to the world', 'breaking . . . with that which he
naturally has his life' – and so has 'emptied himself in the infinite'
(FSE 76; JFY 98; MLW 177, 214; FT 69). This renunciation, this
despair extends to the whole personality (EO 515) – surrendering,
losing, even hating the self (EO 522; SUD 67; MLW 335) – wrest-
ing away self-love in a movement of repentance that dies to the self
and to the world (WL 17; FT 99, 101).

In all of the negation and giving up and 'dying to' of infinite
resignation, one ends up affirming or choosing one thing: oneself

---

16 Kierkegaard's Anti-Climacus describes despair as 'the thoroughfare to faith'
(SUD 67).

17 In *The Concept of Anxiety*, anxiety serves a similar constructive-as-purgative
role – as paving the way for faith (CA 157–9). For example: 'The anxiety of
possibility holds him as its prey until, saved, it must hand him over to faith. In no
other place can he find rest' (CA 158).

18 'Seek first God's kingdom. This is the sequence, but it is also the sequence of
inversion, because that which first offers itself to a person is everything that is visible
and corruptible, which tempts and draws him, yes, will entrap him in such a way
that he begins last, or perhaps never, to seek God's kingdom' (UDVS 209).

'All religion in which there is any truth, certainly Christianity, aims at a person's total transformation and wants, through renunciation and self-denial, to wrest
away from him all that, precisely that, to which he immediately clings, in which he
immediately has his life' (MLW 248).

19 'When every thinkable human certainty and probability were impossible . . .
From the point of view of immediacy, everything is lost' (R 212). When 'a person is
brought to his extremity, when, humanly speaking, there is no possibility . . . this is
the very formula for losing the understanding' (SUD 38).

'in one's eternal validity' as having an 'eternal consciousness' – as being in relation to the infinite, the eternal – as loving God alone (EO 515, 520; FT 46).[20] After one renounces all that is finite one is left with God, with oneself before God – even if before God one is always in the wrong – even if in loving him one is as nothing before him (EO 601–6; R 212).[21] For such a one has renounced even being in the right; God is their only desire.

For Kierkegaard, the second movement of religious faith is that of 'faith'. 'Only when the individual has emptied himself in the infinite', Johannes de Silentio writes, 'only then has the point been reached where faith can break through' (FT 69).[22] After the either/or decision of infinite resignation – choosing the higher and dying to the lower – faith then returns to the lower, for 'it is great to give up one's desire, but it is greater to hold fast to it after having given it up; it is great to lay hold of the eternal, but it is greater to hold fast to the temporal after having given it up' (FT 18). In the double-movement of faith one resigns the lower for the higher (in infinite resignation) and then regains the lower (in 'faith') – this is because the lower is nothing without the higher, for the lower only *is* in relation to the higher – one rightly renounces it as nothing (on its own, as self-existing) in the first movement.

This winning back of the finite that was lost and dead happens, as Johannes de Silentio (alone among the pseudonyms) writes, 'by virtue of the absurd' (FT 36, 40, 46–7, 115). This means that faith makes an affirmation in the midst of despair – when there is no human possibility. It believes (notice de Silentio's gloss) 'by virtue of the absurd, by virtue of the fact that for God all things are possible' (FT 46). For, as Constantius writes, 'when every thinkable human certainty and probability were impossible [and] from the point of view of immediacy, everything is lost' one can come into relation to something other than the human frame of possibility,

---

20 Through the 'act of resignation' one gains one's 'eternal consciousness. . . . My eternal consciousness is my love for God, and for me that is the highest of all. . . . What I gain thereby is my eternal consciousness in blessed harmony with my love for the eternal being' (FT 48).

21 The preacher at the end of *Either/Or* writes that always being in the wrong before God is 'a proof that your love is happy as is only that love with which one loves God' (EO 606).

22 'It is human to lament . . . to sorrow . . . it is greater to have faith' (FT 17).

probability, certainty 'thunderstorm' (R 212).[23] So are the movements of faith the 'movements of finitude' (FT 38) in which one comes to receive, to regain (as a 'repetition')[24] the finite – to 'receive everything' (FT 49), 'to grasp the whole temporal realm' (FT 49), to affirm temporal actuality as divine gift. Faith (re)gains 'everything', the finite 'whole and intact' (CD 146; FT 37) – more fully whole and intact than before in the light of its divine origin – including one's self 'whole in every respect' (CA 106) – regains these as a 'new creation' (FT 40).[25]

With the second movement of religious faith, there is a teleological suspension – suspending one's bonds to the lower and being suspended from the higher (as an inverted foundation, like a suspension bridge). As such a double-movement (negative and then positive) ordered to an end, faith is a foresight that anticipates an arrival, a joyous sight, a fuller understanding that is to come (FT 21, 52, 65). One lives, with divine assistance, in the light of a right relation to God and to oneself (MLW 215). In faith, the self 'rests transparently' in God (SUD 30, 49) and has learned 'the proper self-love' (WL 18). This life is one of security, comfort, harmony and joy (FT 40, 50; EUD 330).

As seen in the second movement above, the higher from the perspective of the lower is seen as absurd.[26] Faith can only be thought, be understood, on the higher plane, in a theological frame. It is seen as 'absurd' because it does not fit within the comprehensive frame of the lower sphere – this is a signal that either I am right and this is wrong (the absurd is false) or I am wrong (my perspective is false). The one in the lower must endure the difficult, the trial, the either/or, the 'absurd' to attain the higher (and regain the lower) (FT 27). The lower (without faith) cannot understand the higher – it cannot 'get a perspective' (FT 33).[27] The absurd is a negative sign

---

23 'What is decisive is that with God everything is possible . . . The critical decision does not come until a person is brought to his extremity, when, humanly speaking, there is no possibility. Then the question is whether he will believe that for God everything is possible, that is, whether he will believe' (SUD 38).

24 This is why '"repetition" is and remains a religious category. Constantin Constantius therefore cannot proceed further' (JP 3794).

25 'Did I not get everything double? Did I not get myself again and precisely in such a way that I might have a double sense of its meaning?' (R 220–1).

26 This, as we will see, is part of the general structure of Kierkegaard's thought.

27 This is why Kierkegaard is unwilling to grant philosophy a position of

that something cannot be narrated from a given perspective. This makes perfect sense from the perspective of the higher (FT 261–3). As Kierkegaard writes in an unpublished reply to a review of *Fear and Trembling*, the paradox marks a 'higher rationality': 'When I believe, then assuredly neither faith nor the content of faith is absurd. Oh, no, no – but I understand very well that for the person who does not believe, faith and the content of faith are absurd' (FT 262 sup).[28]

Christian Faith: The Christian Paradox

Paradox, more generally, for Kierkegaard, comes about when the eternal is brought into relation to an existing individual.[29] This paradox, however, is an 'analog to the paradox *sensu eminentiori*' (CUP 206) – 'the paradox *sensu strictissimo*, the absolute paradox' – 'that God has existed in human form' (CUP 217). Faith in this paradox is the entry, the initiation, for Kierkegaard, into the higher concentric circle of the Christian religion, the Christian way, the Christian truth. Christianity's 'transcendent point of departure' is the person of Jesus Christ.[30] The absurd of Christianity is not any mere nonsense, but 'the absurd' (CUP 558, 568) – namely, 'that the

---

superiority from which it can hold court and pass judgement on religious faith. 'Philosophy cannot and must not give faith, but it must understand itself and know what it offers and take nothing away, least of all trick men out of something by pretending it is nothing' (FT 33). It is with something like this in mind that Vigilius Haufniensis writes: 'When someone asks a stupid question, care should be taken not to answer him, lest he who answers becomes just as stupid as the questioner' (CA 50).

28 In this unpublished piece, Kierkegaard is replying to one Theophilus Nicolaus (the reviewer's, not Kierkegaard's, pseudonym – pseudonyms not being uncommon in nineteenth-century Copenhagen) who says that the doctrines of the Church that are paradoxical or absurd should be rejected in favour of a more universal religion of reason (FT 259 sup) – to 'do away with everything *called absurd*' (FT 261 sup, emphasis added). Kierkegaard writes: 'You throw out all of Christianity and thereupon, with an exultant look, say something like this: Where now is the paradox? More correctly, you should say: Where now is Christianity?' (FT 260 sup).

29 'The paradox emerges when the eternal truth and existing are placed together' (CUP 208). 'The paradox is the boundary for an existing person's relation to the eternal, essential truth' (CUP 220).

30 'Christianity proclaims itself to be a transcendent point of departure, to be a revelation in such a way that in all eternity immanence cannot assimilate this point of departure and make it an element' (BoA 120).

eternal truth has come into existence in time, that God has come into existence, has been born, has grown up, etc., has come into existence exactly as an individual human being, indistinguishable from any other human being' (CUP 210). Part of the paradox of Christianity is that eternal happiness is contingent upon something . . . contingent. As focused on the person of Jesus, Christian faith is placed in something external – on something that happened in history, something actual – something not necessary in its happening, and so in our knowing.[31] Faith in the ordinary sense – as relating to the contingent, the actual – is an ingredient in Christian faith, for when Christ took on flesh, he entered into the human order of human finitude, fallibility, uncertainty, risk. In faith, one is 'venturing everything upon uncertainty, which is to believe'.[32] As proclaiming the impossible (UDVS 237), that there is sin and forgiveness (SUD 100), that an individual human being is the eternal God come into existence, that one's salvation is dependent on one's relation to something about which one can only have, at best, contingent (non-necessary) knowledge – Christian faith is a 'fragile vessel' for it only comes to be in the context of the 'possibility of offense' (PIC 76), forcing an either/or decision (PIC 81).

For Kierkegaard, the possibility of offence exists because comprehension of the object of faith is denied. To comprehend is to place oneself in a position above the subject matter.[33] Yet in relation to the Christian object of faith this is 'conceitedness' (TERE 66). There is no 'going further' than faith without negating it (EUD 27), and attempts to make Christianity probable relative to an external criterion – beyond the transcendent revelation in Christ – serve only 'to falsify it' (BoA 39) – to defend Christianity by measuring it relative to something false.[34] There is here a reversal from philosophy

---

31 The difficulty 'consists in subjectively coveting information about the historical in the interest of one's eternal happiness' (CUP 577).

'Everything that becomes historical is contingent, inasmuch as precisely by coming into existence, by becoming historical, it has its element of contingency, inasmuch as contingency is precisely the one factor in all coming into existence' (CUP 98).

32 'Dead set against an "if" and troubled by this "if," I have ventured out (it is called taking a risk), and now I believe' (CD 240).

33 'The secret of all comprehending is that this comprehending is itself higher than any position it posits; the concept establishes a position, but the comprehension of this is its very negation' (SUD 97).

34 'Under various names and right up to the latest speculative thought, the effort

as theology's handmaid to theology as philosophy's handmaid . . . or worse.[35] This is so because of the difference between God and humans – we cannot understand God 'from above' as under a concept.[36] This difference 'constitutes the possibility of offense, which cannot be removed' (SUD 127),[37] because we, and our thinking, our categories, are from below where 'all thinking draws its breath in immanence, whereas the paradox and faith constitute a separate qualitative sphere' (TERE 94; BoA 175). Kierkegaard writes:

> The human dialectic cannot proceed further than to this admission, that it cannot think this, but also to the admission that this does not imply anything more than that it cannot think this. But the human dialectic, if it wants to understand itself, consequently to be humble, never forgets that God's thoughts are not human thoughts. (BoA 33)

Our understanding of God – of 'the Lord whose wisdom is like the darkness of the night – as unfathomable as the depths of the sea' – is such that the theologian is too often like the enigmatic and lowly figure of Nebuchadnezzar's (Quidam's? Frater Taciturnus'?) 'astronomer', who 'shall be led through the streets and be dressed as an animal, and he shall carry with him his reckonings, shredded like a bundle of hay' (SLW 361–3).

Faith's struggle, however, is precisely 'to believe without being able to understand' (UDVS 273). Faith believes in the paradox.[38]

---

has been to make Christianity probable, comprehensible, to take it out of the God-language of the paradox and get it translated into the Low-German of speculative thought or the Enlightenment' (BoA 40).

35 'Theology sits all rouged . . . ' (FT 32).

36 One should be watchful 'that the gulf of qualitative difference between God and man may be maintained as it is in the paradox and faith' (SUD 99).

37 'The basic meaning of human deliberating is to weigh the temporal against the eternal; in all other human deliberating this basic meaning must be present. Otherwise, despite all the busyness and pompous importance, the deliberating is baseless and meaningless' (UDVS 309).

So Kierkegaard prays: 'Save me, O God, from ever becoming completely sure . . . Is there not bound to be unsureness in fear and trembling until the end if I am who I am and you are who you are, I here on earth, you in heaven, and, alas, the infinitely greater difference, I a sinner, you the Holy One!' (CD 211–12).

38 Faith 'relates itself to the improbable and the paradox, is self-active in discovering it and in holding it fast at every moment – in order to be able to believe' (CUP 233).

Faith as before comprehension, as before the joyous sight (FT 52) 'always pertains to what is not seen' (UDVS 235), to the invisible.[39] Faith brings one into another world – a world larger than the merely human, than the secular and its frame of what is possible – a world revealed in the person of Jesus Christ. Faith as belief in paradox follows the 'the passion of thought', the desire of understanding for that beyond understanding – 'to want to discover something that thought itself cannot think' (PF 37).[40] So the understanding is teleologically suspended in faith as its decentring fulfilment.[41]

Faith's Founding

For Kierkegaard, the methods of modern philosophy for providing a sure foundation for thought, namely Cartesian doubt and Hegelian mediation, have failed to do so. The 'result' of such projects is a fugitive reflection that yields no conclusion – 'a passing through in the continuous process in which nothing abides' (CUP 33).[42] Faith, however, provides a foundation for thought and life. It is, certainly from the perspective of the modern epistemic quest for such, a strange foundation. For the Christian, building on her faith in the Christian paradox(es), faith's foundation is best understood as a suspension – from above, over nothing – 'happy out on 70,000 fathoms of water' (CUP 140). 'Humanly speaking', Climacus writes, 'consequences built upon a paradox are built upon the abyss . . . the whole thing is in suspense' (PF 98). The believer's assurance, the certainty of faith is 'not once and for all', Climacus writes, 'but, with infinite, personal, passionate interest, by daily acquiring the

---

39 'No gaze is as sharp-sighted as that of faith, and yet faith, humanly speaking, is blind; reason, understanding, is, humanly speaking, sighted, but faith is against the understanding. In the same way the downcast gaze is sighted, and what the downcast gaze signifies is humility – humility is the uplifting' (ThDCF 132).

40 'The last thing human thought can will is to will beyond itself in the paradoxical' (CUP 104–5).

41 Climacus uses different forms of love to illustrate this relationship: 'Self-love lies at the basis of love [Kjærlighed], but at its peak its paradoxical passion wills its own downfall. . . . Self-love has foundered, but nevertheless it is not annihilated but is taken captive and is erotic love's *spolia opima* [spoils of war]' (PF 48).

42 'Now he despairs, his life is wasted, his youth is spent in these deliberations. Life has not acquired any meaning for him, and all this is the fault of philosophy.' This is from the planned conclusion of *Johannes Climacus* (JC 235 sup).

certain spirit of faith' (CUP 55). Faith must be continually renewed, repeated, in the midst of the flux of the world. Faith's founding, its certainty, is not false triumphalism of 'another kind of certainty' (CUP 11, 34–5) – is not something one possesses as finished (CUP 86). Its certitude is always a resolution in the face of uncertainty.

Christian faith founds a different understanding. In it one accepts the paradox as '*index* and *judex sui et falsi* [the criterion of itself and of the false]' (PF 51), and so one attains an understanding that is 'not a knowledge' inasmuch as 'all knowledge is either knowledge of the eternal [absolute] . . . or it is purely historical knowledge [contingent]' – for faith affirms a relation between the eternal and the contingent, supremely in the incarnation, in the person of Christ (PF 62). Offence is an acoustical echo of this paradox – an 'acoustical illusion' (PF 49) – for, Climacus writes,

> if the paradox is *index* and *judex sui et falsi* [the criterion of itself and of the false], then offense can be regarded as an indirect testing of the correctness of the paradox, for offense is the erroneous accounting, is the conclusion of untruth, with which the paradox thrusts away. (PF 51)

The offended understanding makes a true observation (that the object of faith is a paradox), yet its conclusion (rejecting the 'absurd') does not necessarily follow from this observation – it has to do with what option one takes, 'when the understanding cannot get the paradox into its head' (PF 53): be it offence or 'that happy passion', faith, in which 'the difference is in fact on good terms with the understanding' (PF 54). The offended understanding's rejection of the paradox as absurd is an inversion of 'the paradox's claim that the understanding is the absurd' (PF 52) – that when such an offended understanding concludes, taking itself as '*index* and *judex sui et falsi*', that whatever is beyond our ken, is false.

In accepting the paradox as a revealed truth, faith is fundamental for 'dogmatics' (MLW 324; CA 18)[43] – which, in turn, is the basis for Christian existence – for a theological ethics (CA 19–21).[44]

---

43 'Christianity teaches that everything essentially Christian depends solely upon faith . . . keeping watch so that the gulf of qualitative difference between God and man may be maintained as it is in the paradox and faith' (SUD 99).

44 'Paradox, faith, and dogma – these three constituents have an agreement and

Christian faith (in the paradox) – continually renewed, repeated, patient, persevering, a 'task for a whole lifetime' (UDVS 238; FT 7) – provides an integrating centre (EUD 27–8) and is so the basis for a new way of being, a new meaning of life (EUD 27–8; PF 96; PIC 120). Faith is

> the divine joint in a human being and that if it holds it makes him the proudest sailing ship, but if it is loosened it makes a wreck of him and thereby makes the content of his whole life futility and miserable vanity. (UDVS 269)

'Christianly', Anti-Climacus notes, 'as you believe, so you are, to believe is to be' (SUD 93).

However, Christian faith, for Kierkegaard, is no mere intellectual assent, not just affirming the content of faith (FT 7). The foundation of and entrance into the Christian way of living is personal and passionate – an active relating to another in trust, in obedience and in love. Christian faith is a personal engagement with the content of Christian belief.[45] Kierkegaard writes: 'For a person to be a Christian, it certainly is required that what he believes is a *definite* something, but then with equal certainty it is also required that it be *entirely definite* that *he* believes' (CD 244). With the 'dialectical' (the issue of the absolute paradox, the claim that Jesus is God Incarnate) there is the 'pathos-filled' (CUP *passim*) – with 'dialectical struggles' is the 'gigantic passion' (FT 32). 'Faith's question', Kierkegaard writes again, 'is to you: Have you believed?' (CD 238). Faith is a matter of resolution, of decision, and so does not come 'as a matter of course' (SUD 58). This is why one cannot give another faith, cannot give them resolution – that here one can have, at best, a Socratic relation (EUD 382). The decision of faith is a passionate, pathos-filled transition. Johannes de Silentio writes that 'the highest passion in a person is faith'. One 'does not come to a standstill in faith', but, as with love, so with faith, 'I am by no means standing still. I have my whole life in it' (FT 121, 122). Faith as a passion is dynamic, in motion, active, alive. Faith, like Platonic *eros* orienting and propelling one towards the Good, is 'a restless thing', a 'seek-

---

an alliance that are the surest solidarity and bulwark against all pagan wisdom' (SUD 96–7).

45 'Faith is related to the personality' (CD 238).

ing', a 'deep, strong, blessed restlessness that drives the believer', a 'health, but stronger and more violent than the most burning fever' (FSE 17; UDVS 218; FSE 18).

Christian faith, finally, is a relation to the divine other – a trust and love that is fundamental to Christian existence.[46] A believer is a lover who 'rests transparently in God' (SUD 103, 82). Such a lover places himself under God's authority – submitting to the transcendent other loved and trusted. 'In the sphere of immanence, authority is utterly unthinkable, or it is only as transitory', but in Christianity, 'between God and a human being there is an eternal essential qualitative difference . . . so that here in this life a human being ought to obey and worship God' (BoA 180–1).[47] The humble submission of faith founds a life of obedience – 'because the object of all faith's works is to get rid of egotism and selfishness in order that God can actually come in and in order to let him rule in everything' (UDVS 259). Faith's obedience, following, conforming oneself to the eternal provides a security in life – faith is 'the fortress' that is 'a world to itself, and it has life within its ramparts . . . and with faith in this fortress lives obedience' (CD 87).[48] Finally, this asymmetrical and founding relationship of faith is one of worship: 'to worship, which is the expression of faith, is to express that the infinite, chasmic, qualitative abyss between them is confirmed. For in faith the possibility of offense is again the dialectical factor' (SUD 129). 'The birth pangs of faith' are 'the beginning of worship' (PIC 135). The life of faith is a life humbly suspended (as over nothing) from the one on high toward whom one longingly ascends on the journey of life's way.

---

46 'I have believed in him – if I am deceived here also, then I am not only the most wretched of all but my life at its deepest root is annihilated, then everything else can neither benefit nor harm . . . If he is a mirage, then my life is lost' (CD 240).

47 'The matter is very simple: will you obey or will you not obey; will you in faith submit to his divine authority or will you take offense – or will you perhaps not take sides – be careful, that also is offense' (BoA 34).

'Doubt and disbelief, which make faith worthless, have, among other things, also made people ashamed of obeying, of submitting to authority' (BoA 184).

48 'Truly, to be face-to-face with its downfall and to have the courage and faith to come into existence in all its beauty – only unconditional obedience is capable of that. . . . Only unconditional obedience can make use of the moment, unconditionally undisturbed by the next moment' (LFBA 28–9).

3

Truth

As there are ascending transitions of faith so are there ascending plateaus of truth on life's way. This chapter on Kierkegaard's understanding of truth is a preliminary or anticipatory sketch to be filled in later from the standpoint of a more robust understanding of Kierkegaard's theological and metaphysical understanding of the way things are (in Chapters 4, 5 and 6) and his understanding of the Christian way of existing (in Chapter 7).

Objective and Subjective Truth

Objective truth (or: selling one's trousers and buying a wig)

The problem with what Kierkegaard calls 'objectivity' or 'objective truth' in relation to being a Christian is that it shifts the 'medium' from 'existence and the ethical to the intellectual, the metaphysical, the imaginational' (PoV 130). In making Christianity a matter of intellectual reflection, of abstract imagination, 'a more or less theatrical relationship has been introduced between thinking Christianity and being a Christian' (PoV 130). The problem with the 'objective' approach to the truth of Christianity is that it ignores existence in favour of something that happens on the level of reflection alone 'as if having thought about something were identical with existing', and so committing the error 'that by coming to know objectively what Christianity is . . . one becomes a Christian' (CUP 253, 570, 577). The problem with 'objectivity' is that, in its abstraction and so isolation from existence, it is not in touch with actuality, not in relation to truth (EO 542). The reality that it has lost contact with is that of the existing person. Objectivity is a truth that 'goes away from the subject' (CUP 193) – a truth that is impersonal and indifferent: 'indifferent to the individual's particular condition. . . . indifferent to its relation to him . . . indifferent to how the individual receives it . . . indifferent to whether the truth becomes a blessing or a ruination to him' (FSE 39; EUD 233–4). A Christianity built around such 'objective' truth is a 'professorial-scholarly Christianity' in which 'the professor is the true Christian' (JFY 195); the problem is 'not that what they say is an untruth, since they say what is true, but the true statement has no truth in them' (UDVS 325) – they are 'rich in truths and poor in virtues' (EUD 350). When truth becomes 'objective', what is lost is the relation between the existing subject and what is seen as true – the appropriation – 'how an existing subject *in concreto* relates himself to the truth' (CUP 75, 192–3). One has lost the relation between one's existence and 'the truth that is related essentially to existence' (CUP 199).

The objective relation is one of abstraction and observation (CUP 21, 32–3, 35, 193). It disengages from life – a 'parenthetical' bracketing (BoA 34–5) – and takes up 'a scholarly distance from life' (SUD 5). In this 'objective orientation' – in the posture of a mere observer – one, as an existing person, becomes 'something such as no existing human being has ever been or can be' (CUP 189) – 'almost like a ghost' (CUP 133). Objectivity, being 'of the opinion that it has a security that the subjective way does not have' (CUP 194), succumbs to 'a phantom of knowledge that fascinates the soul, that there is a security in which one is knowing – and yet deceived' (TDIO 22). Instead of attaining a secure perspective apart from the vagaries of existence, one, 'deceived by much knowledge' (TDIO 22), only succeeds (if temporarily) with an evasion of one's existence – with distracting oneself from reality, from one's life, for 'scarcely any sedative is more effective than abstract thinking' (EO 514; CUP 230; UDVS 82). Such a defection from existence is, for Kierkegaard, a thoroughly 'aesthetic' stance (as the lowest stage on life's way) – that of those fixated on the 'interesting', 'the inquisitive, the idlers' (UDVS 253),[1] and so displaying 'a kind of inhuman curiosity' foreign to ethical engagement in life (SUD 5).

Objective truth, relative to subjective truth is a lesser truth. The 'objective' is a lesser parody of subjective truth – the disengaged curiosity about the way things are is a pale reflection of the desire

---

1 Kierkegaard writes of 'the vile pandering of inquisitiveness' (UDVS 253).

and the end of subjective truth.[2] 'Objective' truth 'fails to express the state of the knowing subject in existence' – it does not reach to the state of the existing subject, to the actuality of the individual (CUP 81).[3] Beyond not being true to the thinking and existing subject, 'objective' truth, insofar as it pretends to be the product of abstract reflection, (is not true to thought itself) – for faith in the ordinary sense, for Kierkegaard, is how one relates to actuality, and this involves a resolution, a decision – the subject is involved.[4] To be honest to thought will make one a subjective thinker. Nevertheless, Kierkegaard diagnoses his present age as reflective – as lacking resolution, engagement. It is 'a sensible, reflecting age, devoid of passion, flaring up in superficial, short-lived enthusiasm and prudentially relaxing in indolence' in which the slackening of one's relation to that which is a necessary concern for human beings, the actuality of one's life – the way one would go through life – is accompanied with an enthusiasm about the interesting and the ephemeral – 'selling one's trousers and buying a wig' (TA 68, 74).

Subjective truth, the truth of appropriation

Subjective truth is a being in relation to, being involved in, the truth. 'The relation of the subject', Climacus writes, 'is precisely the knotty difficulty' (CUP 37). The subjective, for Kierkegaard, is the personal, is related 'to a person present' (FSE 39; UDVS 11). 'Personal consciousness', he writes, 'requires that in my knowledge I also have knowledge of myself and my relation to my knowledge' (CD 194). Central to this personal involvement is one's decisions, one's choices. Choice is, as Judge Vilhelm states, 'decisive for a personality's content' (EO 482). An understanding of truth that includes decision as a necessary component is 'subjective', for 'all decision is rooted in subjectivity' and 'only in subjectivity is there

---

2 As Climacus writes: 'an objective state of mind is an epigram (unless its opposite is an epigram on it) on the restlessness of the infinitely interested subject' (CUP 23).

3 So, Climacus writes, 'that objective thinking has its reality is not denied, but in relation to all thinking in which precisely subjectivity must be accentuated it is a misunderstanding' (CUP 93).

4 'By thus going astray in reflection, the individual really becomes objective . . . reflection cannot be stopped objectively . . . it is the subject who stops it' (CUP 116).

decision' (CUP 33, 129, 203). In resolution one re-engages with actuality (after reflection).[5] The choices one makes in relating to and engaging with the world constitute who one is as a person. <u>Subjective truth is choosing to be in relation to what is.</u> This implies that choosing rightly matters – that the content of the choice matters – for one's life (EO 483). As deciding, choosing, actively relating to the world (to oneself, to others, to God) the thinking subject is involved in an ongoing process of existence as a continual striving (CUP 91–2).[6]

Kierkegaard describes the repeated decision (chosen repetition) to engage in actual life, to express an ideal (as unchanging) in the actual (as changing), in terms of earnestness. The 'succession and repetition' of such decisions yield earnestness as 'the acquired originality of disposition'. 'Earnestness in this sense', writes Vigilius Haufniensis, 'means the personality itself' (CA 149). Though Kierkegaard does not use these terms, it is hard not to describe such earnestness as an ethical disposition (a habit) acquired through repetition as virtue.[7] The subjective truth as earnestness is to be true, in the choices one makes, over time to one's ideals – to incarnate them – to cultivate a state of being true. 'The earnestness of life', writes Anti-Climacus, 'is to will to be, to will to express the perfection (ideality) in the dailyness of actuality' (PIC 190). With such earnestness one acquires the immediacy of 'certitude and inwardness, which can be attained only by and in action', the 'certitude and inwardness' which 'are indeed subjectivity' (CA 138–9, 141).[8]

Subjectivity as an engagement with life entails a certain presence. Subjective truth is an 'acquired originality', a coming back to oneself in a simplicity in which 'the teacher himself is what he is teaching' (LFBA 38). Instead of relating to oneself as from a distance, absent from oneself in reflection, one is 'to become totally present to oneself in self-concern' and so attain a kind of primitivity

---

5 'The true concrete choice is that in which in the very moment I choose myself out of the world I choose myself back into it' (EO 541).

6 'Here erotic love manifestly means existence.... According to Plato, Poverty and Plenty begot Eros, whose nature is made up of both. But what is existence? It is that child who is begotten by the infinite and the finite, the eternal and the temporal, and is therefore continually striving.... Love is continually striving, that is, the thinking subject is existing' (CUP 92).

7 We will return to this in Chapter 7.

8 'Inwardness, certitude, is earnestness' (CA 151).

(BoA 104, 106; TA 74–5).[9] Subjective truth's primitivity or immediacy, however, is an acquired originality, a second immediacy after
reflection.

'Subjective' truth places the emphasis on the 'how' – how one
relates the given reality in one's actual existence as a person (CUP
202). In this way, 'the how of truth is precisely the truth' (CUP
323). 'Subjective' truth has to do with the correspondence between,
not just what one thinks and what is, but between how one lives
and the way things are – whether one is living in reality or not.
Thus, Kierkegaard writes that 'two people can recite the same
creed – the one can be saved, the other is lost' because the right
'what', the right content of belief (however necessary it may be) is
not enough when it comes to the essential truths of human existence (UDVS 291). There must be the right 'how'. Only then, when
one lives as if such a belief is true, does one attain subjective truth
– when one, as a subject, is true to the reality. The ideal (of sorts)
that Johannes Climacus puts forward in the *Postscript* is that of 'the
subjective thinker'. The subjective thinker, as a thinker, has the task
'to understand himself in existence', but, as a subjective thinker, he
'is essentially interested in his own thinking, is existing in it' (CUP
351, 73).[10] The subjective thinker cultivates double-reflection: 'In
thinking, he thinks the universal, but, as existing in this thinking, as
acquiring this in his inwardness' (CUP 73). The second reflection is
the subjective relation to that which is thought in the first reflection.
Such is 'the duplexity [*Dobbelthed*] of thought-existence' (CUP 74).
Kierkegaard's understanding of subjective truth brings attention to
a broader arena of truth, beyond the merely intellectual to one's
ongoing relation to and being in (and as a) reality.

What Kierkegaard advocates is a movement from the 'objective'
to the 'subjective', from reflection to resolution, from abstraction
to action.[11] One of Kierkegaard's characteristic ways of describing
this movement (especially in CUP, but earlier and later as well) is

---

9 'Just as in our business transactions we long to hear the ring of real coins after
the whisper of paper money, so we today long for a little primitivity' (TA 75).

10 The subjective thinker, for Climacus, is like 'the person', in *Upbuilding Discourses in Various Spirits*, 'who wills the good in truth uses sagacity inwardly: in
order to prevent all evasions and thereby to help himself out and to keep himself out
in the decision' (UDVS 93).

11 This follows the movement of *Johannes Climacus*: from the 'objective' and
abstract to the 'subjective' and involved.

as *appropriation*. Appropriation is the movement of incarnating a truth that is not initially your own.[12] It is a receiving that, as a genuine receiving, is a producing; appropriation, *Tilegnelse*, is literally: making something one's own (CUP 21).[13] In appropriation, a thesis, an objective truth to be known, becomes a task – 'something quite different from knowing' (CUP 297; JC 131) – or rather, the ethical and religious 'theses' are given their proper existential resonance as something more than propositions to be affirmed (JC 152–3). Subjective truth is then 'the truth of appropriation' where focus is brought upon 'the subject's acceptance of it' such that, as Climacus famously writes, 'when subjectivity is truth . . . a definition of truth [would then be this]: An objective uncertainty, held fast through appropriation with the most passionate inwardness, is the truth, the highest truth there is for an existing person' (CUP 21, 129, 203).[14] To appropriate a truth (a thesis, a doctrine) is to 'enter into relation to it', to 'embrace' it (JC 146, 148; CUP 16) – such that, as the early (unpublished) Johannes Climacus writes, 'the thesis, to be sure, would be the same, and yet it would become something else . . . In the one case, personality does nothing and in the other, everything' (JC 151–2).[15] The truth of appropriation is truth transformed, transfigured into action (EUD 86, 114) – a truth that is actualized (CUP 138).[16] 'In the world of actuality', writes Anti-Climacus, 'there is this tiny little transition from having understood to doing' (SUD 93–4). This transition whereby one appropriates 'the essential only by doing it' is an essential transition, a leap, from knowing to doing (TDIO 38).[17] The highest truth, the best relation of correspondence between the subject and the object,

---

12 'You cannot appropriate what belongs to you, only what belongs to another' (UDVS 259).

13 'All receiving is a producing' (CUP 78).

14 In the first of his *Three Discourses on Imagined Occasions*, Kierkegaard writes of the need to appropriate one's 'presuppositions' (TDIO 21).

15 Vigilius Haufniensis echoes this: 'For a man to understand what he himself says is one thing, and to understand himself in what is said is something else' (CA 142).

16 As the pastor at the end of *Either/Or* writes, 'for only the truth that edifies is the truth for you' (EO 609).

17 As Kierkegaard writes later in life: 'It is infinitely further from the clearest understanding to doing accordingly than it is from the profoundest ignorance to the clearest understanding, infinitely further – indeed, in the latter case there is only the difference of degree, in the former the difference of essence' (JFY 115–16).

when one comes to exist in the truth, to exist in relation to what is thought, 'to exist in what one understands' (CUP 191, 254–5; PIC 134) – 'to be what he thinks' (CUP 309) – 'to do the truth' (JP 895). In this fuller sense of a correspondence between thinking (about the being of the world, self, God, etc.) and one's own being, one's own existing 'truth becomes appropriation, inwardness, subjectivity, and the point is to immerse oneself, existing, in subjectivity' (CUP 192) – here 'the appropriation is the truth' (CUP 77).

Ethico-Religious Truth

Again moving inward in concentric circles and upward, the transition to subjective truth is a transition to ethical and religious truth. Subjective truth, Climacus tells us, has to do with essential knowing. 'All essential knowing', he writes, 'pertains to existence, or only the knowing whose relation to existence is essential is essential knowing' (CUP 197). 'Therefore', he concludes, 'only ethical and ethical-religious knowing is essential knowing' (CUP 198).[18]

The ethical is fundamentally related to one's individual existence and to what one does, to the kind of person one is becoming. 'The claim of the ethical upon the existing person' is that he is to live, to actively engage – 'that he is supposed to exist' (CUP 315). As operating in the medium of becoming, the ethical has to do with movement, with one's progress toward or away from a goal (CUP 421). Ethical truth then takes the form of a requirement (CUP 358–9), of a standard of what one is to be, namely 'a whole human being' (CUP 346).[19] It is thus that, as Kierkegaard writes, 'only ethics can place a living person in the proper position; it says: the main thing is to strive, to work, to act' (BoA 131).

The ethical dwells in becoming, in the midst of the temporal and the changing, but in relation to the unchanging. Ethical resolution takes a position, makes an either/or; it is not 'Yes and No' (CUP 279). In this way, resolution 'joins a person with the eternal, brings

---

18 'Essential truth' is 'the truth that is related essentially to existence' (CUP 199).

19 'Ethically understood it is every individual's task to become a whole human being, just as it is the presupposition of ethics that everyone is born in the state of being able to become that' (CUP 346).

the eternal into time for him'; it is 'a waking up to the eternal' (EUD 347). It is so that one, in choosing, is brought into relation to 'the eternal power', that one 'encounter[s] God in the resolution' (EO 486; SLW 110).[20] This ethical 'truth' then is not subjective in the sense of being different for each person. The 'subjective', ethical truth is an eternal truth,[21] something universal, if an intimate universal.[22] 'Truly to exist', Climacus writes, is 'to permeate one's existence with consciousness, simultaneously to be eternal, far beyond it, as it were, and nevertheless present in it and nevertheless in the process of becoming – that is truly difficult' (CUP 308). While 'objective' thinking sees truth as either purely philosophical (as dealing with what is necessarily, eternally true) or purely historical (as dealing with what is contingent and so is at best an approximation), ethical existence, however, unifies the eternal and the contingent (JC 139, 142; CUP 30).

Ethical truth, ethical being in truth, is both ideal and concrete. Ethical truth must not be left as an abstract ideal, but is to be manifested, expressed, translated into one's concrete, everyday existence – as Judge William writes in *Stages on Life's Way*: 'The more concrete a person becomes in ideality, the more perfect is the ideality. . . . Abstraction is ideality's first expression, but concretion is its essential expression' (SLW 114). 'The true art of living', writes the same (?) Judge Vilhelm (William) in *Either/Or*, is becoming both 'the only man' (the unique, singular individual) and 'the universal man', both the idiotic and universal (EO 547–8). One participates in the eternal, the idea, the one true way to be, but in such a way that one incarnates it progressively, becoming it over time, striving toward it as a goal, for 'when I join eternity and becoming, I do not gain rest but the future' (CUP 307).[23]

'When ideality and reality touch each other', Kierkegaard writes, 'then repetition occurs' (JC 171). Repetition, for Kierkegaard, is the process of actualizing ethical truth, of becoming true, such that,

---

20 It is in this vein that the good 'elicits a pledge', that such is the 'resolution's solemn agreement with the good' (EUD 359).

21 Kierkegaard writes: 'By *truth* I always understand *eternal truth*' (PoV 109).

22 On the intimate universal, see William Desmond's *Is There a Sabbath for Thought?* (Bronx, NY: Fordham University Press, 2005).

23 'As existing the human being must indeed participate in the idea but is not himself the idea' (CUP 331).

as Constantin Constantius writes, 'repetition is the watchword in every ethical view' (R 149). Repetition, *Gjentagelse*, is a 'taking up again', a returning to the finite, the immanent, the changing – from the perspective of the eternal, the transcendent, the unchanging – with a 'new immediacy' (R 329; CUP 263). This new immediacy is also to be a continuity in time; it is 'to arrange one's life as if today were the last day one lives and yet also the first in a sequence of years' (SLW 384). Repetition is a continuity in movement, in a progression. Indeed, the very idea of progress involves repetition – in having a direction that is the same, that is singular and so gives the progression unity – as an identity of sorts in the midst of non-identity, in the midst of time as a succession of different moments. The true repetition, for Kierkegaard, the only true progression, is a movement that is toward communion with the eternal – for the end of the way makes it a singular way (pilgrim, not nomad) – that teleologically suspends the journey. That the 'only true end' is the eternal entails that there is a theological or metaphysical 'map' or vision that informs, founds, guides the journey. For Kierkegaard, the truth, however, is not merely this vision – not merely a metaphysical correspondence between our thought and being – not merely knowledge. Truth (in this fuller subjective, ethical, religious sense) is correspondence between our existing, our being and such knowledge. This correspondence, this truth, is a way; we enter into it as we progress toward it. Driven by passion,[24] repetition joins the moments of existence together to form a continuity – 'an increasingly established continuity' – over time (CUP 529–31; SUD 106).

Repetition is intimately related to resolution. Ethically being true is continually choosing to relate to the same thing over time, to persevere – repeating the resolution moment by moment – for 'it is the meaning of resolution for human life that it wants to give it coherence' (EUD 364).[25] This process establishes a character, a self

---

24 'Passion', Climacus writes, 'is the momentary continuity that simultaneously has a constraining effect and is the impetus of motion. For an existing person, the goal of motion is decision and repetition. The eternal is the continuity of motion, but an abstract eternity is outside motion, and a concrete eternity in the existing person is the maximum of passion' (CUP 312).

25 This is 'the earnestness of perseverance that sounds to the fleeting and the transitory', for it is 'only gypsies and robbers and swindlers who have the motto: Never go back where you have once been' (SLW 118).

over time.[26] As with marriage, it is 'the union of love through time' (TDIO 44). Its task is 'the long tedious work' of patience, of enduring, of 'remaining on the spot', and to do so 'uniformly but not emptily', for in striving to remain the same, to stay true, in every moment it is ever new (TDIO 51–2, 71). The danger is that the resolution be left aside from one moment to the next, for 'time comes and time goes, it subtracts little by little; then it deprives a person of a good' (TDIO 48). This is why the aesthetic view – without the fixed point/end of the ethical, without something beyond the self and its pleasures to order the self and its pleasures – fails to achieve repetition, to attain continuity over time. 'I cannot rise above myself', says the aesthete Constantin Constantius, 'repetition is too transcendent for me' (R 186). Indeed, the aesthetic viewpoint's consistency with itself is its dissipation in 'infinite possibilities' and its final giving up, saying 'Farewell!' to hope, vigour, resolve, beauty – for 'the journey is not worth the trouble' (R 175–6).[27] Rather, as oriented and ordered to the eternal, repetition is, for Kierkegaard, an essentially religious category (JP 3794). This is so in that only the eternal possesses in truth the stability and the being 'ever new' that repetition would imitate and participate in – so 'eternity is the true repetition' (R 308 sup; CA 18).

Ethical truth, relating to the eternal, is teleologically suspended in the religious – founded from above. The God-relationship, an orientation to God, ends up being central (thinking of the ascending concentric plateaus) to the ethical and so to the subjective, more generally.[28] 'It is really the God-relationship', Climacus writes, 'that makes a human being into a human being, but this is what he would lack' – so that one becomes human, becomes what one is, in their progression toward God on life's way (CUP 244). Religious subjectivity is the highest subjectivity.[29] To see God as merely an object of

---

26 Constantin Constantius writes in the unpublished draft of a long reply to a review by Heiberg: 'If the point is the spiritual development of a self-conscious free will . . . then it [repetition] is a question of nullifying the repetition in which evil recurs and of bringing forth the repetition in which the good recurs' (R 292).

27 It is the aesthete who says of the flux of life: 'Travel on, you fugitive river! You are the only one who really knows what you want, for you want only to flow along and lose yourself in the sea, which is never filled!' (R 176).

28 'This is required of everyone, that he before God shall honestly humble himself under the requirements of ideality' (PIC 67).

29 'For the rigorously religious individual, his life is essentially action' (FSE 11).

knowledge is not religiousness (CUP 76, 199–200). Religiousness is about one's relation to God – such that if one relates wrongly (the wrong 'how'), one does not relate to God. For God is the only proper object of an infinite inwardness, an infinite passion; as Climacus writes: 'God is something one takes along *à tout prix* [at any price], which, in passion's understanding, is the true relationship of inwardness with God' (CUP 194, 200).[30] This proper 'how' of the God-relation – of religious truth, of the relation being true to, corresponding to its absolute object – helps us to understand, in part, how Climacus can say (in his famous statement) that: 'The one prays in truth to God although he is worshiping an idol; the other prays in untruth to the true God and is therefore in truth worshiping an idol' (CUP 201). The 'in truth' or 'in untruth' in this statement refers to the proper religious (so ethical, so subjective) truth – a truth of being-in-relation – and not the mere objective truth referred to when Climacus writes of 'the true God'. But one must not take this as licence; there is a true 'how', a true way. The question of one's relation to God, for Kierkegaard, is tied up with the question of one's immortality, of 'the immortality of a mortal', of one's eternal happiness, for such immortality and whether one must do anything to attain it 'is the subjective individual's most passionate interest' (CUP 171, 174).[31]

Kierkegaard, especially in his later authorship (especially in 1846), characterizes religiousness, the God-relationship, in terms of obedience. One relates to God as one with 'divine authority'. 'The matter', Kierkegaard writes, 'is very simple: will you obey or will you not obey; will you in faith submit to his divine authority or will you take offense – or will you perhaps not take sides – be careful, that also is offense' (BoA 34, 181). Obedience is ingredient to religious truth, 'is so closely related to the eternal truth' that Kierkegaard asks: 'But what is all eternal truth except this: that God

---

30 'The more universal basis of all religiousness; being shaken, being deeply moved, and subjectivity's coming into existence in the inwardness of emotion are shared by the pious pagan and the pious Jew in common with a Christian. On the common ground of the more universal deep emotion, the qualitative difference must be erected and must manifest itself' (BoA 112–13).

31 'There must be several roads, since a person is to choose, but there also must be just one to choose if the earnestness of eternity is to rest upon the choice. A choice in which it makes no difference what is chosen does not have the eternal earnestness of the choice' (UDVS 225).

rules; and what is obedience except this: to let God rule?' (UDVS 255, 257). The obedience of religiousness, of religious truth, is to live in accordance with, to assent to, reality – that God is and calls upon us with authority. Thus, 'in obedience the humble assent, the confident, strengthening yes of devotedness is heard' (UDVS 258).

The Christian Truth

For Kierkegaard, Christianity is the truth.[32] As subjective truth, the essentially Christian is not merely 'a sum of doctrines' – although doctrine is fundamental (CD 214). 'What is decisive', Kierkegaard writes, is 'the relation to Christianity . . . the agreement or non-agreement of the lives of people with this doctrine' (CD 215). Thus, subjective engagement – 'to exist subjectively with passion' – is a precondition, 'an absolute condition for being able to have any opinion about Christianity' (CUP 280). Christianity, then, is not meant to be just an object of intellectual curiosity and scholarly interest, rather it is concerned with building people up, with helping them, with guiding on life's way – 'from the Christian point of view, everything, indeed everything, ought to serve for upbuilding' (SUD 5).[33] It is thus that the driving issue of Kierkegaard's entire authorship is that of 'becoming a Christian' (PoV 8, 63) – to see 'what it is to be a Christian' and what it requires of one (MLW 341; PoV 16).

Christianity, Christian truth, is at the end of a trajectory that begins with subjective truth and ascends and focuses in ethical and religious truth. Given 'that subjectivity, inwardness, is truth', Climacus writes that this 'at its maximum is Christianity' (CUP 279). If 'subjectivity is truth and subjectivity is the existing sub-

---

32 'I wish only to serve the truth, or what amounts to the same thing, Christianity' (PIC 229).

33 'All Christian knowing, however rigorous its form, ought to be concerned, but this concern is precisely the upbuilding. Concern constitutes the relation to life, to the actuality of the personality, and therefore earnestness from the Christian point of view; the loftiness of indifferent knowledge is, from the Christian point of view, a long way from being more earnest – Christianly, it is a witticism, an affectation. Earnestness, on the other hand, is the upbuilding' (SUD 5–6).
'For the Gospel the most important thing is to bring people to be guided by it' (LFBA 20).

jectivity, then, if I may put it this way, Christianity is a perfect fit' (CUP 230). To truly exist humanly is to exist religiously, and to truly exist religiously is to exist Christianly (CUP 249). There is a dialectic, an exigency that leads one along this trajectory toward the paradoxical-religiousness of Christianity.[34] (We will examine this in depth in Chapters 5 and 6.) The religious truth, the relation of one to the eternal, to God, is found to be lacking in us; we fail to achieve it. If we are to be the truth, then this truth must come to us, must enter into existence to give us the truth. Truth, then, as transcendent, as revealed, should be expected as something transcendent, as something from above challenging and frustrating our merely immanent categories here below, as something paradoxical. The trajectory does not lead to paradox or absurdity as such, to nonsense – as if one's 'subjective' passion and earnestness is all that matters – 'as a beatifying universal balm'.[35] The trajectory points to a particular paradox (or cluster of paradoxes).

Johannes Climacus writes in the Postscript: 'The paradox came into existence through the relating of the eternal, essential truth to the existing person. Let us go further; let us assume that the eternal, essential truth is itself a paradox' (CUP 209). At the heart of Christianity is the paradox that 'the eternal, essential truth . . . has come into existence in time' (CUP 213).[36] Christianity claims to present the eternal truth of human life – the truth of what we are

---

34 'Dialectic in its truth is a kindly disposed, ministering power that discovers and helps to find where the absolute object of faith and worship is, where the absolute is. . . . Dialectic itself does not see the absolute, but it leads, as it were, the individual to it and says: Here it must be, that I can vouch for; if you worship here, you worship God' (CUP 490–1).

35 'There are examples enough of a mistaken effort to assert the pathos-filled and earnestness in a ludicrous, superstitious sense as a beatifying universal balm, as if earnestness in itself were a good or something to be taken without prescription; then everything would be good just as long as one is earnest, even if it so oddly happened that one was never earnest in the right place. No, everything has its dialectic' (CUP 525).
'He is essentially deceived if the absurd he has chosen turns out not to be the absurd' (CUP 558).
'Therefore he cannot believe nonsense against the understanding, which one might fear, because the understanding will penetratingly perceive that it is nonsense and hinder him in believing it' (CUP 568).

36 'The paradoxical expression of existence (that is, existing) as sin, the eternal truth as the paradox by having come into existence in time, in short, what is decisive for the Christian-religious' (CUP 270–1).

and what we are to be – but this, Climacus writes, 'is not an eternal truth in the sense of a mathematical or ontological theorem;' rather 'Christianity is the paradoxical truth; it is the paradox that the eternal once came into existence in time' – 'the difficulty and the paradox are that it is actual' (CUP 580; BoA 37).[37]

This eternal truth come into existence is Christ – 'Christ's life upon earth, every moment of this life, was truth' (PIC 203). The teaching, his word about the eternal truth about human life is and how to live it is, most deeply, his own life, his existence – 'he who also was *the Word* in such a way that he was what he said' (JFY 159, 191). Christ's life, then, 'is the essential truth'; he is 'the man who is the Truth . . . the criterion' (CD 122, 278). In Christ, as the heart of the Christian truth, we have the most fundamental human truth, the revelation of what it means to be a human being (MLW 119).[38]

If Christ is this truth, then we are become it, to participate in it. For Kierkegaard, truth, the highest truth that is Christianity, is existing in the reality revealed in Christ. True human being, as living in community with God, with others, and with oneself, is a life 'defined' by Christ; it is the life of a disciple, an imitator of Christ. A disciple is then a non-identical repetition of Christ. In Kierkegaard's writings, repetition (*Gjentagelse*) in his earlier authorship finds its fulfilment, its teleological suspension (its non-identical repetition, its *Aufhebung*?) in imitation (*Efterfølgelse*) in his later authorship.[39] The task of becoming of a self, the forging (the 'taking up again', *Gjentagelse*) of an identity over time in the midst of existence is taken up into the task of imitation, of 'following after' (the *følge efter* of *Efterfølgelse*).

Climacus presents the Christian way, Christian subjectivity as singular. 'The appropriation by which a Christian is Christian', he writes, 'must be so specific that it cannot be confused with anything else' (CUP 609); it is a 'paradoxical inwardness that is specifi-

---

37 Thus, the 'defense of Christianity that understands what it wants' should present Christianity in its paradoxical strangeness, should present 'the improbability of Christianity' (BoA 40). (Improbable from within the frame of immanent and finite calculation.)

38 This will be explored in depth in Chapter 6.

39 Kierkegaard had largely dropped terminology about 'repetition' by mid-1846, by the time he began writing his second, 'religious', signed authorship.

cally different from all other inwardness' (CUP 610). The Christian way is based on Christ.[40] Climacus holds that the Christianity as paradoxical-religiousness is so unique that one, 'just by describing the "how" of his inwardness, can indirectly indicate that he is a Christian without mentioning Christ's name' for 'this "how" fits only one object' (CUP 613–14). Though we will treat this Christian 'how' at length in the final chapter, suffice it to say that Kierkegaard describes this singular Christian way as (among other things) a life of faith, hope and love – of meekness that carries the heavy burden as light – of joy in the midst of suffering.

Kierkegaard in the unpublished but painstakingly written and rewritten *Book on Adler* presents the Christian truth, the distinctively Christian subjectivity as something 'concrete' (being not just some vague emotion) as rooted in and 'controlled by' Christian 'conceptual definitions' or 'conceptual language' – by Christian theology (BoA 111–15). Though it is a 'subjective' truth and the truth of human subjectivity, Christianity is not merely subjective in the sense that its content is a matter of individual caprice – albeit passionate caprice. 'The essentially Christian', Kierkegaard writes, 'maintains its objective continuance outside all believers, while it also is in the inwardness of the believer' (BoA 117–18).[41]

An essential part of the particularly Christian understanding of truth for Kierkegaard – that the truth is 'transcendent', that it comes to us, from beyond us, in Christ – is our state as untruth.[42] Untruth, for Kierkegaard, is the ordinary state for humans, is the 'preceding state' (EO 599; PF 13–14). While, for Christianity, subjectivity is truth, our subjectivity 'at first' is untruth (CUP 213) – that subjectivity is truth, Climacus states, 'begins in this way: "Subjectivity is untruth"' (CUP 207). This untruth is a state of isolation or estrangement – of not being in continuity, in communion with reality – 'inclosed' in one's own false world, at a 'painful distance from the truth' (CA 128; CUP 269). One is self-deceived, not relating to what one is and the way things are as one is and as the way things

---

40 'This "how" can fit only one thing, the absolute paradox' (CUP 610–11).

41 'If the essentially Christian enters into the hearts of ever so many believers, every believer realizes that it did not arise in his heart, realizes that the objective qualification of the essentially Christian is not a reminiscence' (BoA 118).

42 'Christianity, by being the truth, discovered the infinite distance between truth and untruth' (TERE 86).

are, in actuality (TDIO 35). One despairingly misrelates to the self either being tricked out of the self by becoming a finite thing bound to necessity without possibility or freedom (SUD 33) or by becoming something 'fantastic' (SUD 31), 'a mirage' (SUD 36) of infinite possibilities – lacking, not being constrained by actuality and so becoming unreal (SUD 35). This untruth is a despair, an unhappiness, that can manifest itself in a sense of disjunction, a sense that something is wrong with oneself. This despairing untruth, as Kierkegaard's later pseudonym Anti-Climacus describes it in *The Sickness Unto Death*, is not willing to be the self that one is – or (what amounts to the same thing) willing to be a self one is not (SUD 52–3). This misrelation to the self is also a misrelation to God insofar as the self is fundamentally related to God – the self 'is' a set of relations with the relation to God being the most fundamental, as the power that establishes the self – as the one that made the self as it is and against which one rebels in rejecting oneself (SUD 60). The state of untruth is a loss of this God-relationship. As Climacus writes: 'It is really the God-relationship that makes a human being into a human being, but this is what he would lack' (CUP 244). It is being in a state of sin, of rebellion, of mutiny against God (CUP 208) – even to the extreme of the most self-conscious and wilful misrelation to oneself in 'demonic despair' that, 'in hatred toward existence, . . . wills to be itself, wills to be itself in accordance with its misery' (SUD 73).

Being True

Kierkegaard's Christian *theologia viatorum* is a progression from isolation to community, from fragmentation to wholeness, from sin to salvation, from illusion to reality, from untruth to truth. In the transition from untruth to truth, one must first recognize one's untruth. One must be willing to forgo the self-justification that breeds self-deception and confess one's own lack, one's guilt (TDIO 12, 15) – to be honest and transparent to oneself about one's untruth (TDIO 33; PIC 68). With this recognition of one's own untruth, one can be open to receiving the truth from elsewhere, to 'learn' it from another, from a true 'teacher' – not just to 'remember' it as something one had all along (PF *passim*). This is not an immanent enlightenment but being helped by another through a gift – by one who is higher that descends – by that which is beyond and so draws one up (PIC 159).[43]

In Kierkegaard's work, untruth can be seen as leading one indirectly to the truth. In Part Two of *Either/Or*, Judge Vilhelm seems to imply, when talking about ethical existence, that this is less a matter of choosing correctly than just earnestly choosing – of entering onto the ascending way in ethical truth. The important thing to note is that he (and Kierkegaard) does not stay with this subjectivistic stance that is interested in passion but not content. Choosing is rather a matter of getting engaged in existence, of starting to move. He writes: 'So even if a person chose what is wrong, he would still . . . discover what he had chosen is wrong' (EO 485–6). Because there is such a thing as a reality that we are in relation to that is beyond our choosing (a reality to the world, to ourselves, to God) – because there is such a reality, in choosing to live a certain way we are choosing to live a particular way in reality (not merely as a cerebrally contemplated possibility). Because of our being in relation to reality, choosing wrongly will have some effect on us, some kind of dissonance or feedback; we can come to know that the choice is wrong. When we choose and act we are not merely choosing and acting in our own virtual reality in which one can decide what is true – wrong choices probe reality and thus can lead us to truth. Living error can point – in its instructive failure – to the truth.[44]

It is this process of breakdown, the failure of a life-view (aesthetic, ethical, religious) to make sense of existence on its own terms, and making the transition (in faith) to a higher perspective that is the engine that moves the logic of movement, of ascent through the life-views or stages (the existence-spheres). The way that leads to the higher includes turning around – when one is moving in the wrong direction on the way. Kierkegaard writes that 'the road of error . . . leads to the good only in a lamentable way – namely, if the traveller turns around and goes back, for just as the good is only one thing, so all roads lead to the good, even the road of error – if the one

---

43 'What truly can be said to draw itself must be something higher, more noble, which draws the lower to itself – that is, truly to draw to itself is to draw upward, not to draw downward' (PIC 159).

44 It is telling that Judge Vilhelm likens A's writings (in Part One of *Either/Or*) to Ecclesiastes (EO 471).

who turned around goes back on the same road' (UDVS 25).[45] This
subjective way, put briefly, is that if one is properly subjectively oriented, then one is oriented toward finding the right content about
reality as well. 'If only it is altogether definite before God that this
person feels the need to believe', Kierkegaard writes, 'he will very
definitely find out what he is to believe' (CD 246). This is how 'all
things must serve for good those who love God' (CD 191) – this is
the 'unfathomable trustworthiness of the good' (UDVS 25) – that
the 'road of error' is experienced as 'lamentable' and so redirecting
one towards the good that one desires and seeks after.

'The relationship to truth, [humans] relating themselves to the
truth', Anti-Climacus writes, is 'the highest good' (SUD 42). This
fuller truth in Kierkegaard's thought is a transparency, a being in
line with reality – it is to be 'in absolute continuity with the reality one belongs to' (EO 541). Kierkegaard's understanding of truth
has to do with 'an actual relation to the world' (EUD 86). It is not
merely abstract, 'objective' thinking – it 'cannot be mere knowledge
about this world and about himself as a part of it' (EUD 86). The
concern, the desire of the inner being, the built-in orientation of
every human being (though we may defect from this – with dissonance), is for actual relation to the world, to the way things are in
reality.[46] When the pastor at the very end of *Either/Or* proclaims
'for only the truth that edifies is the truth for you' (EO 609), this
is based on a vision of the world that is one way and not another
– that being in accord with reality is thus edifying.

In subjective truth (and so ethico-religious and Christian being
in truth), the reality to which one relates is obstinate – it is the
'obstinacy of truth' that makes it so that *veritas est index sui et falsi*
[truth is the criterion of itself and of the false]' (SUD 42). It is thus
that Kierkegaard writes that 'existence is acoustic' – for being in
opposition to the way things are is not without a dissonant rejoin-
der (MLW 334). For subjective truth, 'to choose is the earnestness

---

45 'There are not, as in confusion, different roads and different truths and new
truths, but there are many roads leading to the one truth and each person walks his
own' (TDIO 38).

46 Thus, what is 'untrue' in the life of a mystic, for Judge Vilhelm, is that he
would 'disdain the existence, the reality, in which God has placed him' – isolating
himself and 'not heeding any relation with the given reality' his untruth is a 'deceit'
against the world and human others (EO 537–9).

of life' – but 'the choice, as the actual, is also restricted in many ways by actuality' (UDVS 248). Subjective engagement in life puts one into contact with that which can push back, as it were. 'So also with the good;' Kierkegaard writes, 'when it puts up with such a deceiver, it is as if it secretly said to him, "Well, have a jolly time with your deception, but just remember, we two will discuss this again"' (UDVS 41).

Truth for Kierkegaard is a matter of being true to one's being. The self has a reality that is independent of one's thoughts and desires – 'the self he is is a very definite something', writes Anti-Climacus, 'it remains itself from first to last; . . . it becomes neither more nor less than itself' (SUD 36, 69).[47] There is something that is 'the original text of individual human existence-relationships, the old familiar text handed down from the fathers' (CUP 629–30). One can either affirm and enter into one's nature, one's actuality or deny it. Truth is a matter of being (becoming) true to the actuality, that one is, 'the only actuality there is for an existing person' (CUP 316).[48] Because there is a reality to the self there is a standard for a proper relation to oneself. Thus Climacus writes: 'That subjectivity, inwardness, is truth . . . but, please note, not every inwardness' (CUP 282–3). One becomes true, becomes more fully actual, when one exists in relation to what one is. One's being, one's actuality, is that of an active relation, an 'existing in', an interestedness – a being-between, 'an inter-esse' (CUP 340, 314).[49] 'Subjectivity is truth; subjectivity is actuality' when one subjectively lives in accord with (one enters into the actuality of) one's actuality as a subject – which is itself a being-in-relation – and so becomes subjective, actual, true (CUP 343).

It is because there is a more-than-merely-subjective reality to our subjectivity that there can be a standard for how one is to be – a kind of intrinsic norm that this reality lays upon one. The proper way of being a self, for Kierkegaard, is to be *as* what one is – to

---

47 'Every human being is a psychical–physical synthesis intended to be spirit; this is the building, but he prefers to live in the basement, that is, in sensate categories' (SUD 43).

48 'All essential knowing pertains to existence' – it is a 'knowledge related to the knower', to the knower's being an existing individual (CUP 197).

49 'As soon as I begin to want to make my thinking teleological in relation to something else, interest enters the game' (CUP 319).

be true to what one is. 'In order to begin to be oneself', he writes, 'a human being first of all must . . . find out . . . what he himself is – in order to be that' (CD 39). Here, the prescription ('in order to be that') depends upon the description ('what he himself is'). One should will to be the self that one is – to live in accord with one's being. As Judge Vilhelm states: 'The I chooses itself – or, more correctly, it accepts itself' (EO 491).

Truth, for Kierkegaard, is becoming what one is.[50] To become subjective is to come to be as one is – 'a very praiseworthy task, a *quantum satis* [sufficient amount] for a human life' (CUP 163). The self's 'task is to become itself . . . to become concrete' (SUD 29–30).[51] In this, all human beings as human beings have 'the same essential task' (TDIO 38). This task, generally, is to conform one's living with one's understanding of one's nature such that for a given person there is a 'continuity with regard to his consciousness of himself' – a conscious and existential 'second nature' that is consonant with the first (SUD 105).

The self, for Kierkegaard (here Anti-Climacus), is 'a relation that relates itself to itself' (SUD 13). As such, it is, among other things, a synthesis of the necessary and the possible. Anti-Climacus writes: 'Insofar as it is itself, it is the necessary, and insofar as it has the task of becoming itself, it is a possibility' (SUD 35). The necessary is the reality of the self, that cannot be otherwise – 'the self he is is a very definite something and thus the necessary' (SUD 36). The necessary aspect of the self is 'that place' (SUD 36) that one is in which one becomes – chooses to relate to the self – possibly rightly, possibly wrongly. The possible is one's possible relation to one's necessary reality. With one's reflective consciousness (with the 'mirror of possibility'), one has freedom with regard to how one relates to oneself (SUD 37). Thus, one can 'become lost in possibility' (SUD 37) – one can conceive of and relate to oneself as other than one is (e.g. not in a fundamental relationship with God as one's origin and end). The proper (possible) relation to one's (necessary) self, the true relation is that of 'taking possibility back

---

50 'Through the decision in existence, an existing person, more specifically defined, has become what he is' (CUP 489).

51 Anti-Climacus writes, 'to venture wholly to become oneself, an individual human being, this specific individual human being, alone before God, alone in this prodigious strenuousness and this prodigious responsibility' (SUD 5).

into necessity' – living as (for one could live otherwise) what one is – of 'submit[ting] to the necessity in one's life', for this is what enables one to become a 'concrete' and actual self (as opposed to an unreal/illusory one) (SUD 36–7). By choosing the possible way of existing that is in accord with our necessary being, one becomes actual – thus, as Anti-Climacus writes, 'actuality is the unity of possibility and necessity' (SUD 36).

Truth is a relationship that could be otherwise, that is rooted in freedom. Thus, Vigilius Haufniensis writes: 'Viewed intellectually, the content of freedom is truth, and truth makes man free. For this reason, truth is the work of freedom, and in such a way that freedom constantly brings forth truth' (CA 138). Truth is not the same thing as reality. Truth is a right relationship to reality (classically, a relationship of correspondence). Freedom is involved inasmuch as the subject judging the truth is actively relating to the given reality (for one could judge the truth to be otherwise). However, beyond such a merely intellectual or 'objective' truth (as a relation of correspondence between one's thought and, say, external being), 'truth is for the particular individual only as he himself produces it in action. . . . [T]he question is whether a person will in the deepest sense acknowledge the truth, will allow it to permeate his whole being, will accept all its consequences' (CA 138).

Kierkegaard sees the more profound 'truth' of human existence as a correspondence between one's existing and one's being – between one's existence and one's essence, perhaps (CUP 190–3). Truth is an honesty – in 'that your life expresses what you say' (CD 167).[52] It is a process of becoming sober – as Kierkegaard writes, '*to come so close to oneself in one's understanding, in one's knowing, that all one's understanding becomes action*' (JFY 115).[53] 'Christianly understood', the goal is 'to be the truth' – and this is achieved when the truth 'becomes a life in me' (PIC 205–6). The truth is incarnated in the way one lives. Bringing all of this together powerfully, Anti-Climacus writes that 'to be the truth is the only true explanation of what truth is' (PIC 205). I quote at length:

---

52 The difficulty is that 'there is nothing as deceitful and as cunning as a human heart, resourceful in seeking escapes and finding excuses; and there surely is nothing as difficult and as rare as genuine honesty before God' (CD 185).

53 'According to Christianity, then, the only person who is completely sober is the person whose understanding is action' (JFY 120).

The being of truth is not the direct redoubling of being in relation to thinking, which gives only thought-being, safeguards thinking against being a brain-figment that is not, guarantees validity to thinking, that what is thought is – that is, has validity. No, the being of truth is the redoubling of truth within yourself, within me, within him, that your life, my life, his life expresses the truth approximately in the striving for it, that your life, my life, his life is approximately the being of the truth in the striving for it, just as the truth was in Christ a life, for he was the truth. (PIC 205)

Anti-Climacus concludes: 'The truth is the way', and 'being the truth is a life – and this is indeed how Christ speaks of himself: I am the Truth and the Way and the Life' (PIC 207).

This lived truth is its own best demonstration. Kierkegaard writes that 'the highest a person is capable of is to make [*gjøre*] an eternal truth true, to make it true that it is true – by doing [*gjøre*] it, by being oneself the demonstration, by a life that perhaps will also be able to convince others' (CD 98). Those who seek to show that Christianity is true in a purely intellectual manner are 'busy in a strange way in the wrong place' (CD 189) – for Christianity is to be true in life and should be shown forth as such, much in the way that 'the resolution of marriage is its own best recommendation' (SLW 156). Christian 'being true' is a making manifest, a concrete showing, of the truth of Christianity in life.[54]

---

54 This is behind Climacus's distinction between a 'doctrine' and an 'existence-communication': 'Understanding is the maximum with regard to a doctrine . . . With regard to an existence-communication, existing in it is the maximum' (CUP 371). 'Let us understand one another. Surely a philosophical theory that is to be comprehended and speculatively understood is one thing, and a doctrine that is to be actualized in existence is something else. . . . When this is now the case, and when, furthermore, it is the case that the nineteenth century is so frightfully speculative, it is to be feared that the word "doctrine" is immediately understood as a philosophical theory that is to be and ought to be comprehended. To avoid this mistake, I have chosen to call Christianity an existence-communication in order to designate very definitely how it is different from speculative thought' (CUP 379–80).

4

Imagination, Theology, Metaphysics

For Kierkegaard, one ascends through faiths (Chapter 2) to progressively higher 'truer' truths (Chapter 3). One climbs toward the higher, the broadest vision of reality. But in doing so, in the ascent of faith, one 'ascends' to the foundation – to the higher that suspends the lower. This suspension – this inverted, paradoxical founding from above[1] – yields the religious, and more specifically the Christian theological, vision as foundational for existence. This founding vision in Kierkegaard's work – the vista from the founding summit – is imaginative, theological, and – in a sense – metaphysical.

Imagination

The imagination plays a central role in Kierkegaard's understanding of thought in general, of the work of theology, and of Christian existence. Kierkegaard is unwilling to relegate the imagination to a secondary role, say behind thought or feeling or the will. While Climacus sees the imagination as 'coordinate', or equiprimordial, with the other faculties (thinking, feeling, will),[2] Anti-Climacus (the later pseudonym) goes so far as to give the imagination a priority – as 'the capacity *instar omnium* [for all capacities] ... the possibility of any and all reflection' (SUD 30–1). The imagination is 'a power that is the first condition for what becomes of a person' (PIC 186).

---

1 Climacus writes: 'humanly speaking, consequences built upon a paradox are built upon the abyss ... the whole thing is in suspense' (PF 98).

2 Climacus writes: 'With respect to existence, thinking is not at all superior to imagination and feeling but is coordinate. ... The task is not to elevate the one at the expense of the other, but the task is equality, contemporaneity, and the medium in which they are united is existing' (CUP 347–8).

Imagination, then, is a first enabling step. It performs something like a transcendental role – as a condition for the possibility of our thinking and living. Our imagination is the basis for what we see as possible, as thinkable and so is the basis for our possibilities for living. Our imagination tells us what can or cannot be so; it is the frame of the possible.[3] This is why, as Climacus explains, 'if actuality is to be understood by a third party, it must be understood as possibility' – 'ethically understood, if anything is able to stir up a person, it is possibility' (CUP 358, 360). If one wants to 'communicate' the fuller truth of an actual state of existence to another (a truth that they are), one must go about presenting the truth 'in the form of possibility' as a possibility, which they can choose to enter into, to become.[4] The imagination helps us to see, to envision, what may be, how we can dwell in the world – such that a restricted imagining limits the possibilities for existence – as Judge Vilhelm complains of the limited visions of the romance novels of his day, of romances culminating in marriage: 'what is pernicious and unhealthy about such writings' is 'that they end where they should begin' (EO 392) – they are no help in enabling us to imagine and so live in the ethical relationship of marriage (which seems to be what is celebrated as the end-goal in the story), because married life is not depicted, not imagined. The imaginative depiction enables one to try a way of being on, as it were, to see what it would be like if such and such was the case and I lived as if this was so. We imagine ourselves as participating in a given reality as a possibility before we do so (FT 32). This is what Kierkegaard himself does, for example, in Johannes de Silentio's use of stories to make the movements of faith imaginable in *Fear and Trembling* (FT 88ff.). It is in this way that a developed imagination (as a potential value of the aesthetic) is a 'presupposition' for an ethical existence, as the ethical is a presupposition for the religious (SLW 430).

For Kierkegaard, the task of imagination, and so the task of the

---

3 'In order for a person to become aware of his self and of God, imagination must raise him higher than the miasma of probability, it must tear him out of this and teach him to hope and to fear – or to fear and to hope – by rendering possible that which surpasses the *quantum satis* [sufficient amount] of any experience' (SUD 41).

4 This is part of what distinguishes an indirect 'existence-communication' from a more direct communication (CUP 358).

poet, is to bring to mind, to make aware, to illuminate, to depict, to make visible (FT 15).[5] Because the fullest 'truth', for Kierkegaard, is not merely a set of propositions but a way of living, imagination is necessary to show and communicate this truth-as-lived (EUD 112–13). Kierkegaard often (for example EUD, FT) takes scriptural statements and, rather than simply depicting the existential fulfilment or incarnation of a given command (for example), imaginatively explores alternative situations where the idea is not, or is only partially, incarnated in life; he imaginatively constructs alternatives in order to help one understand, to throw into relief, the true idea (for example EUD 115ff.). The goal is to evoke a coherent perspective on life – 'a world-view, a life-view' (BoA 8, 16) – to imaginatively bring a world into existence for one (JC 120).

Imagination enables reflection as the second moment of consciousness; it 'is the possibility of any and all reflection' (SUD 31). Imagination is then the fostering nest, the enabling frame for metaphysics and dogmatics as 'presupposed' by ethics (CA 21, 24). The metaphysical and then dogmatic understandings of reality are imaginative world-views that orient one for life's journey. They are reflections funding renewed and meaningful re-engagement with life after reflection.

In Kierkegaard's work, the imagination – as enabling thinking of and living in reality – should be understood in contradistinction to the fantastic – as an escape from reality (EO 386–7). The fantastic, Anti-Climacus writes, is 'generally that which leads a person out into the infinite in such a way that it only leads him away from himself and thereby prevents him from coming back to himself' (SUD 31). The fantastic is a distortion of the imagination – imagination that has become unmoored from reality. The deficient imagination is an escape from reality rather than the proper imagination that functions to enable existing, entering into the real world. In the same way, a deficient metaphysics yields mere speculation, mere abstraction, rather than a proper metaphysics that functions to enable ethics – as its presupposition. In the same way, a deficient theology yields mere abstract doctrine rather than the

---

5 Kierkegaard writes of the stories in *Fear and Trembling*, Problemata III as serving 'to illuminate Abraham, not to explain Abraham directly' (FT 263 sup). Likewise, Kierkegaard writes about *Repetition*: 'I wanted to depict and make visible psychologically and esthetically' (R 302 sup).

proper dogmatics that functions to enable the Christian life. The problem is reflection that does not return to immediacy – imagination, metaphysics and theology that do not issue forth in action, in a life. Imagination (and so metaphysics and theology) is never an end in itself for Kierkegaard – it is a reflective second moment allowing one to step back and survey and evaluate one's life from the perspective of a world that is larger than one's present, immediate experience (in the first moment). Imagination does not, on its own, yield the actual.[6] It is to be a means toward deliberate existence, preceding and enabling the third moment of re-engagement, of immediacy after reflection. Thus the imaginary has a 'being-in-between' (CUP 264).

Founding Theological Vision

Kierkegaard saw his imaginative work as a writer as that of presenting a vision of what it is to be a Christian (PoV 88). As a religious poet, as 'a life-view philosopher', he sought to imagine the world in order that people may then exist in it (R 310 sup). This imaginative project includes theology and metaphysics that serve this end (rather than merely abstract, 'fantastic' theology and metaphysics) – of representing the real world in order to dwell in it. The theology (which we will treat first) which is positive is a 'dogmatics' that is part of the double-reflection – as part of a reflective moment that enables an engagement in life – rather than the more negative 'doctrine' as fixating on the reflective, intellectual moment. Theology makes the real world imaginable – making the unimagined or the unimaginable imaginable – so that one may live in it.

In Kierkegaard's work, Christian theology – or Christian dogmatics or the Christian 'world-view' (CUP 75) – is presented as a guiding vision for human life (a *theologia viatorum*). Human existence, for Kierkegaard, needs a guiding vision – a life-view or world-

---

6 Climacus writes: 'No, however great the efforts of the imagination to make this imagined image actual, it cannot do it. If it could do that, then with the help of the imagination a person could experience exactly the same as in actuality, could live through it in exactly the same way as if he lived through it in actuality, could learn to know himself as accurately and fundamentally as in the experience of actuality – then there would be no meaning in life. In that case, Governance would have structured life wrongly, for to what purpose, then, actuality if with the help of the imagination one could in advance absorb it in a completely actual way' (PIC 188).

view that provides one with a coherent perspective on life (BoA 8). The human passions are guided by more determinate thoughts and words (TDIO 16). In everyone's soul, there is 'a longing like that of erotic love . . . a longing, a wish, that craves . . . a guide and teacher in life' (TDIO 58) – and 'the world never seems to be short of guides' (TDIO 60) – 'the most diverse prototypes appear and disappoint and reappear' (TDIO 59). The Christian claims to be the one guide (after the one Prototype) that is sure and does not disappoint.

The higher and the lower

More generally, Kierkegaard sees the religious as the highest and broadest perspective on life – the final frame advancing beyond, transcending and yet, in some sense, including the earlier stages (the aesthetic and the ethical) as 'presuppositions' (SLW 430, 435).[7] The earlier stages display the 'despair' characteristic of 'any life-view with its condition outside it' and so need to be recentred on what is the ontological, metaphysical centre, on God (EO 531). In the religious, however, one comes to understand and choose oneself in God – to bind oneself to an eternal power – and so 'one receives oneself . . . when in an eternal and unfailing sense one becomes aware of oneself as the person one is' (EO 508). The fundamental place of religiousness is that of orienting us to that which is stable, unchanging, eternal and so orienting us to our own identity and being from that perspective. This is part of what is meant (in the last part of *Either/Or*) by 'always being in the wrong before God' – for the religious, it is God who is the centre, the true to which all else is to be in conformity – we change in order to be true to the eternal reality not vice versa.[8] The religious consciousness is 'a sacred bond that knit humankind together' without which life

---

7 The religious is presented as making sense of the other spheres. As an odd example of this, in *Either/Or* Part One, the 'immediate erotic stages' can be seen, from the perspective of the religious, as a kind of parody of the progression of the spheres to the religious, as having some of the same themes – save the highest sphere is the opposite of the religious, or Christianity, more specifically.

8 Always being in the wrong before God is to be 'hidden in God'. 'This', the pastor at the end of *Either/Or* writes, 'is your divine worship, your religious devotion, your reverence for God' (EO 605); it is 'a proof that your love is happy as is only that love with which one loves God' (EO 606).

would be a lurking ravenous oblivion, 'empty and devoid of consolation' (FT 15). De Silentio writes that it is 'precisely for that reason it [the non-religious perspective] is not so'; it is taken for granted (here) that life is not ultimately cruel and meaningless (FT 15). The religious perspective is a 'higher rationality' above the 'purely human' (FT 262).

The relation of the higher spheres of existence to the lower, in Kierkegaard's work, is that of a teleological suspension, a negating of the lower sphere as absolute and yet an affirmation of it as decentred, as properly located. In *Either/Or*, in relation to the aesthetic sphere, it is shown how the lower sphere cannot hold together on its own, cannot be consistently lived. For the aesthete, other human beings are defined in relation to the aesthete, they are mere functions of the self (like the solar system with Don Giovanni as the sun and all else in darkness) (EO 125). Yet the aesthete cannot both isolate himself from others and use them for his pleasure at the same time; the Seducer who would reduce human others to objects, cannot do without them. See also A's (the aesthetic author of *Either/Or* Part One) speeches to the *Symparanekronenoi*, in which he puts himself in the awkward position of celebrating the persistence of their society that exists, in part, to revel in the lack of persistence, perseverance, continuity in life (EO 167) – the very being and existence of that which wants to deny being and persistence belies, undercuts its denial. The aesthetic operations, even as distortions, in their operation and ability attest to a larger enabling community or endowment – to that which fuels and makes possible self-dissolution – that there was something there, even if wasted, dissipated, distorted – even if coming to a disabled standstill. The aesthete focuses on the fugitive present moment to the exclusion of what sustains it until the present moment disappears, is lost, is emptied out (EO 394–5). Even the aberrant, nihilist, disordered, fleeting desire of the aesthete is only possible inasmuch as it is suspended from a larger order, in something other than its own narcissistic perspective. This is all to say that the aesthetic is presented as teleologically suspended in the higher spheres, in the ethical and the religious. In choosing the higher, one also gets the lower; with the ethical the aesthetic returns truly, as Judge Vilhelm writes: 'only then life is beautiful', only then does one gain 'the whole world' (EO 491–2). The lower immediacy of the aesthetic is repeated, is 'taken up again' (*Gjentagelse*) and 'assumed into a higher concentricity' (EO 403, 406; R 329).

Likewise, the ethical, as the lower, is teleologically suspended in and from the religious, as the higher. Abraham, de Silentio writes, 'transgressed the ethical altogether and had a higher τέλος outside it, in relation to which he suspended it' (FT 59). The religious person 'determines his relation to the universal' – the domain of the ethical – 'by his relation to the absolute' – to God, the domain of the religious (FT 70). The universal, the ethical is not abandoned as such, it is determined, located, relativized in relation to the absolute, to God. Whereas in the movement of infinite resignation, one suspends, renounces the finite world including the concerns of ethical life, in the second movement of faith one is the 'reconciled with existence', one affirms the world, the finite, the ethical as suspended, as dependent upon God 'from whence come all good gifts' (FT 43, 49, 46–50).

From the perspective of the higher, the lower is reconciled, is included, *aufgehoben*, suspended in the higher. The relation of the higher to the lower is a 'both/and': the ethical is both ethical and aesthetic, the religious is religious and ethical and aesthetic. The higher from the perspective of the lower, however, is discontinuous. The lower cannot understand the higher, cannot 'get a perspective' on it (FT 33). The lower speaks of the higher in a 'thieves' jargon', in a lesser, derived way of speaking that sees things in a distorted manner (JFY 114). To the lower, the higher manifests itself as the absurd, as a 'negative sign', as 'speaking in a strange tongue' (FT 262, 119). The lower's relation to the higher is an 'either/or' (FT 19–20); the transition from the lower to the higher is not automatic, but a real transition, a leap. One approaches the higher as a Mount Sinai or a Mount Moriah 'whose peak towers sky-high' – as a challenging height – 'with a *horror religiosus*' (FT 61) – such that one must undergo a breakdown, a constructive 'nihilism', a coming to nothing, for 'only when the individual has emptied himself in the infinite, only then has the point been reached where faith can break through' (FT 69).[9] As de Silentio puts it, only one who works

---

9 See William Desmond's thoughts on breakdown and breakthrough described in Christopher Ben Simpson, *Religion, Metaphysics, and the Postmodern: William Desmond and John D. Caputo* (Bloomington: Indiana University Press, 2009), pp. 39–42.

gets bread; one in the lower must endure the difficult, the trial, the either/or, the 'absurd' to attain the higher (and regain the lower) (FT 27). Taken together, the lower's transition to the higher and the incorporation of the lower into the higher, there is manifest in Kierkegaard's works a logic of 'both either/or and both/and'. One must choose (either/or) between the lower and the higher, between Mammon and God, but for the one who chooses the higher, who seeks first the kingdom of God, the lower is regained, reconciled, renewed as a new creation (both/and) – all these things added.

The truth of the religious generally and the truth of the Christian faith more specifically is evident in its ability to out-narrate lesser perspectives, to include them in itself in a manner that makes more sense of them than they can of it. The mode of argumentation is not to demonstrate Christianity by means of straightforward proofs but of 'assuming' the truth of Christianity and then showing how Christianity understands itself and other perspectives in a superior manner (CUP 15).[10] With regard to Christianity (as it is with any 'higher' position) there is a conflict between the lower, 'immanent' frame and that which exceeds it such that the higher is seen as paradoxical, as absurd. The higher cannot be demonstrated from the perspective of the lower. One 'begins' with a new fundamental, starting place (such as the incarnation) that can only be achieved through faith (PIC 96). In this approach, in this 'out-narration', the best perspective is the one that is shown to be the broadest and most coherent (the most inclusive, the one with the most explanatory power) in the long run (BoA 88, *passim*).[11] The truth is shown in its

---

10 This method can be seen as abductive or retroductive in C. S. Peirce's sense. The demonstration comes afterward. In abduction or retroduction there is 'a surrender to the insistence of an idea. . . . We must throw open our gates and admit it, at any rate for the time being' ('The First Rule of Logic' in *The Essential Peirce*, Vol. 2, Bloomington: Indiana University Press, p. 47). A hypothesis is presented, 'itself an experiment' ('The First Rule of Logic', p. 46), which is then examined to the degree to which it 'is likely in itself, and renders the fact likely' ('On the Logic of Drawing History from Ancient Documents' in *The Essential Peirce*, Vol. 2, p. 95).

11 One can see this mode of argumentation at work in the writings of John Milbank and William Desmond. Indeed, Kierkegaard's approach coheres with so-called Radical Orthodoxy's claim that there is no 'objective', neutral, secular perspective from which one can then judge the merits of religion, of Christianity. This perspective is but one of many perspectives vying for superiority; its objectivity is an illusion. The theologically narrated world is presented as the true world from which one can then explain, can out-narrate the secular. One might say, after Anti-

own coherence – as including accounts of other perspectives – thus, as Vigilius Haufniensis writes, 'orthodoxy . . . is correct when it explains itself more precisely' (CA 93).[12] The religious answers the question of 'meaning in life', of 'returning to himself again, whole in every respect' (CA 106). This is part of Kierkegaard's 'new science of arms', an indirect communication engaging the imagination by presenting alternative imaginative frames rather than simply the inductive or deductive proofs of traditional apologetics, the 'old science of arms' (PoV 52–3).[13]

Theology as foundational

For Kierkegaard, faith founds dogmatics, which in turn founds Christian existence. Faith, as 'constantly being acquired', as 'continually being generated' – faith beyond which one cannot go without negating faith – provides the foundation for dogmatics (EUD 14, 27). Dogmatics as Kierkegaard's term for revealed theology is 'faith's understanding' inasmuch as faith is the 'organ' and 'point of departure' for dogmatics (PIC 78; CA 18; TERE 58; SUD 96). In turn, in *The Concept of Anxiety*, Vigilius Haufniensis presents dogmatics as the basis for what he calls a 'second ethics' – an ethics, a way of existing, based on Christian theology. This second ethics – this 'new ethics' that 'presupposes' or 'begins with' dogmatics – is the 'new science . . . that has as a task for actuality the dogmatic consciousness of actuality' (CA 20). Whereas, traditionally, ethics ('first ethics') was based on metaphysics ('first philosophy'), dogmatics has the corresponding place of a '*secunda philosophia*', a second philosophy which is 'that totality of science whose essence

---

Climacus, that 'the secularization of everything' is, in the end, nothing more than yet another (idolatrous) power-play seeking to hide under a veil of legitimization its nature as one perspective among many – it is 'the deification of the established order' (PIC 91).

12 Thus, the 'essential author' is one that has a more coherent perspective, worldview, narrative (BoA 3–18).

13 Traditional apologetics, for Kierkegaard, in its attempt 'to defend Christianity', ends up 'making Christianity out to be some poor, miserable thing', for 'to defend something is always to disparage it' (SUD 87). The truth, for Kierkegaard, needs no defence. It is rather the attacker; it locates the lesser perspectives, shows them to lack coherence, to lack existential viability (CD 162); as Anti-Climacus writes: 'the enthusiasm of faith is not a defense – no, it is attack and victory; a believer is a victor' (SUD 87).

is transcendence or repetition' (CA 21). Here, for Kierkegaard, theology or dogmatics specifically takes the place and the function of metaphysics; metaphysics is *aufgehoben* – relativized, appropriated, reconfigured – in theology.[14] Haufniensis writes: 'The first ethics presupposes metaphysics; the second ethics presupposes dogmatics but completes it also in such a way that here, as everywhere, the presupposition is brought out' (CA 24). There is a relationship here of mutual dependence inasmuch as second ethics presupposes dogmatics – is founded on a theological vision of reality – and dogmatics is completed, fulfilled by second ethics, which 'brings out' the 'presupposition' of dogmatics by expressing it in actuality, in existence. (From this perspective in *The Concept of Anxiety*, Chapters 5 and 6 of the present work are intended to be a presentation of Kierkegaard's dogmatics, his theological world-view, while Chapter 7 is to be that of Kierkegaard's second ethics, the true way to be in the true world.)

Climacus states that 'Christianity is not a doctrine' (CUP 379). This is a strategic choice of terminology for Climacus, by which he means Christianity is not merely 'a philosophical theory' that is only to engage the intellect.[15] Kierkegaard does not reject theology or theological reflection. As we have seen, Vigilius Haufniensis (before CUP) affirms the necessary place of dogmatics for Christian life. Furthermore, Kierkegaard, in the unfinished *Book on Adler* (written just after CUP) presents 'doctrine' as simply that which is revealed, dropping the negative associations present in the *Postscript* (BoA 181–7).

The foundational place of dogmatics in Kierkegaard's work is due to the divinely revealed and therefore authoritative nature of its content (BoA 3–4). The 'heterogeneous originality of dogmatics' is that it is revealed (CA 19; BoA 181–7). For Kierkegaard, transcendence, revelation and authority come together as a unit in that, as he writes, 'authority is a specific quality that enters from somewhere else and qualitatively asserts itself', whereas 'in the sphere of immanence, authority is utterly unthinkable, or it is only as transi-

---

14 See a similar mapping of disciplines in *Johannes Climacus* (JC 152–3).

15 'It is to be feared that the word "doctrine" is immediately understood as a philosophical theory that is to be and ought to be comprehended. To avoid this mistake, I have chosen to call Christianity an existence-communication in order to designate very definitely how it is different from speculative thought' (CUP 380).

tory' (BoA 180). It is because dogma is divinely revealed, is 'hetero-geneous' to our immanent frames of reference, that it both must be accepted by faith ('must be believed, because it is a dogma') and functions as authoritative in the life of the believer (SUD 96).[16] This is the basis for Christianity's claim to absoluteness and Christian theology's claim to a place of supremacy (PIC 62).

As foundational to Christian existence, Christian theology has a distinctive content. Against 'naturalizing Christianity', making Christianity into something that is either without content or so general it is something everyone already believes – something like belief in belief in general – 'so that in the end to be a Christian and to be a human being are identical' (CUP 367) – against this evacu-ation of Christianity, Kierkegaard takes a definite, militant stance that 'Christianity's meaning' is such that one who 'is to have his life in such decisiveness, is to confess so definitely and publicly what he wants, what he believes and hopes, that it is impossible for all to speak well of him' (CD 230).[17] 'For a person to be a Christian', Kierkegaard writes, while personal involvement is essential, 'it cer-tainly is required [as well] that what he believes is a definite some-thing' (CD 244).[18] The *credo* of Christian belief must have both the personal, the 'I believe', and content, a 'creed'. This theological content of Christian dogmatics – the 'objective qualification of the essentially Christian' (BoA 118) – is the 'essentially Christian' that 'exists before any Christian exists; it must exist in order for one to become a Christian' (BoA 117). Christianity 'maintains its object-ive continuance outside all believers, while it also is in the inward-ness of the believer' such that 'if the essentially Christian enters into the hearts of ever so many believers, every believer realizes that it did not arise in his heart' (BoA 118).[19] The Christian then

---

16 'Every science lies either in a logical immanence or in an immanence within a transcendence that it is unable to explain' (CA 50).

17 Kierkegaard writes: '*I know what Christianity is* . . . That I have understood the truth I am presenting – of that I am absolutely convinced' (PoV 15, 25).

18 Kierkegaard continues: 'To the same degree that one gives the appearance that it will be very difficult to make definite what it is that a person is to believe, to the same degree one leads people away from faith' (CD 244).

19 'One does not become a Christian by being religiously moved by something higher; and not every outpouring of religious emotion is a Christian outpouring. In other words, emotion that is Christian is controlled by conceptual definitions, and when deep emotion is transformed into or expressed in words in order to be com-

needs to understand, to some degree, the content of theology – 'to acquire proficiency in the language of Christian concepts' (BoA 111). Dogmatics, Christian theology, for Kierkegaard, is concerned with 'the clarification of Christian concepts', with instruction, with the removing of illusions (MLW 10, 106; BoA 113).[20]

The limits and perils of theology

While Kierkegaard affirms the constructive and indeed necessary role of theology, of dogmatics, in Christian existence, he is careful to caution theologians against hubristic overreaching. 'Under various names and right up to the latest speculative thought', Kierkegaard writes, 'the effort has been to make Christianity probable, comprehensible, to take it out of the God-language of the paradox and get it translated into the Low-German of speculative thought or the Enlightenment' (BoA 40). Against this tendency, Kierkegaard contends that the foundation of theology for humans (as long as it is a *theologia viatorum*) will always be faith and not our own self-founding and self-justifying comprehension. Such human comprehension lacks the proper frame to grasp the objects of Christian faith (PIC 96).[21] The Christian should thus be concerned with 'keeping watch so that the gulf of qualitative difference between God and man may be maintained as it is in the paradox and faith' (SUD 99). In thinking about God, Christ, sin and human salvation, Christianity has at its foundation 'an utter mystery' that is affirmed in faith (CUP 213).[22] Kierkegaard writes that 'all our language about God is, naturally, human language. However much we try to preclude misunderstanding by in turn revoking what we say – if we do not

---

municated, this transformation must continually take place within the conceptual definitions' (BoA 113).

20 Kierkegaard writes of the value of 'a clarity about and a deft drilling in individual dogmatic concepts that usually are perhaps not so easily obtained' (BoA 3). It is likely in response to this perceived need that Kierkegaard wanted to write a book on dogmatics that is the unpublished *Book on Adler* (BoA 6).

21 Kierkegaard writes: 'To *believe* is to believe the divine and the human together in Christ. To *comprehend* him is to comprehend his life humanly. But to comprehend his life *humanly* is so far from being more than believing that it means to lose him if there is not believing in addition, since his life is what it is for faith, the *divine*–human' (TERE 65).

22 Anti-Climacus writes that 'sin cannot be thought' (SUD 119).

wish to be completely silent, we are obliged to use human criteria when we, as human beings, speak about God' (CD 291). Theology, talk about God, while necessary for the Christian, is limited by our finite human language and thinking. In theology, our language 'seems to burst and break in order to describe' the things of God – our 'words sound very strange' (CD 292, 17).[23]

The other possible failure of theology, for Kierkegaard, is the failure to see the Christian existence, Christian being-in-the-truth, as the proper end of theology. Theology is less a mere 'doctrine' (in Climacus's lexicon) – for which the 'maximum' is 'understanding' – than an 'existence-communication' – whose 'maximum' is 'existing' (CUP 371). 'Surely a philosophical theory', Climacus writes (to quote him again), 'that is to be comprehended and speculatively understood is one thing, and a doctrine that is to be actualized in existence is something else' (CUP 379). Christianity is not just something impersonal and objective, an opinion, a teaching to be comprehended – Christian theology is to be a *theologia viatorum*, to be a foundation and guide for our personal and subjectively involved existence (PIC 106, 141; FSE 35–44). When this mistaken inversion takes place – when theology tries to model itself after a purely speculative philosophy, theology, as de Silentio puts it, 'sits all rouged and powdered in the window and courts its favor, offers its charms to philosophy' (FT 32)[24] – theology has lost its way, has lost fidelity to its purpose as leading one on the way.

A Kind of Metaphysician

Kierkegaard vs 'metaphysics'

Kierkegaard, as a rule, does not have nice things to say about philosophy in general and 'metaphysics' in particular. What, specifically, he is attacking is metaphysics in a restricted sense, a deficient

---

23 Kierkegaard presents Frater Taciturnus, who recovers/creates Quidam, who recounts Nebuchadnezzar. who tells of this vision: 'And an astronomer shall be led through the streets and be dressed as an animal, and he shall carry with him his reckonings, shredded like a bundle of hay' (SLW 362–3). A theologian, thinking of that which is transcendent, though he does not abandon his reckonings (such as they are), is such a humble astronomer.

24 This a quite a reversal: from philosophy as theology's handmaid to theology as philosophy's whore.

metaphysics, as we said before, that yields mere speculation, mere abstraction, rather than a proper metaphysics that functions to enable ethics, as its presupposition. The target (broadly) of Kierkegaard's critique of objectivity, metaphysics, philosophy, the system is not objectivity, metaphysics, philosophy or systematic as such, but rather when they (perhaps all too commonly) get a little too full of themselves (as being after all human enterprises) and go off the rails by denying that which they are dependent upon and which they are to serve – human existence.[25] (Metaphysics was made for man, not man for metaphysics, perhaps.) There are several interrelated charges that Kierkegaard brings against 'metaphysics' – ways in which it loses its way, or ceases to help us on ours.

'Metaphysics', for Kierkegaard, serves to escape from or to deny actuality and, in so doing, removes one from the realm of human existence. The 'metaphysical' can focus on abstraction and so 'flee' concrete reality or see it as an illusion (EO 541). In wanting 'to permeate everything with the thought of eternity and necessity' – in wanting an immanent, self-justifying comprehension – this kind of metaphysics loses sight of actuality, which, for Kierkegaard, is neither purely eternal nor purely necessary (JC 142). Kierkegaard coordinates this kind of metaphysics with the aesthetic sphere, in that, for both the 'scientific' speculator (with her idle speculation) and the capricious 'love-struck fool' (with his idle living), the realms of thought and action are not integrated, not grounded in a vision of existential actuality; both are merely interested in the interesting (EO 385). Kierkegaard also seems to think that metaphysical speculation, as a human way of being, is so disengaged from existence that it is beneath the aesthetic. 'The metaphysical', Frater Taciturnus writes, 'is abstraction, and there is no human being who exists metaphysically. The metaphysical, the ontological, is [*er*], but it does not exist . . . it is the abstraction from or a *prius* [something prior] to the esthetic, the ethical, the religious' (SLW 476).[26]

---

25 Kierkegaard's target seems to be what Desmond calls the univocal (fixing on the immediate sameness between thought and being) and the dialectical (as a developing mediation that reduces all difference to unity and sameness) senses of being. See William Desmond, *Being and the Between* (Albany, NY: SUNY Press, 1995).

26 Climacus echoes his fellow pseudonym: 'Neither is there any individual who exists metaphysically' (CUP 122).

Building on its disengagement from existence, 'metaphysics', for Kierkegaard, proves to be deficient ethically as well. Abstract metaphysics, 'the system', as not concerned with lived human existence is not concerned with the ethical concerns of one involved in existence (SLW 446). The ethical affirms a fundamental reality to the world (it is metaphysical in the broader sense I will suggest) and affirms it toward the end of concretely 'entering into it' (EO 541). Kierkegaard is critical in 'reference to the thesis that metaphysics as such is disinterested', for, Vigilius Haufniensis writes, 'as soon as interest steps forth, metaphysics steps aside' (CA 18). Ethical involvement, engagement, interest stands in opposition to such 'metaphysical disinterestedness', to such 'parenthetical' thoughtlessness (SLW 446; BoA 34–5) – to the extent that Climacus battles against 'the system . . . fighting and cutting through in order to find the way back' to the simple, to becoming a Christian (PoV 94; CUP 155).

Finally, there can be a religious confusion about metaphysics. This confusion arises from not respecting the difference between the kind of metaphysics that works purely from within the frame of immanent rationality and theology or dogmatics that is based on revelation and faith, reducing the latter (transcendent revealed theology) to the former (immanent speculation). This is the mistake that happens 'when metaphysics and dogmatics are distorted by treating dogmatics metaphysically and metaphysics dogmatically' (CA 59). It is thus that 'faith begins precisely where thought stops' (FT 53). Christian faith, as ever attended by risk, as always accompanied by 'the dialectical', keeps things from being too 'firm and fixed', helps one avoid a false triumphalism built upon the false foundations of a metaphysics that is not concerned with the difficulties of human existence or with the transcendence of God or with the paradox of the God-man (CUP 34–5).

Kierkegaard as metaphysician

Kierkegaard's rejection of metaphysics is not a simple rejection. It is rather the first step in an appropriation – a teleological suspension (an *Aufhebung*) in which metaphysics is decentred (as a self-founding, comprehensive and abstract enterprise unto itself) and recentred or located in the midst of existence – in relation to the ethical, the religious, the Christian. Kierkegaard's thought is metaphysical in a broader sense; he is a kind of metaphysician, even if he rejects metaphysics as something with the more restricted meaning outlined above.

For Kierkegaard, actuality is a reality beyond appearances, in that, as Anti-Climacus writes, 'however great the efforts of the imagination to make this imagined image actual, it cannot do it' (PIC 188).[27] This can be seen in his affirmation of a metaphysical order – that reality has a certain stable and universal order. For Kierkegaard, the cosmos is an orderly whole; there is 'an order in the world' and 'a law within [humans] also' (EO 61; EUD 84) reminiscent of Kant's starry skies above and moral law within. Reality is not merely a chaotic flux, 'a passing through in the continuous process in which nothing abides' (CUP 33). There is an eternity to which this changeable world is ordered, that gives life order, such that faith orders us to that which orders the world. As God creates the world and the world is dependent upon, suspended from and ordered by and to God, so does our faith in God found our relation to the world as so created, dependent, suspended, ordered (EUD 24). As Anti-Climacus writes: 'The physician has a defined and developed conception of what it is to be healthy and ascertains a man's condition accordingly' (SUD 23). There is an objective reality to the self, to what one is – it is not merely the product of subjective projection.[28]

The broader understanding of metaphysics that one finds in Kierkegaard can be seen as what William Desmond calls a metaxological metaphysics. The metaxological (from the Greek *metaxu*, between) is a 'fourth' beyond univocal simple unity, equivocal unmediatable difference and dialectical self-mediating unity. As a step beyond, as a redeeming of the dialectic (such as is evident in Kierkegaard as well), the metaxological sees being as a community of different singularities in relation to each other – not a univocal or

---

27 He continues: 'If it could do that, then with the help of the imagination a person could experience exactly the same as in actuality, could live through it in exactly the same way as if he lived through it in actuality, could learn to know himself as accurately and fundamentally as in the experience of actuality – then there would be no meaning in life' (PIC 188).

28 'The physician, precisely because he is a physician (well informed), does not have complete confidence in what a person says about his condition' (SUD 23).

dialectical monism, nor an equivocal dispersed utter plurality.[29] It is not that Kierkegaard explicitly shares (anachronistically) Desmond's concept of metaphysics, but that Desmond's metaphysics is compatible with Kierkegaard's thought such that Kierkegaard's thought can be constructively rendered in Desmond's terms – as metaxological – and this against Desmond's own version of Kierkegaard as individualist, irrationalist, acosmist, anti-philosophical.[30] There is a strong similarity between the metaxological and Kierkegaard's understanding of repetition: both present a dialectic that allows for transcendence, genuine difference and genuine movement, not penultimate difference on the way to an ultimate immanent unity. Repetition, Constantin Constantius writes, is 'the new category' which 'precisely explains the relation between the Eleatics and Heraclitus, and that repetition proper is what is mistakenly called mediation' – as the metaxological presents the 'relation between' the univocal (sameness) and the equivocal (difference) that the dialectical (the same Hegelian 'mediation' that Kierkegaard refers to) misunderstands (R 148). When Vigilius Haufniensis sees 'mediation' as possibly meaning both 'the relation between the two and the result', the former (the relation 'between' rather than the unified result) can be seen as the metaxological (CA 11). For both Desmond and Kierkegaard, the best metaphysics must attend to the *inter-esse*, the being-between (as changing, as in relation) of being. It is thus that we can read that: 'Repetition is the interest [*Interesse*] of metaphysics and also the interest upon which metaphysics comes to grief' (R 149). To deal properly with actuality as involving difference, relation, freedom and transcendence (especially from a religious frame) – as involving both flux and stability, without reducing one to the other – we need another metaphysics, a metaphysics other than univocal or dialectical metaphysics as the dominant but not exclusive modes of Western metaphysics hitherto. We need a metaphysics of the between of being (*interesse*), a metaxological metaphysics.[31]

---

29 For an introduction to and explication of Desmond's metaphysics, see Chapter 2 of my *Religion, Metaphysics, and the Postmodern*.

30 '(Kierkegaard, less so)' (William Desmond, *Is There a Sabbath for Thought?* Bronx, NY: Fordham University Press, 2005, p. 18).

31 I will make reference to Kierkegaard's thought in terms of Desmond's metaxological metaphysics throughout the rest of this work.

Veritas: The Truth is the Way

The proper function of metaphysics in human existence, in Kierkegaard's *theologia viatorum*, is that of orienting us toward reality so that we might come to live in accord with reality, to be true. Metaphysics plays a part in guiding us on life's way. For example, in life we must deliberate, we must weigh in order to choose which way we should go. This necessary task of deliberation is guided, either overtly or tacitly, by some understanding of the way the world is, what we are and the place of God – in short, a metaphysic (EUD 187–8). Deliberation, Kierkegaard writes, 'ultimately states what is essential about human nature, states its composition and its preeminence' – that it involves a relation between the temporal and the eternal (UDVS 307). To deliberate (*overveie*) is to weigh (*veie*) these relative magnitudes: 'The basic meaning of human deliberating is to weigh the temporal against the eternal; in all other human deliberating this basic meaning must be present' (UDVS 309). Deliberation in human existence is based on a broader metaphysical frame of the relation between the temporal and the eternal.

The proper use of 'sagacity' – of 'the power of thought' in general – is not to escape from or to ignore one's life, but is its being used 'inwardly: in order to prevent all evasions and thereby to help himself out and to keep himself out in the decision', to help, 'in the service of truth', one to be aware of what is happening within and without that they may 'will the good in truth' (UDVS 93–4; CD 28). Such an orientation for metaphysics makes it 'another kind of knowledge' of 'concerned truths' – that has to do with 'the relation of knowledge to himself' – 'that does not remain as knowledge . . . but is transformed into action' (EUD 86, 233). One's knowledge has to be linked to 'an actual relation to the world', to the way things are; it is to be 'about the meaning the world has for him and he for the world, about what meaning everything within him by which he himself belongs to the world has for him and he therein for the world' and thus 'cannot be mere knowledge about this world and about himself as a part of it' (EUD 86). Metaphysics thus plays a part for the 'subjective thinker' being 'a thinking person' who 'thinks the universal' – who is interested in the nature of reality, human being, etc. – but is also 'essentially interested in his own thinking, is existing in it', in living in the world as she has come to understand it (CUP 73–4, 351).

The place of metaphysics in involved, ethical existence, for Kierkegaard, is that of a presupposition to be appropriated. These are the two moments of the double-movement or 'double-reflection' of the subjective thinker: (1) the moment of reflection, of stepping back in order to examine, to deliberate over the way things are and (2) the moment of immediacy after reflection, of re-engaging with life anew with the benefit of the perspective gained in the prior moment (CUP 73–4).[32] Metaphysics has a place in this first moment that then becomes the 'presupposition' that is appropriated in the second moment (TDIO 21). The transition from the 'metaphysical' to the 'ethical', for Kierkegaard, is not a simple rejection of the former in favour of the latter. Ethics, generally, 'begins with' and 'presupposes metaphysics', as Vigilius Haufniensis writes, in a parallel manner to the way in which Christian ethics ('second ethics') presupposes dogmatics (CA 20, 24). Metaphysics is then the presupposition that is 'brought out', is appropriated in ethics (CA 24). The problem comes when one never makes the transition; for Kierkegaard, metaphysics (and the dogmatics that comes in its place) is not properly utilized if it is not appropriated.

Ethical engagement in existence (and so religious and Christian existence as well), as intent on being true to the way things are, needs a true conception of life, of oneself, of God. 'The first condition for a resolution', Kierkegaard writes, is 'a true conception of life and of oneself' and of God (TDIO 52, 63).[33] The particular nature of the ethical life is built on a foundation of one's life, one's self and God being a certain way (TDIO 68). There is an 'ethical order of things' – a 'law of life' – a 'way things are' that impinges on how we are to live (SLW 478, 479). 'A person', Kierkegaard writes, 'must certainly know his soul in order to gain it', and know 'that his soul does not belong to him, that there is a power from which he must gain it, a power by whom he must gain it'; 'but this knowing', he cautions, 'is not the gaining' (EUD 173, 174). A right under-

---

32 In relation to the moments of faith 'in the ordinary sense' as presented in Chapter 2, the first moment here (of reflection) corresponds to the second moment there, and the second moment here (of immediacy after reflection, of the resolution, of the appropriation of the presupposition) corresponds to the third moment there.

33 'Neither does the conception of God come as an incidental addendum to that conception of life and of oneself. On the contrary, it comes and penetrates and crowns everything and was present before it became clear' (TDIO 63).

standing of the right metaphysical presuppositions is necessary for existential progression but is insufficient, on its own, to bring this about. There must be both a true presupposition (a 'world-view') and an appropriation of the presupposition.

Even Kierkegaard's seemingly anti-metaphysical gestures – against the system, the advocacy of subjective truth and faith – are grounded in his metaphysics. A system of existence cannot be given because empirically experienced being – actuality, that which exists in time – can never attain to the nature of a logical system (CUP 109). Only with ideal being – and not temporal existence – can the truth be fully possessed and complete as with a tautology (CUP 190). With everything that 'has come into existence' there is a fundamental uncertainty (PF 80–1), for what comes into existence in the movement of time, for actuality, is contingent and does not have the necessity of the eternal and so can only be grasped by faith 'in the ordinary sense' (PF 83–4). To see this in its proper perspective, we need a fuller explication of Kierkegaard's metaphysics – his understanding of the nature of God, of the world and of human beings – provided in the next chapter.

PART 2

Theologia Viatorum

5

The Truth: God, World, Humans

Kierkegaard's work as *theologia viatorum* is a guide for living in the light of the way things are. As such, its guidance is ordered to his theological and metaphysical understanding of reality, his world-view. This chapter is a gazetteer of sorts, an albeit brief systematic description of Kierkegaard's understanding of the nature of time and existence, of God, of God's relation to the world, of human beings and their relations and misrelations to God.

The World: Existence and Time

There is, for Kierkegaard, 'an order in the world', a certain stability to temporal existence, but this is a strange order (EUD 84; PIC 232). While it is difficult, if not impossible, to render actuality univocally 'in the language of abstraction' due to its fluid nature (as we will see), this spacing (between one's imaginative rendering and the actual), for Climacus, affirms that the actual, the reality of the world, is independent of our imaginative projections (CUP 314; PIC 188).[1] Climacus describes the actual, the way the world around us is, in terms of existence (*Tilvaerelse*) (CUP 84). Existence as temporal is in process, not a complete, closed whole or coherence (CUP 123). Climacus also describes existence as a spacing – 'the spacing that holds apart' – that entails 'contradiction' in the sense of othernesses, transcendences not reducible to a unity (CUP 119, 421). It is because of this that Climacus writes: 'Existence itself is a system – for God, but it cannot be a system for any existing [*existerende*] spirit' (CUP 118).

For Kierkegaard, 'time itself' is 'an infinite succession' of moments, of a ceaseless quantity of discrete points that are passing by (CA

---

1 See the section on imagination in Chapter 4.

85–6). As such, temporality is characterized in terms of becoming and plurality. Time is not a simple progression, but a 'growing progression' – its succession entails movement (EO 465). Existence, the 'dialectic' of space and time, is not static but in motion, in becoming – as Climacus writes: 'to exist is to become' (CUP 199, 109; CA 13).[2] This becoming is not necessary but contingent. All finite, temporal actuality for Kierkegaard is contingent 'inasmuch as precisely by coming into existence . . . [it] has its element of contingency, inasmuch as contingency is precisely the one factor in all coming into existence' (CUP 98). All that has come to be could have been another way if another possibility would have been actualized. (This, as we will see, is rooted in Kierkegaard's understanding of creation.) It is for this reason that, as Vigilius Haufniensis writes, 'every deliberation about the nature of actuality is rendered difficult'; human understanding or knowledge of events in time, in history, involves an irreducible uncertainty due to the contingent status of its objects (CA 10).

In the midst of the 'fugitive river' of time, of 'the alteration, which existence is' (R 176; CUP 176), 'the changefulness of earthly things', the, at least seemingly, 'random' changing of 'everything' in the finite realm is manifest (MLW 269; BoA 83; CA 18). Temporal actuality, for Kierkegaard, is a fluid impermanence, fleeting and transitory, always passing from one moment to the next (CD 27; CA 89, 105). As such, its being is an ever-unfinished between-being, an 'inter-esse' (CUP 86, 314). The temporal is fragile and perishable – not lasting but dissolving – soon passing away after its coming to be (EUD 266; UDVS 8–9, 202–3).[3] This is why, for Kierkegaard, earthly possession is ultimately a delusion, why 'wealth essentially cannot be possessed' (CD 28, 31), for it comes and goes, as do all things in time.

In this fleeting impermanence, as an 'infinite vanishing', any given being in time – from the perspective of time alone – does not remain, 'is not', but 'is' only 'to a certain degree' (CA 86; UDVS 76–7). The temporal world 'is', Kierkegaard writes, 'the nonessen-

---

2 Kierkegaard writes in unpublished papers: 'Movement is dialectical, not only with respect to space . . . but also with respect to time. The dialectic in both respects is the same, for the point and the moment correspond to each other' (R 309 sup).

3 'Such is the life of nature: short, full of song, flowering, but at every moment death's prey, and death is the stronger' (UDVS 203).

tial', not one subsisting thing in itself (UDVS 29). There is nothing temporal that is 'one thing' that is 'the same amid all changes – on the contrary, it is the continually changed' (UDVS 26). The temporal realm is that of the plural, of the 'multifarious', of dispersal in plurality (UDVS 29–30; EUD 192).

Time is 'the most difficult mystery' because time itself, simply as an infinite succession, has no 'ecstases', no present and thus no past or future (SLW 384). The differentiation and distinction into present, past and future only arises in the relation of time to another order – to the eternal. As Vigilius Haufniensis writes: 'If time is correctly defined as an infinite succession, it most likely is also defined as the present, the past and the future. This distinction, however, is incorrect if it is considered to be implicit in time itself, because the distinction appears only through the relation of time to eternity and through the reflection of eternity in time' (CA 85). In the moment as 'an atom of eternity', as 'the first reflection of eternity in time' – 'whereby time constantly intersects eternity and eternity constantly pervades time', where 'time and eternity touch each other' – as Haufniensis writes, 'the concept of temporality is posited' (CA 87–9). In the moment, human consciousness becomes 'the place where the eternal and the temporal continually touch', where time is made into a meaningful succession of present, past and future (UDVS 195). In this way, in the 'strange entity' of the moment, 'the eternal is refracted in the temporal' (UDVS 195); meaningful time 'hangs' from eternity (CD 98–9).[4]

God and God's Relation to the World

The three main ways that Kierkegaard describes God, the three principal attributes of God for Kierkegaard, are these: that God is eternal, that God is love and that God is good. Kierkegaard's understanding of the relations between God and the world generally (creation and orientation/sustenance) arise from these attributes. This section then falls in five parts: God as eternal, God as love,

---

4 The moment, Vigilius Haufniensis writes, is a 'strange entity ... that lies between motion and rest without occupying any time, and into this and out from this that which is in motion changes into rest, and that which is at rest changes into motion. Thus the moment becomes the category of transition' (CA 83).

God's creation of the world, God as the good, and God's orienting and sustaining the world. It will be seen that Kierkegaard's understanding of God and of his relation to the world generally follows a classical *exitus–reditus* schema: that God as transcendent to the temporal world (eternal) is the loving, gift-giving Creator of the world and the good end to which the world is ordered and from which the world is sustained and suspended.

God is eternal

God, for Kierkegaard, is eternal. The eternal, in contradistinction and dialectical relation to the temporal, is understood as an eternal present (SLW 361; PIC 63). (In a sense, the present is eternal before it is temporal.) God's nature, for Kierkegaard, is one of changelessness in the sense (analogically) of constancy, of faithfulness and stability (UDVS 77; MLW 271–2). As the sailor looks to the unchanging stars, and not the changing sea, for guidance, so God is 'the constant who remains the same, whereas everything else changes' (EUD 19, 40). 'Eternity is the true repetition'; it is the same that does not change (R 221, 305; CA 18, 151). God 'is' – he is as he is – is 'transparent' (UDVS 90). This is why Climacus writes that 'God does not exist' – as one changing, becoming in time, as is the character of existence – 'God does not exist, he is eternal' (CUP 332).

As eternal, God is fundamentally different from the temporal world of finite existence[5] – as beyond the order that frames finite probability (JFY 100). Yet, Kierkegaard continually holds together the transcendence, the otherness of God with His nearness – as Climacus writes of God: 'it is he who himself is outside of existence yet in existence' (CUP 119). This relationship of fundamental difference – of being 'outside of existence' – and of an enabling presence to the world – being 'in existence' – is expressed in Kierkegaard's

---

5 It should be noted that, in the passages where Kierkegaard is emphasizing this difference, he is writing specifically about the difference between humans and God. Between God and humanity there is: 'the eternal essential difference of infinity' (CD 63), an infinitely greater distance (CD 212; ThDCF 123), 'an eternal essential qualitative difference' (TERE 100; BoA 181), a 'qualitative difference' (SUD 99, 117, 121), an 'infinite qualitative difference' (SUD 126–7), 'an absolute difference' (CUP 412).

affirmation of God's omniscience. God knows the world as other, but as other can know the world truly. 'Existence itself is a system – for God', Climacus writes, 'but it cannot be a system for any existing [*existerende*] spirit' because the 'existing spirit . . . is in the process of becoming' – because we cannot make the ever-changing flux of our thinking to fully agree with the ever-changing flux of the empirical world (CUP 118, 190). God, however, as eternal, as 'outside of existence', 'comprehends actuality itself, all its particulars' (SUD 121) – 'God in heaven, who from the blessedness of this sublime eternity, without the least tremor of dizziness, surveys these countless millions and recognizes each and every individual' (PoV 107). For Kierkegaard, God as eternal is not merely other than and absent from the temporal world – not a distant eternity that has nothing to do with existence – but knows the world, is in relation to the world. Indeed, God acts to change the world 'himself unchanged' – is the 'one restless disturber that nevertheless is the true rest' (MLW 271; CA 152). To understand the nature of God's activity in relation to the world (for Kierkegaard), we must see that God is not merely an eternal, unchanging being but is also and equally loving and the good.

God is love

In 1840, the year before he begins *Either/Or*, Kierkegaard writes in his journal while overlooking Sæding (his father's birthplace): 'divine fatherly love, the one single unshakable thing in life, the true Archimedean point' (JP 5468). For Kierkegaard, love is one of the defining characteristics of God, or as he often writes:[6] 'God is love' (FT 34; UDVS 101, 267–8, 274, 277; WL 264–5; CD 191, 194, 198). God is not motivated by need, by compulsion to acquire something lacking in himself – is not 'self-loving' – but moves out of a love that gives, that communicates itself – God 'seeks his own, which is love; he seeks it by giving all things' (EO 539; PF 24–5; WL 264). Kierkegaard's God is agapeic.[7] God's love (*Kjerlighed*) is 'older than everything else', and its goal (as far as we humans are concerned) is our good, our blessedness (TDIO 47; EUD 46–8).

---

6 This phrase is found especially in Kierkegaard's writings of 1846–8.
7 In Desmond's terms, Kierkegaard's God is not erotic but agapeic.

God's love is communicative, giving forth; he says, '"Become something even in relation to me"' and so seeks a 'reciprocal relationship' with that which he has given, has created (CD 127). God is the prior giver, 'the ground of all things [that] is before all things' and whose 'heart . . . issues the life in everything' (WL 225; UDVS 277). God is the 'benefactor' who wants nothing else but to 'send good and perfect gifts' and the patient provider whose abiding love 'sustains all existence' (CD 16–17; MLW 269; LBFA 31; WL 301). As loving, God makes possible what is other than himself, opening a space for other (SUD 38–41; MLW 271). As such, God is the agapeic source of each one in their own singularity, creating each with a 'distinctive individuality' and enabling them to stand by themselves 'through God's help' (WL 271–2, 274–5, 278).

Though transcendent, though qualitatively different, Kierkegaard's God is also intimate, near, 'the closest of all' (TDIO 9). God is 'in existence', 'in the creation, everywhere in the creation, [though] he is not there directly' (CUP 119, 243) – so that 'to make God so lofty that his existence becomes a delusion, becomes meaningless – that, too, is blasphemy' (UDVS 208). God's omnipotence, for Kierkegaard, is understood in the context of God's love – of God's agapeic giving and intimate concern for the least and smallest – 'even his omnipotence is in the power of love' (CD 127; SLW 144). The 'incomprehensible omnipotence of love' – God's 'omnipotent love' – does not dominate the other, does not subsume it into itself, but makes something truly other, something singular even in relation to God (CD 127; PF 32; WL 272). God's greatness, for Kierkegaard, is seen in God's love, in his mercy and grace (CD 289–95).

Both the eternality and the love of God are central in Kierkegaard's thought from the beginning to the end of his authorship – from the journal entry overlooking Saeding (in 1840) to *The Changelessness of God* (written in 1851). Indeed, God's eternality and God's love are interrelated. God 'is eternal love' (UDVS 268). The changelessness of God for Kierkegaard is the changelessness of God's love – God is 'changeless in love' (MLW 268). God's love 'abides' and 'sustains all existence' (WL 301). God's unchanging eternality is, as also loving, a comfort. God's loving, agapeic eternality is not that of a static object but of an eternal spring, 'fresh and everlasting', an eternal giving forth: 'Your faithful coolness', Kierkegaard writes, 'O beloved spring, is not subject to change' (WL 10; MLW 280). The eternality of God as conjoined with the love of God is not cold and distant, but near, intimate – a refreshing coolness (as of a spring) or a warm presence, as Kierkegaard writes: 'this changelessness is intimate and warm and everywhere present; it is a changelessness in being concerned for a person' (EUD 393).[8]

Creation

For Kierkegaard, God is the creator, the origin of the world as other than God. 'The wonderousness of creation', Climacus writes, is 'not to produce something that is nothing in relation to the Creator, but to produce something that is something' (CUP 246). In creation, God lets there be something other than himself; 'God's creator-words' are 'Let there be [*blive*]' (WL 308). God's creation is a coming into existence from nothing (CA 83). Such creation is, as Climacus writes, 'an absolutely freely acting cause' (PF 76). This 'transition [that] takes place in freedom' is the transition from possibility ('a being that nevertheless is a non-being') to actuality ('a being that is being') (PF 75, 74).[9] This change of 'coming into existence' is a change unlike any other – for all other change presupposes existence (PF 74).[10] Creation is God's repetition; as Constantin Constantius writes: 'If God himself had not willed repetition, the world would not have come into existence' (R 133). As with ethical repetition, God's repetition is not necessary, but the actuality it yields – here, actuality as such – is the fruit of decision – here God's act of creation.

God's creation of the world, for Kierkegaard, is a work of love. God, as Kierkegaard quotes often (from James 1.17–22), is the giver of 'every good and perfect gift' – that every good and perfect gift comes down from God with whom there is no variation (EUD 32ff., 79, 90). God's love, 'older than everything else', gives plural

---

8 This is related to God's intimate omniscience – that 'God in heaven, who from the blessedness of this sublime eternity, without the least tremor of dizziness, surveys these countless millions and recognizes each and every individual' (PoV 107). See the parallel between Kierkegaard and Desmond on God's immutability (William Desmond, *God and the Between*, Oxford: Blackwell, 2008, p. 299).

9 It is thus that human acting is an analogue of the agapeic creation of the agapeic origin.

10 Compare Kierkegaard's 'coming into existence' with Desmond's 'coming to be'.

and singular being as a gift (TDIO 47; WL 274). Creation as God's loving gift explains, as Kierkegaard writes, 'both the what and the whence', both the goodness of being and the agapeic origin (EUD 129).

Kierkegaard presents the natural world, the created order, as the product of God's loving ordering of the world in creation. God in his loving creation has made the world and every creature in it good (EO 435). The world was created good, was intended to be in a state of peace and beauty and glory (EUD 62, 125–6) – whose particulars are more and more beautiful the closer one looks (SLW 141; UDVS 162).[11] This is why one is to learn from the birds and the lilies. Kierkegaard writes that it is God 'who rules and he alone to whom wisdom and understanding are due' and that it is from nature, from the wondrous and 'obedient' harmony of nature, that this is seen. 'The bird and the lily', Kierkegaard writes, 'serve only one master and, what amounts to the same thing, serve him wholly . . . there is only one master whom one can serve wholly', and this because the world is ordered to him as the good (CD 82). God, for Kierkegaard, is indirectly 'known in his works', which bespeak their Creator (CD 291; UDVS 192). The love of God is manifest in the goodness of the world.[12] 'All nature', Kierkegaard writes, 'is like the great staff of servants who remind the human being, the ruler, about worshipping God' (UDVS 193) – such that 'nature's visible glory sighs' (UDVS 194) – so is the natural world's hyperbolic testimony about God.

God is good

God, for Kierkegaard, is the good, the highest and true (independent, substantial) good (CA 134; TDIO 18; EUD 133). 'God', he writes, 'is the only good, that no one is good except God' (EUD 133).[13] The good is one, is a unity; it is 'one thing in its essence and

---

11 God is 'the artist who weaves the carpet of the field and produces the beauty of the lilies. . . . [T]he wonder increases the closer one comes' (UDVS 164).

12 'When God had created everything, he looked at it and behold, "it was all very good", and every one of his works seems to bear the appendage: Praise, thank, worship the Creator' (CD 291).

13 'What thinkers call the idea, is the true, the good or more accurately, the God-relationship' (WL 339).

the same in every one of its expressions' (UDVS 36, 30). In its simplicity, as 'one thing', the good has a 'transparency', an 'unchanged clarity'; it is 'pure' and 'knows nothing of evil' (UDVS 90; MLW 272; CA 112). God as the good is the end to which the created world is ordered and oriented. 'The good', Kierkegaard writes, 'is its own reward', that toward which one strives (UDVS 39). The good is the eternal end ordering the finite, the goal and criterion (EUD 260). As the good, God is that ordering end to which the lovingly created world strives.

The goodness of God and the eternality of God are interrelated. The simplicity of the good is 'the transparency of the eternal' – 'in being good [God] is unchanged' (UDVS 90; CD 224). The eternal is the true repetition as the sought repetition that orders human repetition (CA 18, 151) – 'one can be only by being in the one who is in himself' – in God who is eternally one and the same (CD 40). The good is the sought continuity – 'the good signifies continuity' (CA 130). The good as that sought, that toward which one moves is such that 'only the good is the unity of state and movement' (CA 135). God as the eternal good is 'the ground of the future' and the 'one restless disturber that nevertheless is the true rest' inasmuch as his drawing forward disturbs and calls to change (EUD 19; CA 152). Thus, 'God is the constant who remains the same, whereas everything else changes' – and specifically here is drawn to be changed in relation to God as the eternal good (EUD 40).[14] The eternal is the non-transitory *regula*, the rule that 'applies' or 'pertains' to all things (UDVS 9).[15] As 'the Holy One', God is the good, the standard, that is eternally other (CD 212).

God's nature as being love and as being the good are also intimately connected. God is the good end that is also the loving origin; the love of God is 'the unfathomable fountain of goodness in God's goodness' (WL 271). God is the originating love that is also the desired end of finite being; 'the only true object of a human being's

---

14 Kierkegaard observes that James exhorts us 'to love God in such a way that our nature might become like his, that we might gain God in constancy and rescue our soul in patience' (EUD 40).

15 'What, then, is the eternal? It is the difference between right and wrong. All else is transitory: heaven and earth will collapse; all other differences are evanescent; all differences between one human being and another are a part of the interlude of human life on earth and therefore something terminating' (CD 207–8).

love', Kierkegaard writes, 'is love, which is God . . . he is Love itself'
(WL 265). 'The power that governs human life', Anti-Climacus
writes, 'is love' – it is 'Loving Governance' – a 'Governance, who is
compassionate love' (PIC 189, 87). God in creation and as present
in creation orders all things to himself (SUD 121).

God's creating love issues in 'the life in the tasks', in a life so
ordered toward God as the good end (UDVS 277). The conjoining
of the good and agapeic love of God is seen, for Kierkegaard, in
God's allowing freedom in relation to himself (as good end). 'God',
Anti-Climacus writes, 'who constituted man a relation, releases it
from his hand, as it were' (SUD 16). Seeking God as one's good end
is not compulsory: 'Compel you, no, the God of love will not do
that at any price' (MLW 294). The relation to God always includes
the possibility of offence (SUD 126–7). The good 'in its love for
the free . . . will not use power' and so 'in its compassion it is long-
suffering' (UDVS 62).

Because of this loving ordering of the world in creation, our end,
the good we are ordered toward (though we may defect from this
ordering), is our own blessedness, our own happiness, our own joy
(EUD 48). 'The thought that God is love', Kierkegaard writes, 'contains all joy in itself. . . . The thought that God is love contains all
the blessed persuasion of eternity. Then the road, even if it is the
most difficult, and the condition, even if it is the most bitter, are
unconditionally joyful' (UDVS 282). It is God (as the good) that
satisfies us, that satisfies our desire with blessing, and it is God (as
love) that orders us toward himself as the good.[16] In this, God, as
love and as the good, receives back differently, and given freely (by
us), what he gave (to us). In seeking the good we 'exist for the God'
who is our 'benefactor'; the individual 'exists for God [as the good]
and God [as love] for him' (CD 16).[17] Kierkegaard, in some of his

---

16 Kierkegaard writes of 'the heavenly Father, he who opens his gentle hand
and satisfies with blessing everything that lives' (UDVS 173).

17 Kierkegaard (reminiscent of C. S. Lewis's 'sixpence none the richer') writes of
'a child who gives its parents a gift the parents have given the child. Oh, but what
parents would be so cruel as to take the gift from the child and say, "Why, this is
ours!" instead of smiling at the child and going along with its idea that it is a gift
– so also with God; he is not that cruel when someone brings him as a gift – his own'
(PoV 89). Earlier, in the *Postscript*, Climacus has God speak: 'Do you have anything
of which you can give me some? Or when doing your utmost, are you not simply
returning my property to me, and perhaps in rather poor condition?' (CUP 139).

last writings concludes, addressing the reader, that God 'loves you and he wants to be loved by you, both out of love', that 'he is love and out of love he wills that you should will as he wills' (MLW 177, 294). God wills, wants that we should love him because reality is structured such that our loving God is our only true end, our blessedness.

Sustenance, suspension, orientation

God, after the creation of the world, relates to the world in terms of sustenance, suspension, orientation. 'In relation to the lily and the bird [in relation to the finite order generally], God is the fatherly Creator and Sustainer' (LFBA 31). God's love is 'the love that sustains all existence' – 'he changes everything – himself unchanged' (WL 301; MLW 271). 'Certainly everything that exists', Kierkegaard writes, 'is by grace' (CD 81, 85). The temporal world hangs, is suspended from, the eternal – is dependent upon it as a 'refraction' (CD 98–9; UDVS 90, 195). The world is oriented toward God – 'the lily and the bird seek God's kingdom, nothing else whatever' (LFBA 19; EUD 39) – the created order is good and is ordered to its own good. Kierkegaard describes this orientation, this ordering, of the natural world toward God in terms of obedience. 'In nature everything is obedience, unconditional obedience', Kierkegaard writes, 'here in nature "God's will is done on earth as it is in heaven"' (LFBA 25).[18]

Human Being

What a human being is

The human being, for Kierkegaard, is fundamentally *dependent upon and in relation to God*. As created out of nothing, a human being is dependent upon God: one receives the agapeic gift of one's own being from God (EUD 236). Beyond this, humans are structured to be actively relating to that beyond themselves, to others

---

18 In nature, Kierkegaard writes, 'every sound [*Lyd*], every sound you hear is all compliance [*Adlyd*], unconditional obedience [*Lydighed*]. Thus you can hear God in it just as you hear him in the harmony that is the movement of the celestial bodies in obedience' (LFBA 25).

and to God, communicating; as Kierkegaard writes: 'A person is not an exclusively receptive relation; he is himself communicating' (EUD 45). Humans have what Desmond calls agapeic being;[19] they are made to be agapeic, giving, themselves; as Judge Vilhelm writes: 'only he who loves has a proper conception of what he is and what he is capable of' (EO 452). Essential to the human self is the self's relationship to God or God-relationship, the self's 'eternal consciousness', being a self 'before God'; as Climacus writes: 'It is really the God-relationship that makes a human being into a human being' (CUP 244; FT 15; SUD 79).

In the task of understanding human nature,[20] Kierkegaard sees human beings as being in a state of *existence* (CUP 81–4, 193, 230). As existing, human life is in a constant process of becoming, of change, in which, as Anti-Climacus writes, 'there is no standing still' (SUD 94); as Climacus puts it: 'to exist is to become' (CUP 199, 80, 180). This process of becoming makes human existence 'illusive', 'a very difficult matter to handle' (CUP 83, 309) – in that existence is 'the spacing that holds apart' – a state of change and incompleteness that 'separates thinking and being' and keeps thought from attaining an identity with one's ever-changing being (CUP 118, 332, 196). However, human existence also entails the process of 'joining together' the 'motion' of becoming and the 'motionless' in one's striving 'continually "forward"' in relation to something that is not changing (CUP 529–31, 411); as Climacus writes: 'The motionless belongs to motion as motion's goal [*Maal*], both in the sense of τέλος [end, goal] and μέτρον [measure, criterion]' (CUP 312). As being in relation to a goal and a standard that is other to the becoming of finite human existence, there is thus 'a continuity that holds motion together' (CUP 312). Existence as so 'teleologically' oriented and so 'continually striving' (a motion in an unmoving direction, hence the continuity of the striving) is a between-being, an *inter-esse*, interested in a particular goal and so

---

19 See William Desmond, *Perplexity and Ultimacy* (Albany, NY: SUNY Press, 1995), pp. 199ff. and my *Religion, Metaphysics, and the Postmodern: William Desmond and John D. Caputo* (Bloomington: Indiana University Press, 2009), pp. 43, 115–17.

20 The task of, as Climacus puts it, 'once again to read through solo, if possible in a more inward way, the original text of individual human existence-relationships, the old familiar text handed down from the fathers' (CUP 629–30).

making choices in life accordingly – 'the walking itself is a continual differentiating' (CUP 413, 85, 313, 319).

The interested striving of human existence, for Kierkegaard, is a relation, a being-between, the finite and the infinite, the temporal and the eternal. This striving relation is *passion* – modelled in part after Platonic *eros*. 'Erotic love', Climacus writes, 'manifestly means existence'. He continues: 'According to Plato, Poverty and Plenty begot Eros, whose nature is made up of both. But what is existence? It is that child who is begotten by the infinite and the finite, the eternal and the temporal, and is therefore continually striving' (CUP 92).[21] The passion (the *eros*) of human existence – that is 'the essentially human' – is an interested striving movement in the midst of temporal and finite becoming that moves toward and is moved by (as the will that is 'the mover but that it itself is to be moved') the infinite and the eternal (FT 121; UDVS 75; CUP 92). In this way, movement of passion is the 'unity' of the finite and the infinite, of the temporal and the finite (CUP 92, 197). 'Passion', Climacus writes, 'is the momentary continuity that simultaneously has a constraining effect and is the impetus of motion. For an existing person, the goal of motion is decision and repetition. The eternal is the continuity of motion, but an abstract eternity is outside motion, and a concrete eternity in the existing person is the maximum of passion' (CUP 312). Human existence, as such a passionate 'unity', is the forging of a continuity over time in the midst of the temporal – 'where everything is in a process of becoming' – in relation to the eternal, which at once motivates (as a desired end) and has 'a constraining effect in the passionate decision' (CUP 307). In this, one moves not out of the finite and the temporal, but in them into the future; as Climacus writes: 'the eternal relates itself as the future to the person in the process of becoming. . . . In other words, when I join eternity and becoming, I do not gain rest but the future' (CUP 307). 'Truly to exist', Climacus continues, is 'to permeate one's existence with consciousness, simultaneously to be eternal, far beyond it, as it were, and nevertheless present in it and nevertheless in the process of becoming – that is truly difficult' (CUP 308).

---

21 Cf. Desmond's rendering of this passage from Plato's *Symposium* (*Religion, Metaphysics, and the Postmodern*, pp. 36–7). Also, following Plato's *Phaedrus*, Climacus presents the relation between the eternal and the temporal in human existence as 'if a Pegasus and an old nag were hitched to a carriage' (CUP 311–12).

This 'true' existence is, again, religious – the 'absolute passion' of the 'hidden inwardness' 'guarded as a sacred fire' that 'hold[s] out with the eternal' (EUD 392; CUP 510; UDVS 256).

The passionate striving of existence, in Kierkegaard's work, intimates the structure of the self as a *synthesis*. Anti-Climacus defines human being in this way (SUD 13–14):

> A human being is spirit. But what is spirit? Spirit is the self. But what is the self? The self is a relation that relates itself to itself or is the relation's relating itself to itself in the relation; the self is not the relation but is the relation's relating itself to itself . . . The human self is such a derived, established relation, a relation that relates itself to itself and in relating itself to itself relates itself to another.[22]

Spirit is the 'third' that is the relation between the 'two' elements in the synthesis (CA 43). 'The self', Anti-Climacus writes, 'is the relation to oneself' (SUD 17). One's self is one's relation to the synthesis that is what one is as a human; or, alternatively, the character of one's self is determined by the manner in which one relates, and relates to, the constitutive elements in the synthesis of the self. The synthesis is a 'joining together', 'a relation between two', a bringing together of 'a duplexity [*Dobbelthed*]', of a 'contradiction', a 'self-contradiction' (CUP 519–31; SUD 13; PIC 159; EUD 163, 166). What is the synthesis of human being? Initially, Kierkegaard describes the human as a 'synthesis of the psychical and the physical', 'of psyche and body', of 'the external and the internal' (CA 43, 85; EUD 166). Second, the existing human being, for Kierkegaard, is also a synthesis of the eternal and the temporal or 'the becoming' (EUD 166; CA 85; CUP 56, 89; CD 71, 141). There is 'something eternal in the human being' that makes human life different from animal life (UDVS 9–11). Third, the self is a synthesis of 'the infinite and the finite' (CUP 89, 391; SUD 29–30). The infinite here is the relating – via the medium of the imagination – to God, to the eternal as one's 'infinite interest', regarding the 'infinite reality' gained 'by being conscious of existing before God, by becoming

---

22 'And what, then, is it to be a self? It is to be a redoubling [*Fordoblelse*]. . . . [T]he self is a redoubling, is freedom' (PIC 159).

a human self whose criterion is God' (CUP 89; SUD 30, 69, 79). Finally, the self, for Kierkegaard, is a synthesis between necessity and possibility. In relating to oneself, to what one is, to the 'constituents of which the self as a synthesis is composed' – where one has the freedom to relate variously in possibility to what one necessarily is – 'the self he is is a very definite something and thus the necessary' (SUD 29, 36).

For Kierkegaard, this human synthesis is the ground for *anxiety*. As a synthesis of possibility (of the ability to choose between different imagined options) and of necessity (of what one is), the human is able (in freedom) to actualize various non-necessary possibilities in the future (CA 91). One may, however, choose wrongly, may fail. Anxiety, for Kierkegaard, has to do with the inherent possibility of failure (of failing to be in accord with what one is and in relation to the way things are). As such, anxiety is an intermediate term between possibility and actuality; realizing one has possibilities, has the freedom to choose, one, in 'the anxious possibility of being able', is anxious about making the wrong choice (CA 44, 49). Anxiety, then, is an uneasiness, a 'dizziness'; as Vigilius Haufniensis writes: 'anxiety is the dizziness of freedom' before the 'yawning abyss' of possible failure (CA 61; EUD 91; SUD 16). What is more, the experience of anxiety manifests an ambiguity in one's desire; one fears moral failure, yet one also desires it. One exhibits 'a sympathetic antipathy and an antipathetic sympathy' (CA 42); one desires what one fears and fears what one desires (JP 94). This deformed desire is an 'entangled freedom' (CA 49).

Finally, the human being, for Kierkegaard, is fundamentally communal, is oriented toward community. There is something in human desire, in human love that opens one beyond the self toward a mutuality, toward the deeper reality of agapeic community.[23] Judge Vilhelm writes of the fundamental place of love in human life as revealing the meaning and fulfilment of life as being in joyous communication, 'openheartedness' and honest 'phanerogamous' (flowering, reproducing) revelation over and against sorrowful isolation, withdrawal and 'cryptogamous' secretiveness that has so lost touch with reality; as he writes, 'it is the meaning of life

---

23 It is from this perspective that Johannes the Seducer writes, perhaps despite himself, referring to the *Phaedrus*, that 'Plato really understood love' (EO 351).

and reality that man be revealed' (EO 582; 169, 386, 436, 439, 443–8, 542). This is echoed by Vigilius Haufniensis who presents the 'demonic' in terms of that which 'closes itself up within itself', 'the sudden', the momentary versus 'the good' that is described as 'continuity', 'transparency', 'the expansive', and communicating (CA 123–4, 127–30). 'The good of the spirit', Kierkegaard writes in *Christian Discourses*, 'is communication', is 'sharing' (both translations of *Meddelelse*) – is participating in a community of giving and receiving – a treasure whose acquisition makes others rich (CD 116, 118, 120).[24] To be true to what one is as a human being, for Kierkegaard, is to be in community; 'a person', he writes, 'is not an exclusively receptive relation; he is himself communicating' (EUD 45) – 'communicating the goods of the spirit, by communicating what in itself is communication' (CD 122).[25]

The aesthetic and the ethical

The human person, for Kierkegaard, can relate to his or her self in different ways; one can be more or less true to oneself. The aesthetic and the ethical ways of being represent two such less or more (respectively) relatively true self-relations. 'Esthetic existence', Climacus writes, 'is essentially enjoyment' (CUP 288). The aesthetic way is one focused on the immediate, present, the sudden (against the ethical way's becoming a unity over time) (EO 492) – either of thoughtless living in the moment or getting lost, paralysed in possibility (EO 485, 525). The only repetition the aesthete is interested in is that of pleasure, the sustaining of 'the blissful security of the moment' (R 132). If, however, as Climacus writes, 'the essential esthetic thesis, [is] that the moment is all' – that the highest desired object is that of the immediately pleasurable and 'the interesting' – then to the extent that 'the moment is all' it is, 'in turn, essentially nothing' (CUP 298; EO 311). The aesthetic way is one of distrac-

---

24 Kierkegaard writes, 'the true way, the way of perfection, to make others truly rich, must be: to communicate the goods of the spirit, in other respects to be oneself solely occupied with acquiring and possessing these goods' and thereby 'communicating and immediately makes others rich' with 'the true riches, the nature of which is communication' (CD 120).

25 As Judge William writes of marriage: 'We are what we are in union' (SLW 93).

tion, of deception, of fantasy (CUP 254). Its 'eccentric' centre is the insular and ever-vanishing, and so ultimately empty, moment of time (EO 384).

Corresponding to the aesthetic 'selving', for Kierkegaard, is an instrumental understanding of community.[26] The aesthetic relation to others is primarily predatory, acquisitive, seeking to conquer, to take what one wants from the other (EO 229–30, 458–9). As such, aesthetes are anti-community; they live 'aphoristically' like 'solitary birds in the stillness of night' (EO 212). The aesthete cannot abide with the 'congregation', with 'personal relationships' (EO 436–7). However, one may follow the trajectory of aesthetic desire for momentary pleasure beyond itself, toward love of the other, toward the pleasure of relation.[27]

Relative to the restlessness of the aesthetic, the ethical way of being – the ethical way for the self to relate to itself – is stable, it seeks the still, deep waters over (or beneath) the turbulent sea (EO 466–7). Rather than the momentary, the ethical seeks the universal, the 'law within', seeks to be truly human, to model one's life after 'the universal man', to be 'simultaneously himself and the whole race' (EUD 84; EO 552; CA 28).[28] One affirms and incarnates this universal ideal in resolution, in ethical choice or faith, as was presented in the second chapter above. As Judge Vilhelm writes, 'the act of choosing is a literal and strict expression of the ethical' (EO

---

26 See Desmond's work on the relation between ethical selvings and ethical communities in *Ethics and the Between* (Albany, NY: SUNY Press, 2001). I see strong affinities between Kierkegaard's existence spheres and Desmond's ethical selvings and communities. Kierkegaard's aesthetic sphere covers similar ground as Desmond's second and third ethical selvings: the selvings of equivocal liberty and its 'freedom from' the other and the instrumental community of serviceable disposability. Kierkegaard's ethical sphere roughly corresponds to Desmond's fourth and fifth ethical selvings (those of 'dialectical autonomy' and 'erotic sovereignty') – with their 'freedom to' become in accord with some project striving toward excellence as guided by an ideal – and the community of erotic sovereignty. Kierkegaard's religious sphere strongly resonates with Desmond's sixth and seventh ethical selvings, of agapeic service and suffering – with their 'freedom toward' the other – and the corresponding community of agapeic service.

27 See here again Johannes the Seducer's comment about love in the *Phaedrus* (EO 351).

28 Climacus writes that 'ethics and the ethical, by being the essential stronghold of individual existence, have an irrefutable claim upon every existing individual' (CUP 134).

485).[29] Ethical resolution takes a position. In the ethical way of being, 'the main thing is to strive, to work, to act' concretely for one's choices change things in reality (BoA 131; EO 551). The ethical is ideal but is also concrete; it does not deny the flux of becoming, nor does it fixate on the fleeting moment, but it actively engages in life in relation to an ideal; the ethical person intentionally becomes (EO 492).[30] The ethical is a coherent becoming, a 'continued striving' that is, as Climacus writes, 'the expression of the existing subject's ethical life-view' (CUP 121–2). The ethical actuality is the choosing and acting upon an ethical ideal in life; it is 'the developed possibility of the subjectivity's first possibility' (CUP 130).

Ethical choice, ethical resolution in relation to a universal ideal becomes concrete and intends to forge an identity through the discontinuity and becoming of time through the process of repetition; as Kierkegaard writes, 'it is the meaning of resolution for human life that it wants to give it coherence' (EUD 364). While everything else finite changes, while finite reality is fleeting and non-substantial, in ethical repetition [*Gjentagelse*] one 'takes up again' each fleeting moment, 'filling out' one's existence so as to acquire a 'solidity', a consistency over time; in repetition, one seeks to establish a continuity persisting through time (CA 18; CUP 121; EO 460–3). Ethical becoming is no Dionysian revelling in a meaningless flux; rather, as Climacus puts it, 'for an existing person, the goal of motion is decision and repetition' (CUP 312). In ethical repetition, one lives at once in both hope and recollection – thinking about the future and the past in relation to an ideal – thereby gaining for one's life 'true, substantial continuity', thereby 'acquir[ing] a history' (EO 465, 542). Repetition is 'a development', an establishing of character, of a self – of a concrete way of being in relation to what you are – over time (R 292, 307).[31] Kierkegaard describes 'the acquired originality of disposition' that is repetition (or perhaps is the result

---

29 Choice, the ethical Judge Vilhelm writes, is 'my watchword, the nerve of my life-view' (EO 514).

30 Climacus writes: 'A person can be both good and evil, just as it is quite simply said that a human being has a disposition to both good and evil, but one cannot simultaneously become good and evil. . . . [A]s soon as he is again in the process of becoming, he becomes either good or evil' (CUP 420–1).

31 Kierkegaard writes: 'If the point is the spiritual development of a self-conscious free will . . . then it [repetition] is a question of nullifying the repetition in which evil recurs and of bringing forth the repetition in which the good recurs' (R 292).

*yet the
very fallacy.*

of) as 'earnestness', as 'the earnestness of existence' that perseveres
and endures and is faithful in the task of life that is 'not over until
life is over' (CA 149; SLW 118, 143; CUP 158).[32]

The ethical self chooses itself, affirms itself – as Judge Vilhelm
writes, 'the I chooses itself – or, more correctly, it accepts itself' (EO
491, 540). One can either affirm or deny one's self and one's nature;
the ethical chooses the former.[33] To choose oneself 'absolutely' is
both to choose oneself ideally, 'in one's eternal validity' – to affirm
the universal reality of human being, one's reality as a finite being
in relation to the eternal, to God (EO 515–20) – and to choose oneself concretely (as a 'rich' and 'diversely determined concretion') as
this particular, singular person with this particular, singular history
(EO 518, 523, 543; CUP 254). 'The true art of living' is to be both
'the only man' (the individual) and 'the universal man' (EO 547–8).
In the ethical way one seeks to be or to become what one is (EO
491; CUP 489). In this 'redoubling' one existentially appropriates
the metaphysical reality of the self, one takes from the description
of what one is the prescription to be what one is, to be as one in
reality is (R 133; CD 41).[34] As such a concrete individual, as being
'in absolute continuity with the reality one belongs to', the ethical
person has the goal of being transparent to oneself and thus 'to be
totally present to oneself' – to have, so to speak, 'himself outside
himself [one's reality] inside himself [as appropriated]' (BoA 106;
EO 540–1, 549–51). In this way, the ethical person has the goal of
ethical truth.[35]

Ethical community, for Kierkegaard, is intentional. Ethical being
with others is not merely immediate but is sustained by resolution,
by commitment (SLW 148). Resolution is the 'abiding place', the
sustaining 'vessel' for immediate erotic love, such that immediate
desire and aesthetic pleasure can undergo 'resolution's rebirth'

---

32 Climacus continues, writing that one is not 'finished with life before life is
finished with him' (CUP 163).

33 Climacus writes that there are 'two ways for an existing individual: either he
can do everything to forget that he is existing and thereby manage to become comic
. . . because existence possesses the remarkable quality that an existing person exists
whether he wants to or not; or he can direct all his attention to his existing' (CUP
120).

34 As Judge Vilhelm writes, 'the greatest thing is not to be this or that, but to
be oneself' (EO 491).

35 See Chapter 3 above.

and so achieve a second immediacy (TDIO 57, 62–3; SLW 148). Marriage is the ethical relationship *par excellence*. In marriage there is a teleological suspension of immediate 'falling in love' where the loves of the lower, the aesthetic (individual, self-oriented) order fit within marriage as the higher, communal, reciprocal order such that 'only in marriage does being in love have its true expression' (EO 383; SLW 126). Ethical repetition manifests itself in the community of marriage as a 'continual rejuvenation', at once uniform and rich in change (EO 387, 467). Indeed, Kierkegaard describes the wedding ceremony, as the beginning of a relationship that is sustained through continual repetition, as a kind of invitation to conflict – not conflict with the beloved but with oneself, continually struggling and fighting the good fight of the ethical.[36]

Ethical human community (and marriage in particular), for Kierkegaard, arises from our very being as communal. A 'husband' (*Aegtemand*) is a 'genuine man' (*aegte Mand*) – one who is in intentional, committed community with others is truly human – inasmuch as the human is ordered toward freely giving agapeic community, as the human is fundamentally relational (EO 428, 453). Ethical community is the concrete 'being true' to the communal and communicative nature of human being (as described above). One finds oneself in community, for the self is 'not just a personal self, but a social, civic self' and sympathy is an essential human quality (EO 444, 553; SLW 113).

Finally, like the aesthetic before the ethical, the ethical can open beyond itself to religious. Even Judge William admits that marriage is not the highest life (SLW 169). Ethical community must be grounded in something beyond itself – 'the secret of earthly love', Kierkegaard writes, 'is that it bears the mark of God's love, without which it would become silliness or insipid philandering' (EUD 75). The ethical itself is teleologically suspended, is founded from above, from the religious, is dependent upon the God-relationship, for before God all humans are revealed to be equal (SLW 230; CUP 53, 455–6). Thus, 'the religious is eternity's transfigured rendition of the most beautiful dream of politics' (PoV 103).

---

36 Kierkegaard goes on to describe marriage as 'a conflict that must be fought to the finish, toil that must be endured, danger that must be encountered, a curse if it is not jointly borne as a blessing' (TDIO 48).

The Human Being's Relation to God: The Established Relation (The Religious)

Human relation to God

First, we are *related to God as eternal in terms of God's otherness.* God to us is other, transcendent. Between God and humans there is, for Kierkegaard, an incommensurability, a qualitative difference,[37] a distinction in the midst of relation such that God is alien, other to natural man (PIC 62–3; SUD 117; CUP 162; WL 244). As such, God is invisible to humans; our relation to God as indirect, as 'distinguished by the negative', is a relation to a higher realm that is ultimately a mystery to us who are blinded by eternity (CUP 246, 263, 432; PIC 155; WL 5; CD 35). Before such a transcendent God – whose 'thoughts are not human thoughts', 'whose wisdom is like the darkness of the night – as unfathomable as the depths of the sea' – our human thinking is humbled (BoA 33; SLW 361).

Second, we are *lovingly created and sustained by God.* Humans, for Kierkegaard, are created in their very essence as good and as glorious – as 'creation's wonderwork' with a 'dowry of good nature' such that Kierkegaard praises 'the glory of human nature' (UDVS 165, 171, 189–91; WL 159; EUD 182; CUP 182). This glorious essence is our God-relation as what makes us truly human (CA 109–10; CUP 244). Regarding human being, Kierkegaard writes: 'I am responsible for none of it, but glorious it is.' But 'how', he asks, 'should we speak about this glory?' The best way to speak of this glory is to say that: 'God created the human being in his image' (UDVS 192). Human beings are created in the image of God and bear this likeness as an 'invisible glory' (UDVS 192–3; CUP 261; CD 41; WL 264). As created, we are dependent on God (EO 151; UDVS 177, 181). God is the source of what benefits us, of 'every good and perfect gift', and is thus a 'Loving Governance' that willingly gives that which provides for our good, our true end, our blessedness (EUD 39, 48; PIC 189; MLW 177, 294). God is not only our loving origin but is also the 'source of all love', the source of our being in loving community which is our good and end (WL 3, 216). Anti-Climacus writes: 'Just as the quiet lake originates deep down in hidden springs no eye has seen, so also does a person's

---

37 See Note 5 above.

love originate even more deeply in God's love' (WL 9). The God-relationship, for Kierkegaard, sustains and supports human exist-ence – strengthening and assisting (UDVS 7, 16; WL 333; CD 130, 268, 286). One's 'eternal consciousness' gives life meaning; it is 'a sacred bond that knits humankind together' without which life would be 'empty and devoid of consolation' (FT 15).[38]

As lovingly created by God, humans, for Kierkegaard, are given freedom in relation to God. 'God', Kierkegaard writes, 'who cre-ates from nothing, omnipotently takes from nothing and says, "Become"; he lovingly adds, "Become something even in relation to me"' (CD 127).[39] Kierkegaard's God is a loving omnipotence that does not coerce, does not compel, does not take away the voluntary (UDVS 62; MLW 294; CD 179).[40] Though we are utterly depend-ent upon God for our existence, he has made us independent from him, agents in our own right (WL 38–9). This freedom to choose or not to choose God, indeed, Kierkegaard writes, is the glory of humanity (UDVS 206).

For Kierkegaard, God as loving is present to us. God is not merely distant; he is lofty yet near, present everywhere and on every occa-sion (EUD 199; CD 166; CA 140; CUP 87, 243). 'His intimacy', Kierkegaard writes, 'surrounds you everywhere; it is offered to you at every moment' (UDVS 107). God as loving is ever-present to the human in inwardness (CUP 243; TDIO 64; CD 108); when one turns inward to one's relation to God (as other to the world, to whom one is intimately related) 'then it is possible to see God everywhere' (CUP 246–7).

Third, we relate to God as the *good in terms of God being our desired end*. God is the good that we desire, that we love, that we long to be in communion with in blessedness. In Kierkegaard's vision, human beings have a fundamental desire for the transcend-ent and eternal God (PF 37, 44). God, for humans, is the one thing needful (EUD 133; CD 13). Thus to need God 'is a human being's

---

38 Kierkegaard writes that, 'a human being cannot in the deeper sense live with-out relating himself to the unconditional' (PoV 20).

39 Desmond also makes a connection between God's loving omnipotence and the creation of free humans (*God and the Between*, p. 320).

40 Kierkegaard writes: 'Do you know any more overwhelming and humbling manifestation of God's complaisance and indulgence toward human beings than that in a sense he places himself on the straight line of choice with the world just in order that the human being can choose' (UDVS 206).

perfection' (CD 64); the need for God 'is a good and perfect gift from God' in that this need orients us toward our good (EUD 139). This orientation of desire – 'this loving understanding, resolution's solemn agreement with the good' (EUD 359) – is a guide, a need that draws us toward what is needful (TDIO 58–60). As Kierkegaard writes: 'The need brings the nourishment [*Næring*] along with it – oh, so near [*nær*] (the word indeed says it) it is, so near it is, if only the need is there. The need brings the nourishment along with it, not by itself, as if the need produced the nourishment, but by virtue of a divine determination that joins the two' (CD 244–5). Our desire for God orients us, points us to God – such that God 'is in the longing that is for him' (CD 260) – 'God is negatively present in the subjectivity' that is our interest in our eternal happiness (CUP 53, 316, 393). God is the 'proper object' of human love, of our infinite desire (WL 130; CUP 194), and human love leads to God, 'points beyond itself to something higher' (EO 399, 351). This is manifest in the religious horizon of marriage as a continual resolution, a commitment in which one 'discover[s] God' in 'the infinitude of the ethical' (CUP 244; EO 398–9; SLW 100, 122).

God as the good is the higher that draws us to itself (PIC 151–2, 159). God as the good is the end that orients us towards himself – 'the weight of the good is elevating' (SUD 110). This orientation to the eternal God makes other orientations right; it *'will help a person to understand himself in temporality'* for it is 'a criterion that is always valid and valid in itself; by means of this goal and this criterion he will always understand himself in temporality' (EUD 259–60).[41] The end of the good, of God, is 'built in' to thus oriented desire and willing, for willing the good, for Kierkegaard, is to follow the self-correcting orientation of our desire whose only ultimate fulfilment is God.[42] This is the 'unfathomable trustworthiness of the good': that 'wherever a person is in the world, on whatever road he is travelling, if he wills only one thing, there is a road that leads him to you!' – to God (UDVS 25). This orientation of desire is related to conscience as a kind of intrinsic judgement – the criterion, the good, as other, is the end desired and so known, and so

---

41 Kierkegaard writes that 'only by loving God above all else can one love the neighbor in the other human being' (WL 58).

42 'A person begins', Kierkegaard writes, 'and then little by little is transformed into willing one thing in truth by willing the good' (UDVS 35).

nt, if negatively (EUD 350–1; SUD 124).[43] The end sought is of communion with God. Being with God is the end, 'the good is its own reward', the reward that beckons and encourages (UDVS 39, 49). This communion, for Kierkegaard, as 'the highest good' is our happiness, our blessedness (*Salighed*) (CD 222, 225).

Human relating to God – religiousness, the religious

For Kierkegaard, *one relates to God as the eternal, transcendent other in faith*. Our subjectively being true to our relationship with the transcendent God is to see him as 'the eternal being, who is the object of faith' (FT 51). The eternal, the absolute, is always 'an occasion for offense' for finite humans and our relation to the eternal God happens in the 'supreme passion' and 'divine madness' of faith in the context of the possibility of offence (PIC 119; FT 23). In faith (in the first movement of the double-movement of faith), we are faced with an 'either/or' decision to choose God over the finite, either to be devoted to God or to despise him, to seek God's kingdom first, for 'the person who does not seek God's kingdom first is not seeking it at all' (LFBA 19–22; MLW 233–6).[44] This is faith's difficult beginning, its leap – as dying to or 'losing the temporal temporally' in order to gain or grasp the eternal (UDVS 209; CD 72, 141–2). The resolution of faith – as the only way 'in which God will involve himself with a human being' – 'joins a person with the eternal' (EUD 347; TDIO 63). It is the relation to the eternal God in faith that then (in the second movement of faith) comes to structure and orient one's existence in finitude, 'express[ing] the sublime in the pedestrian' (FT 41). Faith – as constantly, daily being acquired and repeated – works to join all of one's life together with the eternal and so establish a continuity, a constancy in life given stability with the ballast of the unconditional (EUD 14; CUP 55, 535; SUD 105; PoV 19–20). The eternal grounds repetition. At the same

---

43 It is perhaps with this in mind that Quidam writes of God speaking to a person by speaking through himself (that person) (SLW 316).

44 Kierkegaard writes: 'There is an either/or: either God – or, well, then the rest is unimportant. Whatever else a person chooses, if he does not choose God, he has missed the either/or, or through his either/or he is in perdition. . . . Thus it actually is God who, by being himself the object of the choice, tightens the decision of choice until it in truth becomes an either/or' (LFBA 21).

time, as in the process of becoming, we encounter the eternal with fear and trembling; faith so challenges all of our relative stabilities – as Anti-Climacus writes, 'fear and trembling signify that there is a God – something every human being and every established order ought not to forget for a moment' (PIC 88).

We are lovingly created (as good, glorious, free) and sustained (in God's presence) by God. We live as if this is true – we are religious – when we *gratefully affirm and strive to be what we are created to be*. We should relate to ourselves as we are in relation to God. In that we, for Kierkegaard, as human beings are created by God, this understanding should affect our self-understanding; it should found our way of existing (EUD 32, 76; CUP 249). When one comes to understand and to choose oneself in God – 'when', as Judge Vilhelm writes, 'in an eternal and unfailing sense one becomes aware of oneself as the person one is' – 'one receives oneself' (EO 509). This is to choose oneself, to take possession of oneself, 'in one's eternal validity' (EO 515).[45] In this process – in which 'it is as if his self is outside him and is to be taken possession of' – a person comes 'to relate himself to himself in his religious idea' (EO 519; SLW 428). In choosing oneself as originated – in relation to 'the originality that was his eternal source' (CUP 153; EO 518) – one seeks to attain a 'religious transparency' in which 'he has seen his self over against the eternal power, whose fire has permeated it without consuming it' (SLW 428; EO 529). One 'rests transparently in God', in the changelessness of God's love (SUD 30; UDVS 121; MLW 278). This transparency is a sober coming to oneself, to be oneself before God (UDVS 137; SUD 5; LFBA 17).[46] Here the religious self is a theological self – 'the self directly before God . . . whose criterion [that directly before which it is a self] is God' (SUD 79).

To be religious, to be in relation to God as loving creator is to recognize our dependence upon the gift of God and to affirm the goodness of God's loving creation in gratitude. To be true to ourselves, to choose, to affirm ourselves as we are, for Kierkegaard, is to affirm that we are fundamentally dependent upon God, such that, as Kierkegaard writes, 'the person who is not before God is

---

45 'But', the Judge clarifies, 'I do not create myself, I choose myself' as created (EO 517–18).

46 Kierkegaard writes: 'Only by being before God can one totally come to oneself in the transparency of soberness' (JFY 106).

not himself either, which one can be only by being in the one who is in himself' (CD 40, 13–16; UDVS 181–2). In affirming one's relation to God as loving creator, one is thankful for one's life, thankful beyond the finite distinctions that would limit one's vision of the good that one has received. To see all of life as a good gift is 'always to give thanks' (CUP 178). To give thanks to God as one's 'benefactor' – to gratefully recognize 'that one has received what one has' – is, as Kierkegaard writes, to 'be reminded of one's Benefactor, that is, of one's God, one's Creator, one's Provider, one's Father in heaven, thus of the love for which alone it is worth living and which alone is worth living for!' (CD 16–17).

God is the good that we desire, that we love, that we long to be in communion with in blessedness. We are true to this in *our loving God – in our passionate concern, our worship, and our obedience.* The God-relationship, for Kierkegaard, is a relating to God with an infinite passion – its 'how' is 'the passion of the infinite' (CUP 203). Having gone through infinite resignation (in the double-movement of faith), one is assured that what one relates to in truly infinite passion, in a desire for one's eternal end beyond finite, is God (CUP 201). 'The inspecting resignation', Climacus writes, 'discovers no irregularity, this shows that the individual at the time of inspection is relating himself to an eternal happiness' (CUP 395). Such is the intimate connection between the form and content of religiousness – that 'the person who in truth wills only one thing can only will the good, and the person who wills only one thing when he wills the good can will only the good in truth' (UDVS 24). God is one's eternal end, and so the God-relation at once 'consists precisely in being religiously, infinitely concerned about oneself' (CUP 200; SLW 486). One desires God as one's own eternal happiness.[47] One's 'eternal happiness' is the 'highest τέλος' that is 'willed for its own sake' in 'the moment of resignation, of collecting oneself, of choice' (CUP 394, 400). Religiousness, for Kierkegaard, is for a person so 'to relate himself with pathos to an eternal happiness' – 'simultaneously to relate oneself absolutely to the absolute τέλος

---

47 Kierkegaard writes: 'Just as the shipwrecked person who saved himself by means of a plank and now, tossed by the waves and hovering over the abyss between life and death, strains his eyes for land, so indeed should a person be concerned about his salvation' (CD 220).

and relatively to the relative ends' – that his existence is transformed (CUP 393, 414). Kierkegaard describes this religious 'pathos-filled transformation of existence' as a 'humble, obedient enthusiasm', as 'be[ing] shaken', as being 'infinitely, unconditionally engaged' before God (CUP 581; UDVS 62; BoA 112–13; JFY 104). Yet this strenuous, passionate engagement brings 'a tranquility and a restfulness' for there is 'no contradiction . . . to relate oneself absolutely to the absolute τέλος' – in doing so one is acting in accord with reality, for God is the end of human being. To relate oneself absolutely to God is 'the absolute reciprocity in like for like', while it is 'demented . . . for a being who is eternally structured to apply all his power to grasp the perishable' (CUP 422). Only God comports with our infinite passion . . . our *eros*, perhaps.

Suffering, for Kierkegaard, is an (or 'the') essential expression of religiousness, of religious infinite passion; it 'belongs essentially to the highest life' (CUP 434, 440). This is so because the end of eternal happiness is not yet achieved. One desires absolutely something that one is still approaching. When one is oriented to God as the good in infinite passion, 'the continuance of suffering', Climacus writes, 'is the guarantee that the individual is in position and keeps himself in position' (CUP 443).

This austere picture of suffering, however, is not the centre of our being unto God in Kierkegaard's thought. The 'primus motor', Kierkegaard writes, is love – such that 'anyone who loves God . . . forgets the suffering in the love' (JP 2383; FT 120). One's religious being in relation to God, one's 'eternal consciousness' is one's 'love for God' (FT 48).[48] For Kierkegaard, to love God is the fulfilment of human existence; it is 'the highest good' (CD 200). As such, as arising from our very being as made for this end, 'the only way in which a person can truly love God' is 'to love God because one needs him' (CD 188). We love God for loving God is our own greatest good. Our love of God is not outside the fundamentally asymmetrical relationship of dependence between ourselves and our loving Creator. We do not love God for God's sake. To love God is at once to love the supremely other, to become as nothing before him, and to also fulfil oneself. It is at once self-giving and

---

48 Johannes de Silentio writes: 'my eternal consciousness is my love for God, and for me that is the highest of all' (FT 48).

self-receiving – 'selfless' and 'selfish' – for this orientation toward the other is our own greatest good.[49]

The love of God, for Kierkegaard, is manifest in worship and obedience. Worship is the fulfilment of our being; it reflects the truth of what we are: in our being the image of God, in our dependence upon or our being nothing without God's loving creation, and in our orientation toward God as the good. In worship we 'reflect the image of God', are 'transfigured [*forklaret*] in God' for, as Kierkegaard writes, 'only when he himself becomes nothing, only then can God illuminate him so that he resembles God' (EUD 399–400).[50] In worship, one is as nothing before God – one recognizes one's being utterly dependent on God as lovingly creating one from nothing – and is so transparent to one's source (the spring, the power that establishes) and so reflects, illumined, transfigured, by God (JFY 104). To love God is to worship God, to minimize oneself in order to magnify him, to submit to always being in the wrong before God, and so be 'hidden in God' (EO 604–5). 'This', the preacher at the end of *Either/Or* declares, 'is your divine worship, your religious devotion, your reverence for God' (EO 605).

True worship, for Kierkegaard, however, is 'obeying God's will – when his will is certainly my only true good' (CD 86). The higher worship that is obedience – the true existence that is 'the only true hymn of praise' – is orienting oneself toward that which 'is simply and solely my own good' (CD 86). To love God in obedience is to be true, to live in accord with the reality that God, as the origin and end of all things, is the Lord. Obedience, Kierkegaard writes, 'learns to let God be the master, to let God rule. But what is all eternal truth except this: that God rules' (UDVS 257). In obedience one is 'educated for the eternal', one 'appropriates' the eternal and the rest of the eternal in 'sheer simplicity before God' (UDVS 258–9; LFBA 32). Such obedience, such being in accord, in harmony with the eternal God, communicates (in one's worshipful transparency) 'the peace and rest of the eternal' for 'wherever the eternal is, there is rest' (UDVS 258). In so doing, one 'participates in the good . . .

---

49 'God', Kierkegaard writes, 'is so close to [the one that loves God] that between him and God there is an area of reciprocal relationship' (CD 127).

50 Indeed humanity's uniqueness (as 'erect, upright') is that ability to prostrate oneself in worship (UDVS 193).

which is from above'; one participates in the eternal God, in loving communion with him (EUD 134).

The Human Being's Relation to God: The Deformed Relation and Repentance

The demonic way of isolation

For Kierkegaard, there are two ways to travel on the road of life: the way of the 'eternal through being before God in faith' – the way of unity unto life and rest – and the way of sin that leads to separation and death (SUD 105; PIC 18). Each of these ways has an 'increasingly established continuity' – as if one's movement in one direction or another has an inertia, a momentum forming into a habit of being, be it virtue or vice (SUD 106). As fixating on the 'multifarious', the passing, the finite, 'the way of damnation' is (also) a 'narrow' way (UDVS 29–30; FSE 66).[51]

The wrong way on the road of life, in Kierkegaard's work, is a way of isolation. On this way, one turns in on oneself in an inward circle 'from which he cannot escape' (EO 252)[52] – in an isolating selfishness in which one only takes, only receives (like a bag, as Judge Vilhelm writes), unable to love (CA 79; EO 402, 465, 480). Such a person dwells 'like a ghost' among people, 'roam[ing] like an inconstant spirit, like a ghost among the ruins of the world yet lost to [them]' (EO 520, 452). They are full of (and yet empty in) a self-indulgent melancholy, an anguished egotism, that cuts itself off from community (CA 43; EO 212, 236, 395, 436–8) – suspicious and mistrustful (WL 228). This melancholy, this withdrawing sorrow, is the spirit's taking revenge for one's ab-use of it, the dissonance one experiences for one's treating one's spirit as something other than it is (EO 169, 507) – for, as Judge Vilhelm writes to the aesthete A, 'the spirit is not mocked, and the darkness of melancholy thickens about you' (EO 508).

---

51 It is 'easy from the beginning but becomes more and more dreadful. It is so easy to trip the light fantastic of desire, but when, after a while, it is desire that dances with the person against his will – that is a ponderous dance!' (FSE 66).

52 The aesthete A writes: 'I can imagine nothing more agonizing than an intriguing mind which has lost the thread and then turns all its wits upon itself . . . pursued by despair . . . constantly seeking an exit' (EO 252).

Kierkegaard calls this being closed in on oneself an 'inclosing reserve' (*det Indesluttede*) – that which 'closes itself up within itself' and 'makes itself prisoner' (CA 123–4). This inclosing reserve of melancholy self-isolation is a cutting across, a going against, a defecting from one's being as communicative. Defecting from living communication and continuity, one makes oneself into a 'closed machinery', a perpetual but monotonous movement (like a pendulum that is the illusion of true motion), a 'monotonous sameness' that is a 'pseudocontinuity' (EO 590, 170; CA 130).[53] This inclosing reserve is 'an inwardness with a jammed lock' that wishes to have 'a world exclusively for itself' (SUD 72, 73; SLW 197); it is, as Anti-Climacus writes, 'a carefully closed door, and behind it sits the self, so to speak, watching itself, preoccupied with or filling up time with not willing to be itself and yet being self enough to love itself' (SUD 63).

Kierkegaard identifies 'the demonic' as just such an isolating, inclosing reserve.[54] The demonic seeks 'to close itself off completely and hypostatize itself',[55] but in so doing traps itself such that the demonic nature is a deformed one, like 'witches, nisses, trolls, etc.' (CA 137; FT 88, 105). This is so because the demonic 'wants to close itself off', but this is an 'impossibility' for one 'always retains a relation' (CA 123). The demonic self goes against what it is; it is untrue,[56] suffering from a 'tormenting self-contradiction' of denying what one is and needs (CA 138; SUD 67). The demonic fixates on the single moment, on 'the sudden' that, as lacking continuity, is the 'boring' and 'dreadful emptiness and contentlessness of evil' (CA 129, 132–3) – as evil, for Kierkegaard, is 'at odds with itself, divided in itself', 'without continuity' (UDVS 34; JC 154). The demonic self, as fixated on the momentary and the empty, dissolves into a 'disorganization', the 'wild flight' of a multitude, a demonic 'legion' (CA 122; EO 479–80).

---

53 Vigilius Haufniensis writes that 'inclosing reserve maintains itself in the person as an abracadabra of continuity that communicates only with itself and therefore is always the sudden' (CA 130).

54 'The demonic is inclosing reserve' (CA 123).

55 The demonic, which 'shuns every contact', says: 'Leave me alone in my wretchedness' (CA 137).

56 As Vigilius Haufniensis writes, the 'truth is for the particular individual only as he himself produces it in action. If the truth is for the individual in any other way . . . we have a phenomenon of the demonic' (CA 138).

Despair

In isolating oneself from God, the self of the deformed relation fails to relate to the self as it is.[57] Kierkegaard describes this misrelation to the self and to God as despair. Despair is 'not to will to be oneself'; it is not relating to oneself as it is (SUD 23, 52). Yet this is a 'double-mindedness' – one is unhappy with one's self and wants to be rid of it, but one cannot rid oneself of oneself – the phenomenon of this unhappiness, of this disjunction point to a persistent self that cannot be imagined away (UDVS 30; SUD 17).

Part of this misrelation to the self, as Anti-Climacus describes it in *The Sickness Unto Death*, is a misrelation to one's being a synthesis – of over- or under-emphasizing one element of the synthesis (SUD 15, 30). Infinitude's despair is to be caught up in the fantastic – of losing relation to one's finite self (SUD 31) – while finitude's despair is the 'despairing reductionism, narrowness' that lacks infinitude (SUD 33). Possibility's despair is to become unreal by running away from the constraint of necessity, of one's limitations, of the 'very definite something' that one is (SUD 35–6) – in possibility's despair 'everything seems possible, but this is exactly the point at which the abyss swallows up the self' and 'the individual himself becomes a mirage' (SUD 36). Finally, necessity's despair is that of 'the determinist, the fatalist' to whom 'everything has become necessary . . . or . . . everything has become trivial' (SUD 40); one simply is what one is, things are as they are, and nothing can change at all.

Ultimately, despair for Kierkegaard is to lack the eternal; it is to despair of the eternal, of God (WL 40–1; SUD 60–1). Despair is 'giving up on God' – on a relationship with God (UDVS 101). Despair does not see itself in an established relation to God – does not see itself in the midst of God's loving gift in creation. Despair is 'to deny that God is love' (UDVS 101). Here despair stands in contradistinction to the human affirmation of God's loving creation in acknowledging what one is (as presented above). Despair is ultimately defiance against God; it is 'severing the self from any relation to a power that has established it, or severing it from the idea that there is such a power' (SUD 68). 'At its maximum', this

---

57 As so ignoring God, it is a 'life-view' that does not take account of its 'condition' (EO 531).

despair is absolute defiance, a 'rebelling against all existence', being 'offended at all existence', and so being defiant against God as creator (SUD 42, 71-3). One does not thankfully affirm the gift of the world as lovingly created by God, one defies the way things are and their Maker. One defects from reality.

Despair's misrelation to the reality of the self is sin. The one who despairs is not necessarily aware, however, that it is sin. One needs revelation. Sin, then, is an 'intensification of despair' (SUD 77), an intensification with regard to one's consciousness, one's awareness. As an 'intensification', sin is not ultimately something different from despair. One's despair was in fact rebellion against God – it was sin.

Sin

Sin, for Kierkegaard, is something that must be revealed by God to human beings. 'To sin', Anti-Climacus writes, 'is: "after being taught by a revelation from God what sin is, before God in despair not to will to be oneself or in despair to will to be oneself"' (SUD 101). 'There has to be', Anti-Climacus writes earlier, 'a revelation from God to show what sin is' because sin is a qualitative leap that has no rational precursor (SUD 89). Natural reason cannot understand the coming-to-be of sin; it must be revealed. Sin, for Kierkegaard, is a qualitative leap, an incomprehensible 'position', 'an unwarranted actuality' appearing 'with the suddenness of the enigmatic' that 'has no place' and belongs to no 'science' (SUD 98; CA 111, 30, 14, 16). Sin is a going against reality that has, in itself, no logical explanation – it is 'a paradox that must be believed' (CA 50).

The 'leap' of sin is a breach of continuity, a separation, a difference caused by the individual between the individual and God (UDVS 7, 154; PF 47). This break, this striking against – standing in contradistinction to our love of God as our proper end – is sin's rebellion, is sin's 'insubordination' as an unwillingness to acknowledge the authority of anything higher (EO 532; BoA 5). Sin is the presumptuousness that one either does not need God or that one superstitiously has God at one's disposal (CD 66-9).[58] Thus, despair

---

58 This presumptuousness is 'to be spiritlessly ignorant of how a person needs God's help at every moment and that without God he is nothing' (CD 63).

is, more deeply, sin in that despair's 'wanting to be another self' is a rebellion against God for in so doing one 'wants to tear his self away from the power that established it' (SUD 20).

For Kierkegaard, sin is an independence that is a slavery. In it one seeks independence (to not be dependent, to be secure and sufficient unto oneself) – one 'wants to entrench himself', but 'in this entrenched security he is living – in a prison'.[59] This entangling is the 'sophistry of sin' (CA 117). For sin gains an 'impetus', a momentum in the wrong direction and so one is bound, enslaved to it (SUD 105; PF 17). Thus sin is like a sickness that, if untreated, gets worse, of itself.[60] The leap of sin then enters one into 'the circle of the leap' in which 'sin presupposes itself' (CA 112). Here sin becomes a 'coherence', an 'encompassing nature', a 'second nature', a corrupted disposition (TDIO 32, 34; SUD 105; FT 100; CUP 161). This 'weed of corruption . . . that . . . sows itself' – 'the rust' that 'can consume the soul' – degrades and corrupts the aesthetic, the sensual, and the temporal – making them incorporated functions of sin's coherence (TDIO 55; CD 102; CA 57–9, 63).

Untruth

The person on the way away from God has a trajectory of untruth – of being at odds with what is. Such a person has forgotten what it is to be human (UDVS 165; EUD 85). For Kierkegaard, it is only by being before God that one can be 'essentially' oneself (CD 44). In falling prey to 'the temptation, by doing away with God, to cease to be a human being' such that one becomes a 'traitor to oneself' by 'breaking faith with the eternal', one becomes a self that fails to relate 'itself to itself, by relating itself to that which has established the entire relation' (CD 35; UDVS 318; SUD 14).[61] Such a person – deluded and 'intoxicated' (PoV 51; JFY 113) – 'fools himself' with a cunning self-deception (FT 100; CD 185–7; UDVS 25). He sees things upside down and backwards: that the good needs humans,

---

59 One 'has cunningly shut himself in and thereby trapped himself, has in fact . . . trapped himself unto death' (UDVS 178).

60 Thus, Anti-Climacus writes, 'every unrepented sin is a new sin and every moment that it remains unrepented is also new sin' (SUD 105).

61 Thus Climacus writes: 'It is really the God-relationship that makes a human being into a human being, but this is what he would lack' (CUP 244).

that the temporal is what is trustworthy while the eternal is uncertain, that 'that with which busyness fills up life' is preferable to the emptiness of the eternal (UDVS 87; CD 134, 172). Turning from an engagement with actuality – 'poetizing instead of being' (SUD 77; EO 385, 391, 485) – the 'person who does not fight with reality' gets to 'contend with' the 'phantoms' and anxieties of worldly care (EO 582; CD 57–8).

This path of untruth, in Kierkegaard's thought, is a way of disintegration. In this way, one is in self-contradiction, at odds with oneself, double-minded (FT 87; TA 97) – for one is seeking (impossibly) to be rid of oneself – one defiantly wills to assert oneself as independent, as self-sustaining (which one is not) while willing to be rid of oneself as dependent (which one is) and is so 'divided in himself' (UDVS 27, 31).[62] As so double-minded – as at odds with one's reality – one becomes 'a kingdom divided against itself, a kingdom in continual rebellion, where one tyrant succeeds another' (CD 87). Against repetition, this way is one of dispersal into mere plurality, mere sequence – of scattering, of 'parcel[ling] out yourself' by constantly being different people – of dissolving into a disordered multitude, a demonic 'legion' (EUD 192, 194; MLW 319; EO 319). Instead of being in accord with one's being, such a person is eccentric – 'he has his centre at the periphery' (EO 528). This self-centred yet centre-less way is actually a futile 'endless detour' experienced in a 'ruinous' boredom that manifests – as much as one would seek amusement to avoid the experience – the ruin of the selfish self (EO 227ff, 390).

The way of untruth is a way of impatience, of an unrest without perseverance (EO 387; BoA 9). Fixating on the 'sophistical' and anxious moment, on 'impatience's short, hasty, precipitous, frivolous, arrogant, shrewd, comfortless "maybe",' this impatience is a distorted dwelling in time (EUD 217, 344–6; BoA 9; CD 100; UDVS 309–10). 'To live only for the moment, to covet the moment first and foremost', to take the 'moment's view', is to fixate upon the momentary, upon the immediate, the proximate, such that one seeks to intensify the actual present to such a degree that one at once 'chokes' on it and 'loses' it – it remains opaque and yet fleet-

---

62 One here has 'two wills, one that he futilely wants to follow entirely, and one that he futilely wants to get rid of entirely' (UDVS 30).

ing and transitory (CD 227; UDVS 90; EO 394–5; CA 105). Such a fixation on 'the moment as abstracted from the eternal' is to be a slave to the moment and to take time – the moments passing in becoming – as an enemy (CA 93; EUD 347; UDVS 195).

A person embarked this way seeks from the moment the fruit of fleeting, passing, fragile and anxious pleasure (SLW 24, 27, 72; TDIO 66).[63] Such a person is inconstant and incontinent, desiring in the moment and desiring no continuity, no stability (EO 236, 389) – a 'hater of second nature', who avoids sameness and stability as 'boring', as 'worse than death' (EO 305, 466, 453; PoV 92). Kierkegaard describes this desire as a futile 'craving' (EUD 117; CD 152); 'desire's fiery moment' of 'the purely momentary' is a 'consuming passion', a 'burning restlessness' (UDVS 135; EUD 117). Seeking greedily to secure oneself in and secure for oneself the objects of one's 'worldly appetites', one secures oneself indeed in the 'glittering bondage of pleasure' (CD 21–2, 34–5; EUD 84). For Kierkegaard, this is so because being independent and being only beholden to one's own desire – one's futile and unquenchable desire, one's greed – is slavery.[64] Kierkegaard describes this impatience, this 'desire in its boundless extreme', as vanity and nausea (EO 485; EUD 195; UDVS 29, 135). This momentary desire for the interesting, for diversion seeks constant change (EO 384–7; UDVS 185) – revels in the accidental changes of the world (without) and in changing oneself, one's mind, arbitrarily (within) in order to avoid the boredom that 'rests upon the nothingness that winds its way through existence' (EO 232, 239–40). Attributing 'infinite worth to the indifferent', such 'an inconstant spirit' wanders aimless on the surface of life – a 'fantast' in a boat built for one 'skim[ming] along with the infinite speed of restless thoughts, alone in the infinite ocean' – 'escap[ing] into meaninglessness' (SUD 33; EO 520, 426; UDVS 107).

For Kierkegaard, the world – the established order of the human social world – is structured according to this untruth such that the deformed relation is the norm. The world 'wants to be deceived'

---

63 Such a moment is 'the moment of sensual pleasure . . . a moment of time filled with emptiness' (CUP 422).

64 Kierkegaard writes: 'To be dependent on one's treasure – that is dependence and hard and heavy slavery; to be dependent on God, completely dependent – that is independence' (UDVS 181).

and is ruled by 'illusions' (PoV 59, 63; JFY 91, 139–40). The crowd, Kierkegaard writes, 'is untruth if it is supposed to be valid as the authority for what truth is' (PoV 106). The crowd's 'untruth' lies in making 'the numerical' the authority (PoV 126; FSE 19). The mechanism for the untruth of the crowd or the world is in making 'human approval' and human comparison (and thus envy and fear) – 'the way others regard one' – to be the criterion for human value (UDVS 166, 188, 190, 327; CD 230; SUD 56; FSE 86), such that one 'is what "the others" make of him and what he makes of himself by being only before others' and so 'sinks under comparison's enormous weight' (CD 44–5).[65] This view 'assumes that on average most people, the majority of people, are of the truth' (UDVS 338) – and thus 'we are governed, educated, and brought up according to mankind's conception of what it means to be a human being' (FSE 86). But this view, for Kierkegaard, is an inversion: it sees sin as a joke (EUD 343); it does not esteem humanity's eternal end (UDVS 320); it has (relative to Christianity) 'completely opposite conceptions' of sanity and wisdom (JFY 97); 'the noble act is regarded as stupidity, the evil act of sagacity' (CD 29).[66] Kierkegaard describes the fallen social world (comprised of sinful humans and thus not properly ordered to God) in terms of 'the deification of the established order', which is 'the secularization of everything' (PIC 91), the evacuation of the relation to the divine. Such deification yields secularization because 'the established order wants to be a totality that recognizes nothing above itself' (PIC 91) and so idolatrously worships its own invention in 'a mutiny against God' (PIC 92; WL 117). The paradox here is that the world (which would seem to be more expansive) is an 'untruthful extensiveness' enclosed in itself and will see nothing beyond itself whereas the religious singularity (which would seem the more insular) is in communication with itself, with God, with other actual persons (MLW 42).

---

65 The crowd bases value on 'what "they" will say and judge', on 'the majority, the crowd, its approval – its disapproval. Imagine such an assembly or crowd of worshipers and devotees of the fear of people' (CD 232).

66 Kierkegaard even goes so far as to say that the world is 'immersed in evil'. He would have us see 'how deeply humanity has fallen, sorrow over the fact that gold is virtue, that might is right, that the crowd is truth, that only lies make progress and only evil is victorious, that only selfishness is loved and only mediocrity is blessed, that only sagacity is esteemed, that only half measures are praised and only contemptibleness succeeds' (ThDCF 118).

Perdition

For Kierkegaard, the end of the human being's deformed relation to God – the end of the way of sin, of despair and untruth, of isolation – is perdition (*Fortabelse*). This perdition is intrinsic to reality and to one's being; it is inherent in the way.[67] 'There is', Judge William writes, 'no need to impose a penalty, for life always asserts itself and knows how to punish anyone who wants to emancipate himself' (SLW 106). This 'punishment' is an 'involuntary self-appraisal' in which one becomes the 'place' in which one must live in eternity, be it 'a solitary prison or a delightful room of eternal happiness' (EUD 351; UDVS 134). For Kierkegaard, disordered desire and worldly care are their own punishment – are a doleful 'self-consuming' and a 'self-torment' (EUD 85; CD 77, 80). Such a self-tormentor futilely 'devours himself' – 'desouls his self' (CD 78–9; EUD 185; SUD 32–3). This self-torment arises because one has come to hate oneself and yet one cannot be rid of oneself (CD 79).[68] The self in this 'impotent self-consuming' becomes a hell – 'the self at the root of despair whose worm does not die and whose fire is not quenched' (SUD 18) – such that eternal perdition is an extension and a making permanent of one's present self-torment. 'Eternity', Anti-Climacus writes, 'nevertheless will make it manifest that his condition was despair and will nail him to himself so that his torment will still be that he cannot rid himself of himself' (SUD 21). One wills one's own isolation, one's own perdition – 'in the world of the spirit', Kierkegaard writes, 'the only one who is shut out is the one who shuts himself out' saying 'Let me be what I am' (EUD 335; CD 89).

The expression for this 'state of deepest spiritual wretchedness' is death (SUD 6). The life of perdition, the way of perdition comes to have death as its end (as *telos* and *terminus*), and yet the torment is 'precisely the inability to die' (SUD 17–21) – 'this tormenting contradiction, this sickness of the self, perpetually to be dying, to die and yet not die, to die death' (SUD 18). As with the

---

67 Reality, like the good, says: 'Well, have a jolly time with your deception, but just remember, we two will discuss this again' (UDVS 41).

68 Anti-Climacus explains: 'a person cannot rid himself of the relation to himself anymore than he can rid himself of his self, which, after all, is one and the same thing, since the self is the relation to oneself' (SUD 17).

Symparanekromenoi in *Either/Or*, the inability to die is the 'greatest misfortune' – that life, a tormented life of not being what one desires, is a greater misfortune than death (EO 211–12). Such a person – experiencing 'death in life' – is 'like a baleful spirit that found no rest in the grave, he lives like a ghost – that is, he is not living' (TDIO 53; CD 79).[69] Perdition, for Kierkegaard, is that one cannot escape oneself. It is the hell of hating one's being and wanting to be free of it – to flee [*flye*] in an inward circle in order to escape [*undflye*] from oneself from which one cannot escape as long as one is what one is (EUD 211; EO 252; SUD 92; TDIO 39). That which one rejects in oneself is the relation to God, which is unbearable for the person that would have nothing above them and their desires. By wanting to do away with the eternal or reducing the eternal to the temporal, one is alienated from one's source; one comes to bring about the loss of the eternal in the midst of the temporal (CD 136–7). 'The eternal', Kierkegaard writes, 'is always in agreement with itself, and its agreement shuts out only that which shuts out itself' (EUD 267). And this, the reality of divine being, combined with the nature of human being and the futile human defection from one's being, establishes the abyss, the greatest distance between God and a human being – enclosed in one's own private room of sovereignty and torment (CD 69).

Repentance

What is the way out for the one in the midst of this deformed relation? How does one get back on the way from which one has departed – back from the downward slope? As faith and truth have several different, interrelated (ascending and nested) meanings in Kierkegaard's writings, so does the 'turning' of repentance. The initial repentance is the repentance of turning from the world, from the finite to the infinite, to God. This is the repentance that is at the beginning of the religious as such – one's turning to God in infinite resignation, in 'the infinite movement of repentance' – whose (repentance's) 'infinite annihilating power' is a dying to immediacy (FT 99; SLW 477).

---

69 Kierkegaard continues: 'Our Lord cannot throw light around him, because it remains just as dark around him and just as unblessed whether he lives or dies, he who neither lives nor dies and yet lives – yes, as in a hell' (CD 79).

Once 'within' the religious, one comes to a further repentance. Climacus writes that suffering is the essential expression for one's relationship with God – of Religiousness A (pre-Christian religiousness) in that, in relating to an eternal happiness while in the midst of becoming, one becomes aware of the contradiction between the two[70] and so of one's failure to unite them – the religious person 'wills to do everything; he wants to express this relation absolutely, but he cannot make the finite commensurate with it' (CUP 484, 453–5). Indeed, the deeper one's engagement in an active relationship with God, the more one becomes aware of one's failure (CUP 525).[71] It is thus that guilt is the 'decisive expression' of Religiousness A (CUP 525ff.) – that 'the essential consciousness of guilt . . . expresses that an existing person relates himself to an eternal happiness . . . expresses the relation by expressing the misrelation' (CUP 531). This guilt as an awareness of failure, of breakdown, is a necessary negative moment that prepares one for the breakthrough of repentance – for 'if repentance is to arise, there must first be effective despair, radical despair, so that the life of the spirit can break through from the ground upward' (SUD 59; UDVS 279).[72] This repentance, then, is the repentance of turning, not from the finite, from the world, but from one's failed, deformed God-relation – the repentance that is at the end of Religiousness A.[73] This repentance 'seeks to return to its beginning so that it might rebind what is separated'; it is a turning that seeks a correcting, a healing (UDVS 7, 13, 15; SLW 468).

In the consciousness of sin a deeper disordering is revealed. Beyond 'guilt-consciousness', 'sin-consciousness' is an awareness of the true depth of one's sickness – that there is not just something wrong with a relation external to the self, but that one's self – one's 'identity', oneself as a 'subject' – is 'broken' (CUP 534, 584). Sin is not merely something one can stop 'doing', it is a state that is

---

70 Climacus writes: 'Suffering is precisely the consciousness of contradiction' (CUP 483).

71 'The more', Climacus writes, 'he, acting, striving, immerses himself in existence . . . , the further he in the task is from the task' (CUP 527).

72 So such a despair is called a 'salutary terror' that gives 'some comfort' for with it one 'is always somewhat closer to his salvation than he was as long as he went on living secure in an illusion and a delusion' (CD 220–1).

73 It is in this sense that, as Vigilius Haufniensis writes, 'as soon as guilt is posited . . . repentance is there' (CA 103).

securely established in the self (SUD 100). This distortion *of* the self is something that needs to be revealed *to* the self from *beyond* the self – for, Anti-Climacus writes, 'invariably, what error needs most is always the last thing it thinks of – quite naturally, for otherwise it would not, after all, be error' (SUD 92). Sin is a lack of a sober perspective on the self (JFY 113).[74] God must reveal to us, in the work of the Holy Spirit, 'what sin is' and that this is our state (SUD 89, 95; ThDCF 127); as long as we think we are sober (though we are not), our intoxication must be made manifest to us (JFY 114). For Kierkegaard, this understanding of the depth of human brokenness is unique to Christianity, to Religiousness B; it must be revealed (in Christ and in the work of the Holy Spirit) and cannot be known immanently as with Religiousness A (SUD 90).

'With regard to sin', Kierkegaard writes, 'a turning around is required' (CD 153). Repentance, one might say 'Christian repentance', is 'formed in the expression of repentance' (CA 114). The consciousness of sin is the awareness that one's state is such that one cannot fix oneself – that one needs help – that one is untruth. So this repentance, turning from one's state but unable to fundamentally change it, seeks forgiveness – seeks help from beyond the self (SLW 482). One sorrows over one's sin, and this sorrow is not only a negative appraisal of one's current state but is an orientation toward another state. Repentance's sorrow is a seeking – its turning from sin is a seeking for forgiveness (UD 150–2; TDIO 29).

Consciousness of sin and repentance, for Kierkegaard, come together in the act of confession. In confession – as a 'biding place on the road of salvation, where one pauses and collects one's thoughts' (TDIO 15) – one 'collects' oneself in stillness and solitude (apart from distraction and confusion) and honestly considers and understands oneself in the consciousness of one's sin (TDIO 9–10, 32–3; UDVS 19–21, 152) – and so hearing as a singular individual 'God's voice delivering judgement in stillness' (TDIO 11). In confession, one is honest, transparent to oneself, 'comprehending before God that [one's own] sin has a coherence in itself' – that one is in a state of sin – so being true to one's untruth (TDIO 32–3). It is from this honest and contrite place that one not only recognizes one's sin

---

74 Climacus writes: 'The individual is therefore unable to gain the consciousness of sin by himself' (CUP 584).

but seeks forgiveness – turning from one's sorry and sorrowed-over state toward help from beyond oneself. To confess, Kierkegaard writes, is 'to gather all, most concisely and most truthfully, into one thought: *God, be merciful to me, a sinner*' (ThDCF 133).

6

The Truth: Christ

The First Dynamic

For Kierkegaard, the eternal is not merely the origin and the end of the temporal way/journey. For on this journey we have become lost along the way. The eternal, in Christ, meets us here – entering into time to help, to save, to show the way. The solution, then, to the problem of the deformed relation or misrelation to God, for Kierkegaard, comes in the person and work of Jesus Christ. In this chapter, I will present the principal portraits of Christ in Kierkegaard's authorship (the Absolute Paradox, the Object of Faith, the Sign of Offence, the Truth in Existence, the Saviour/Teacher, the Pattern/Prototype) organized into two 'dynamics' (comprised of the first three portraits and then the last three portraits respectively). The first dynamic is made up of three portraits of Christ: the Absolute Paradox, the Object of Faith and the Sign of Offence.

Christ as the absolute paradox

For Kierkegaard, one of the defining marks of Christianity is the absolute paradox (CUP 540). This 'absolute paradox' is identified with the person of Jesus Christ. To understand how the descriptive 'absolute paradox' applies to Christ and its significance in Kierkegaard's thought, one must first understand what Kierkegaard means by 'absolute paradox' generally.

As a coincidence of heterogeneous entities, a paradox is an apparent contradiction. The question arises as to whether this 'contradiction' is in fact a logical contradiction or something else. The way that this question is answered by many Kierkegaard scholars is that the paradox is a contradiction but not a formal logical contradiction. In the Johannes Climacus literature (PF, CUP), 'contradiction' appears in many places as describing the paradox. But Climacus's use of 'contradiction' does not necessarily entail a formal logical contradiction but rather follows a broad Hegelian usage that refers to a tension between ideas. It can be seen that Climacus explicitly distinguishes between a 'meaningless' contradiction or 'self-contradictory' statement and a paradox in that he says, in contrast to a meaningless statement, 'our hypothetical assumption of that fact [the paradox] ... contains no self-contradiction' (PF 101). While the paradox is described as unthinkable, 'meaninglessness [nonsense], however, is unthinkable in a sense different from our stating that that fact [the paradox] ... [is] unthinkable' (PF 101). Climacus distinguishes between the incomprehensible, which one can believe, and nonsense, which reason protects against. Looking to Climacus's general strategy in his books, we see that he considers the absolute paradox to be unique. If the paradox were a formal contradiction, this would not be the case.

Kierkegaard's paradox is not as much in the proposition itself, but in the proposition's relation to the human understanding. This can be seen in Climacus's assertion that the paradox is not a paradox from a divine (God's) point of view (CUP 212). At its heart, the contradiction of the paradox is relational; it challenges the paradigm of human understanding – vs a divine standpoint. So, there is a view from nowhere where the paradox is not paradoxical, but we are not privy to it. We, as temporal and finite beings, are always conditioned by a (or many) definite 'somewhere(s)'. If the individual chooses the paradigm over the paradox then the paradox becomes – given the assumptions of the totalizing paradigm – absurd.

There are three primary senses in which Christ is seen to be paradoxical in Kierkegaard's existential Christological reflection. First, the general idea of the unity of God and man, being fundamentally distinct from one another, is paradoxical. Second, the idea that God existed as one particular person in history is paradoxical. Third, the idea that one's eternal destiny is contingent upon one's relation to a particular historical (temporal) person is paradoxical. It can be seen that Climacus summarizes the dialectical, paradoxical 'issue' in his Postscript as including all three of these senses (CUP 385):

The individual's eternal happiness is decided in time through a relation to something historical [the third point and the second point by implication] that furthermore is historical in such a way that its composition includes that which according to its nature cannot become historical [the first point] and consequently must become that by virtue of the absurd.[1]

In Kierkegaard's thought, the designation 'absolute paradox' refers to the incarnation. In *Philosophical Fragments*, Climacus states that the God-man has the unique quality of being a self-contradiction (PF 87) – of being, as Anti-Climacus writes, 'absolutely the paradox' (PIC 82). In his journals, Kierkegaard writes that the fact 'that a simple human being is God' is 'the most absurd, humanly speaking, of all absurdities' (JP 1642). This paradox is central to Christianity (CUP 540; SUD 129).

The paradoxicalness of the incarnation, for Kierkegaard, is ultimately rooted in an 'infinite qualitative difference' between God and humanity (PF 45–6; SUD 99, 126) – 'the absolute difference by which a human being differs from God' (CUP 217). For Kierkegaard, it is only with an infinite *qualitative* difference (not quantitative) that there can be an incarnation; Christ is not God because he is the greatest human, or the greatest finite being. 'If to be God', Anti-Climacus writes, 'is nothing else than that, then God does not exist at all' (PIC 28). There is a metaphysical distinction between God and humanity.

Another important sense in which the incarnation is paradoxical for Kierkegaard is that it is the existence of the eternal in time (CUP 271–2, 570, 578–9; PF 62). Christianity, he writes, 'is the paradox that the eternal' or 'God once came into existence in time' (BoA 37, 40). That an eternal reality that is not bound, limited or mortal – as all finite, temporal realities are – should come into existence in time is absurd from a human point of view; it confounds our categories. Paradox inheres in 'the fact that the god has existed' (CUP 326).

---

1 These three loci of the paradox of Christ are also present in the three dialectical contradictions of Religiousness B in the Postscript: 1. 'The Dialectical Contradiction That Constitutes the Break: to Expect an Eternal Happiness in Time through a Relation to Something Else in Time' (CUP 570); 2. 'That an Eternal Happiness is Based on the Relation to Something Historical' (CUP 574); 3. 'That the Historical under Consideration Here Is Not Something Historical in the Ordinary Sense But Consists of That Which Can Become Historical Only against Its Nature, Consequently by Virtue of the Absurd' (CUP 578).

Kierkegaard considers the idea of the incarnation as such to be absolute paradox in relation to Hegelianism. While both Kierkegaard and Hegel hold to the Chalcedonian view of the two natures of Christ and see him as the contradictory God-man, for Hegel, and Strauss under his influence, not only is the contradiction of the incarnation resolvable by speculative philosophy, the incarnation reveals the true unity between God and all of humanity. In relation to orthodox Christianity, Kierkegaard saw this to be 'the most dreadful of all blasphemies' (SUD 117). Thus, as Anti-Climacus sees it, instead of God paradoxically and miraculously becoming man in Christ, Hegelianism, like Christendom, 'brazenly turns it around and foists kinship on God' (SUD 118). To fend off the Hegelian idea of God and humanity being one, Kierkegaard focused on the paradoxicalness of the incarnation stemming from the infinite qualitative difference between the human and the divine.

While the emphasis on the metaphysical distinction between God and humanity is present in Kierkegaard's works, another significant distinction that he focuses on is a moral one. In *Philosophical Fragments*, the 'absolute difference' is identified as sin (PF 47). Here the distinction is not ontological, but is something that an individual deliberately causes. God's pure, selfless love shown in Christ is seen as paradoxical insomuch as we – as sinful creatures – have never experienced and are not capable of such love.

From the standpoint of seeing the radical difference between God and humanity, the paradoxicalness of the incarnation is brought more clearly into focus. Through the insistence upon 'absolute distinctions' that makes one 'a good dialectician' (PF 108), Kierkegaard sees in the doctrine of the incarnation the profound tension 'between being God and being an individual human being' (PIC 125). Anti-Climacus states further, that '[i]n the first period of Christendom ... even aberrations bore an unmistakable mark of one's nevertheless knowing what the issue was, the fallacy with respect to the God-man was either that ... "God" was taken away or ... "man" was taken away' (PIC 123). More specifically, Climacus, in *Philosophical Fragments*, identifies the Paradox as, 'the duplexity by which it manifests itself as absolute – negatively, by bringing into prominence the absolute difference of sin and positively, by wanting to annul this absolute difference in absolute equality' (PF 47).

In short, God and humanity are shown to be separated by humanity's sin yet are united in the incarnation. Kierkegaard emphasizes both the distance between God and humanity and God's nevertheless entering into relationship with humanity. In order to reunite humanity to himself, God in Christ not only became human, but took on the lowest common denominator, the form of a suffering servant (CUP 339–40, 537–44).

(2) The second sense in which Kierkegaard considers Christ to be the Absolute Paradox pertains to the historical particularity of Christ as a 'specific historical person' (PIC 23). Above and beyond the paradoxicalness of the idea of God becoming man, the claim that a particular human individual in history, Jesus of Nazareth, 'under Emperor Augustus', was in fact God, 'that the god, the eternal, has come into existence at a specific moment in time', adds another level of paradox and offence (BoA 38; CUP 578). Climacus states that 'the heart of the matter is the historical fact that the god has been in human form' (PF 103). In this matter regarding the person of Jesus and the idea of the incarnation, 'the historical is precisely its essential aspect, whereas in other ideas this is the accidental' (PF 182).

That a particular human being who lived in history was also God is scandalous and absurd to the human understanding. 'Was it not terrifying', Johannes de Silentio writes, 'that this man walking around among others was God? Was it not terrifying to sit down to eat with him?' (FT 66).[2] The scandal lies in the actuality of God's existence as a human being – that the incarnation is something that actually happened (CUP 326, 580). Climacus, in *Fragments*, fleshes out the scandal of the coincidence of the majesty of the Deity and a particular common human being: 'it is indeed less terrifying to fall on one's face while the mountains tremble at the god's voice than to sit with him as his equal, and yet the god's concern is precisely to sit this way' (PF 35). This, Anti-Climacus writes, is 'too shabby a glory' (PIC 31).

Nevertheless, it is the scandalous historical particularity of Christ's life that is at the heart of the Christian religion. As Kierkegaard writes in his journals, 'the real issue is that Jesus Christ be presented

---

2 As Anti-Climacus states, 'the contradiction in which the possibility of offense lies is to be an individual human being, a lowly human being – and then to act in the character of being God' (PIC 97, 26).

as he walked and tarried and lived 1,800 years ago' (JP 321). This vision enables one to perceive better the ambiguity or contradiction between the concrete, overt humanity of Jesus and his claims (implicit and explicit) to unique – yet covert – divinity and thus to see more starkly the paradoxicalness of Jesus. Jesus was a common, lowly human being and yet there were signs or traces that he was, in fact, much more than this (PIC 65–6, 126). So, while the God-man was incognito he also revealed himself – albeit only to a certain degree (PF 56). Among these partially revelatory signs were: a predecessor to announce his coming (PF 55), an unconventional lifestyle (PF 56), his appearance in a context in which people would be attracted to him (given a messianic expectation) (PIC 44) and his performance of miracles (PIC 44). Kierkegaard comments that, 'Christ's whole life here on earth would indeed have become a game if he had been so incognito that he had gone through life totally unnoticed – and yet he truly was incognito' (PoV 16). It is here that we see that historical information (mostly contained in Scripture) is necessary for the reconstruction of the 'immediate sensation' of the phenomena of Jesus' life, in that all of our knowledge of his life is mediated to us by the reports of others (PF 103–4). Yet, it must be recognized that such a reconstruction alone will never lead one to the conclusion of Jesus' identity (PIC 30–1). This is what Anti-Climacus means when he writes that Christ as the God-man 'historically can be neither proved nor disproved' (PIC 250).

One of the primary ways that Kierkegaard speaks of the paradox of the incarnation is in the unity of such disparate qualities as the temporal and the eternal – the actual and the ideal. Climacus identifies the paradox as 'the eternalizing of the historical and the historicizing of the eternal' (PF 59). The historical incarnation is 'no simple historical fact' (PF 92).[3] Unlike simple historical facts, the event of the incarnation is an 'absolute fact' (PF 99–100). This 'absolute fact' is the unity of a simple historical fact, which is historically/temporally conditioned, and an eternal fact, which is universally true and not temporally conditioned. In the incarnation

---

3 Kierkegaard writes in his journals and papers: 'Christ's story always is ideality and not like history, which usually is not pure ideality, and therefore the poet can add ideality to it. But here the ideality is the historical, the greatest contradiction possible, again an expression of the fact that Christianity in its pure ideality explodes all existence, just as the graves burst, and the veil' (JP 1645).

both the historical element and the trans-historical, eternal element are necessary.

The third sense in which Christ is seen to be paradox is in the scandalous idea that one's eternal salvation is based upon one's knowledge of and relation to a particular historical event or person, or as Climacus puts it, 'to expect an eternal happiness in time through a relation to something else in time' (CUP 570; see CUP 570–7). In the *Postscript*, Climacus addresses the question of how something historical can be decisive for one's eternal destiny (CUP 94). He later sets forth the thesis of the book and the summary of the paradoxical elements of the incarnation, 'The individual's eternal happiness is decided in time through a relation to something historical that furthermore is historical in such a way that its composition includes that which according to its nature cannot become historical and consequently must become that by virtue of the absurd' (CUP 385). The paradox is that 'this historical event' is 'the condition for [one's] eternal happiness' (PF 58).

The paradoxical nature of salvation being dependent upon historical knowledge owes much to the nature of historical knowledge itself. Climacus states, 'the historical intrinsically has the illusiveness of coming into existence' (PF 81). Given the illusiveness of the historical, part of which being the inherent ambiguity of knowing anything that happened in history, belief ('the organ of the historical') in something historical always risks error (PF 83). Belief implies an uncertainty and hence a need to venture, to risk (to venture on a certainty is to venture nothing); this movement from uncertainty to belief is what Kierkegaard calls the 'leap' (CUP 93, 211, 424). For Climacus, the contradiction is to base one's eternal happiness – the most extreme passion of subjectivity, the most important thing in life – on an approximation (CUP 574).[4]

In the *Postscript*, it is seen to be paradoxical that faith as the most inward, personal passion finds its object in something outward. The ultimate relation between a person and God is not immediate – just between God and me in the here-and-now. It is based upon and mediated by one's relation to an external, historical event (CUP 561, 574). That faith, as the most inward passion, has as its object

---

4 Climacus writes regarding the fact that eternal blessedness is decided in time that all Christian principles 'inhere in this one qualification and can be consistently derived from it' (CUP 369).

something external and historical is the paradox (CUP 323–4). In Christianity, the divine is not known as immediate to the self, but comes to the self as something external, foreign. This paradoxical-ness of one's relation to God being contingent upon one's relation to the historical person of Jesus is evident in Christianity's primary focus upon the person of Jesus (who is historically located) rather than upon his teaching (which is not historically located).

Eternal happiness is so heavy a consequence that no amount of probability will suffice to make the decision secure, comfortable or – by any means – easy. Climacus holds that the biblical reports, being as reliable as other historical reports, are still not reliable enough to base one's absolute end on them (CUP 96). In *Works of Love*, Kierkegaard states that Christianity has 'no infallible signs' (WL 70). Christianity 'venture[s] everything upon the "if"' (CUP 429).

Christ as the object of faith and sign of offence

Christ as the Absolute Paradox is encountered by human reason as a limit. The furthest that human reason can go in understanding this paradox is to admit that it cannot think it (PF 37; JP 3026). Insomuch as knowledge entails the idea of control or mastery, the transcendent God who is encountered in the paradox of the incar-nation remains unknown. The Absolute Paradox is encountered only at the limit of human reason.

This encounter with the Absolute Paradox posits what Kierke-gaard calls the possibility of offence. Anti-Climacus identifies this possibility of offence as 'the negative mark of the God-man' (PIC 143). The possibility of offence 'accompanies the God-man at every moment in one way or another' (PIC 121); it is the 'halt' that calls for a decision on the part of the encountering individual (PIC 39). Thus, in the incarnation, God reveals himself 'in such a way as to bring about the most terrible decision' (PF 34). This possibility of offence is 'the crossroad. . . . From the possibility of offense, one turns either to offense or to faith' (PIC 81). It is 'the repulsion in which faith can come into existence – if one does not choose to be offended' (PIC 121).[5] The God-man – being, as Anti-Climacus

---

5 Thus, Anti-Climacus entreats, 'fear not anything that can damage only the outer person . . . but fear yourself, fear what can kill the faith and in that way kill

designates him, 'the sign of contradiction' – 'discloses the thoughts
of hearts' (PIC 126). He is a watershed; he confronts the individual
with choice. This decision is between the mutually exclusive stances
of faith and offence. As we have seen earlier in Kierkegaard's
thought more generally, the higher is encountered by the lower as
a 'stumbling-block', as a sign of offence (EO 484). The difference
between faith and offence is not as much in the 'what' – they both
agree that the paradox is the limit of human reason – but in 'how'
they relate to it.

Offence sees the Absolute Paradox as a Sign of Offence and
summarily rejects it. Climacus postulates that if there is no mutual
understanding in the encounter between the individual's passionate
reason and Christ as the Absolute Paradox, then the result is an
unhappy relation or 'offense' (PF 49). The offended understanding,
when it 'cannot get the paradox into its head', simply rejects that
which is beyond its comprehension, that which it cannot 'digest', as
absurd (PF 52–3; PIC 30). Thus, the offended understanding makes
a true observation – regarding the nature of the paradox as 'that
which conflicts with all (human) reason' (PIC 26) – yet its conclusion – rejecting the paradox as 'absurd' – does not necessarily
follow from this observation; it is a choice driven by a passionate
impulse. Here the Absolute Paradox is seen as the Sign of Offence
in that, wanting to fully comprehend, 'reason becomes conceited'
and concludes that the paradox is nonsensical (TERE 66; JP 1033).
The paradoxical truth of Christianity is 'the nettle' that stings when
one grasps it in the wrong way (CUP 46–7).

Faith sees the Absolute Paradox as the Object of Faith and summarily accepts it. Climacus states that, 'if the paradox and the
understanding meet in the mutual understanding of their difference,
then the encounter is a happy one' (PF 49).[6] It is in faith that the
Absolute Paradox and limited human understanding are 'on good
terms' with one another (PF 54). Faith is not a conclusion regarding
the Absolute Paradox that one comes to through reflection, but a

---

Jesus Christ for you. . . . Fear and tremble, for faith is carried in a fragile earthen
vessel, in the possibility of offence' (PIC 76).

6 Anti-Climacus writes: 'The person who does not take offense worships in
faith. But to worship, which is the expression of faith, is to express that the infinite,
chasmic, qualitative abyss between them is confirmed. For in faith the possibility of
offense is again the dialectical factor' (SUD 129).

resolution whereby doubt is excluded and the paradox is accepted (PF 84). The response of faith follows human reason's desire to go beyond itself and accepts the limitation of human reason as implied by the Absolute Paradox. In *The Sickness Unto Death*, Anti-Climacus describes the way of faith as when 'through the aid of the eternal the self has the courage to lose itself in order to gain itself' (SUD 67).

Faith in the Absolute Paradox for Kierkegaard is an affirmation of that which is other to the understanding that follows a negation of human understanding's totalities. In his journals, Kierkegaard writes:

> Faith is, quite rightly, the 'point outside the world' which therefore also moves the whole world.
>
> It is easy to perceive that what bursts forth through a negation of all points in the world is the point outside the world. (JP 2803)

Similarly, Kierkegaard explains in another section of his papers:

> The absurd is the negative determinant which assures, for example, that I have not overlooked one or another possibility which still lies within the human arena. The absurd is the expression of despair: that humanly it is not possible – but despair is the negative sign of faith. (JP 9)

Finally, it should be recognized that for Kierkegaard faith in the Absolute Paradox is not irrational. Faith provides the plausibility structure in which the Absolute Paradox fits harmoniously. Kierkegaard explains the relation between faith and the 'absurd':

> When the believer has faith, the absurd is not the absurd – faith transforms it, but in every weak moment it is again more or less absurd to him. . . . To a third person the believer relates himself by virtue of the absurd; so must a third person judge, for a third person does not have the passion of faith. (JP 10)

It is in what Kierkegaard calls 'the moment' that Christ as the absolute Paradox is taken to be either the Object of Faith or the

Sign of Offence. In the moment of decision, the individual encounters Christ as a present actuality. For Kierkegaard, Christ as the Absolute Paradox must be encountered, in some way, as a present reality. In this contemporaneity there takes place an 'I–Thou' encounter, in which one is able to relate to the personal reality of Christ and not just an intellectual distillation thereof. Christ is here encountered as a present, living reality. Anti-Climacus explains (PIC 64):

> But that which has actually happened (the past) is still not . . . the actual. The qualification that is lacking – which is the qualification of truth (as inwardness) and of all religious is – for you. The past is not actuality – for me. Only the contemporary is actuality for me. That with which you are living simultaneously is actuality – **for you.**

This contemporaneity is possible in that the incarnate Christ is both temporal (human) and eternal (divine), and, as such, can encounter temporal human beings hundreds of years after his earthly life as a contemporary – as God incarnate 'his life on earth has the eternal contemporaneity' (PIC 64; PF 69). This is why contemporaneity with Christ is 'essentially Christian' (PIC 65; BoA 43) – for one can only be contemporary with the incarnate Christ, who can be present in time (as temporal) but be present at any time (as eternal). The encounter in the present necessarily builds upon one's knowledge of the historical person of Jesus. While 'eminent faith' is indeed of a different order than direct or ordinary faith (in that eminent faith's object is unique), it is clear that eminent faith is based upon ordinary faith in the historical facts regarding Jesus (PF 87–8). It is in this context that one sees the report of the contemporary witness – as preserved in the New Testament – as being the occasion for the encounter in which faith is acquired. Here historical knowledge becomes more than historical knowledge, as the occasion for an encounter with Christ in the present.

For Kierkegaard, this encounter – contemporaneity with Christ – is the occasion for decision. The occasion for decision arises as one becomes aware of the tension or ambiguity regarding Christ's identity. It is here that one encounters Christ as the sign of contradiction – as something that is different than immediately appears

(PIC 124–6). It is here – in 'the possibility in the tension of contemporaneity of having to be offended or to lay hold of faith' (BoA 44) – that Christ is properly seen as 'the sign of offense and object of faith' (PIC 24). It is thus that the Absolute Paradox as the sign of contradiction is presented as a 'dialectical knot' in which 'if anyone wants to have anything to do with this kind of communication, he will have to untie the knot himself' (PIC 133). So, in contemporaneity with Christ, a decision is necessary in addition to (not over and against) the historical information one is presented with. To encounter Christ, the Absolute Paradox, as a contemporary is not simply a matter of seeing him as he is (given the historical data) but one of seeing him as either the Object of Faith or the Sign of Offence. Thus, given the historical report, one chooses to respond in the moment, in contemporaneity, to Jesus Christ, the Absolute Paradox, as either the Object of (one's) Faith or the Sign of (one's) Offence.

Another way that Kierkegaard describes the moment relative to the Absolute Paradox is that the moment is the eternal in time. Climacus describes the moment as the point in time at which the eternal, paradoxically, 'came into existence' (PF 13). The moment is 'the fullness of time' that is in time yet is 'filled with the eternal' (PF 18). It is the moment in which the eternal 'came into existence' (PF 13). In Kierkegaard's work, the moment is described as the eternal in time in two senses: as involving a temporal decision with eternal consequences, and as an analogue of the incarnation.

One of the central issues addressed and answered affirmatively in *Fragments* is whether 'a historical point of departure can be given for an eternal consciousness' (PF 1). For Kierkegaard, it is in the moment that one chooses to accept or reject Christ, the Absolute Paradox, and consequently one makes a decision regarding one's eternal destiny (PF 59). In the *Postscript* the moment is described as that in which the believer 'becomes eternal' (CUP 507). As Christ is a composite of eternal truth (God) and temporal existence (man), the moment is a historical point of departure for eternal happiness.

The second sense in which Kierkegaard sees the moment to be the eternal in time is in its being an analogue of the incarnation itself. Thus, using one of Climacus's descriptions of the paradox, the moment of incarnation involves 'the historicizing of the eternal' while the moment of faith involves 'the eternalizing of the historical' (PF 59).[7] Both involve a qualitative leap, one ontological and one epistemological and existential. Both involve a free (not necessary) choice – one being God's choice to become a human and one being a human's choice to risk to trust in Christ. Here, the distinctive 'how' of Christian faith is structurally similar to the distinctive 'what' that is its object (Christ as the Absolute Paradox). The incarnation – as both eternal/divine and historical/human – can only be encountered and appropriated in a manner like unto its nature – God giving the condition and the historical report giving the occasion. Thus, the moment is the eternal in time insofar as faith is an incarnational event – a retracing of the road from heaven to earth pioneered by Jesus, the Incarnate One.

The relation between the absolute paradox and the object of faith/sign of offence

Having examined Kierkegaard's portraits of Christ as the Absolute Paradox and the Object of Faith/Sign of Offence, we will now turn to see how these portraits interact with one another to form a single Christological dynamic. The first point of interaction lies in the fact that the Absolute Paradox corresponds with human reason's limit. The paradoxicalness of Christ reveals the limitation of one's reason in that paradox is precisely that which is encountered at the limits of human understanding and implies that which is beyond understanding. It is from this signalling of the limit inherent in the Absolute Paradox that the individual is brought to choose between one of the two response portraits.

The second point of interaction is that the Absolute Paradox is the occasion or provides the tension out of which comes the individual's decision to accept or reject Christ. It is this 'seeing as' that constitutes the passionately motivated decision of how to deal with the Absolute Paradox and the idea of the limitation of human understanding. After one sees Christ as the Absolute Paradox (translated into subjective terms) one then chooses to see Christ, the Absolute Paradox, as either the Object of Faith or the Sign of Offence. It is

---

7 'This is the consequence of the appearance of the god in time, which prevents the individual from relating himself backward to the eternal, since he now moves forward in order to become eternal in time through the relation to the god in time' (CUP 583–4).

out of the qualities of both the individual's human reason and the portrait of the Absolute Paradox that the portraits of Object of Faith/Sign of Offence come into existence.

The third point of interaction between the portraits is in the idea of contemporaneity. The 'contemporaneity' in which one sees Christ as he existed and taught in first-century Palestine (giving rise to Christ's paradoxicalness) is logically prior to the 'contemporaneity' that comes about in the present moment (in which one encounters Christ) and is the occasion for one's decision between either faith or offence. 'Contemporaneity then' is necessary for 'contemporaneity now'. We encounter the scandalous divine–human Jesus as he was then yet in the living here-and-now.

The final point of interaction is in the concept of the eternal in time. In the incarnation (the Absolute Paradox) the eternal God ontologically took on temporal humanity, while in the moment of decision (between seeing Christ as the Object of Faith or the Sign of Offence) the temporal individual existentially makes a decision with eternal consequences. Thus, the moment of decision is a reverse analogue of the moment of the incarnation.[8]

The first Christological dynamic

The portraits of Christ in Kierkegaard's thought – as Absolute Paradox, the Sign of Offence and the Object of Faith – form a dynamic that functions in several different, yet interrelated, ways. The first function of this dynamic is that of emphasizing God's distinctness/transcendence from humanity. There is here a 'distancing' of the subject (the individual) from the object (God in Christ) that maintains a sense of holiness and mystery. Here the paradox preserves the transcendent character of Christianity over and against distortions in which the qualitative difference between God and man is 'pantheistically abolished' (SUD 117; see also PIC 140). The emphasis on the absoluteness of the paradox of Christ points to the 'chasmic abyss between the single individual and the God-man over which faith and faith alone reaches' (PIC 139). Here also the

---

8 The moment of decision is then paradoxically both temporal (it happens at a certain point in history) and atemporal in that in it one encounters the incarnate Christ in the person of Jesus of Nazareth 1900 years ago yet also in the living present.

emphasis on the uniqueness and finality of the incarnation makes Christianity a religion of 'transcendence'.

The second function of this dynamic is that of eliciting an existential either/or response that initiates one into Christian existence – ensuring the existential character of Christianity and establishing its authority. With this commitment of faith, one takes on a new paradigm of existence. Central to this new paradigm is submission to God's authority. In this first Christological dynamic, the act of faith subjectively establishes the authority of God in one's life. The acceptance of the divinity (and thus authority) of Christ inaugurates a new ethics for the individual. As such, this function of the first dynamic lays the existential foundation for the ethical character of the second dynamic.

The third function of Kierkegaard's first Christological dynamic is that of preserving human freedom. With the possibility of offence that is inevitably present when one encounters the Absolute Paradox, one always has the choice to accept Christ or reject him – neither conclusion is inevitable.

The fourth function of this dynamic is that of establishing egalitarianism. The paradox guarantees human equality by reducing intellectual differences among individuals to insignificance. Before the Absolute Paradox, being faced with the choice of faith or offence, every individual is equal (CUP 217, 227, 596).

The final function of Kierkegaard's first Christological dynamic is that of keeping the road to God a way of humility and of reverence. Built into the structure of this dynamic is the fact that the proud, arrogant person will never come to have faith in Christ as long as he remains in this posture. As Anti-Climacus states, 'Christianity insists on having absolute respect' (PIC 68). The elements of Christianity that are offensive, such as the paradox and 'the absurd', guard the way to it against those who are not interested in the impassioned subjective appropriation of faith (CUP 214, 218; WL 70). Christianity is not a religion for the strong, for the arrogant, for the self-justifying, for those who put ultimate trust in their own abilities. Christ allows only those who know they need him to approach him: the weak, the humble, the penitent, those who put their ultimate trust in an-Other.

The Second Dynamic

The second dynamic, the second and largely later set of interrelated portraits of Christ in Kierkegaard's thought, is primarily comprised of three figures: Truth in Existence, the Saviour or Teacher and the Prototype or Pattern.

Christ as truth in existence: the way, the criterion, and the cross

For Kierkegaard, Christianity looks beyond mere truth or mere knowing to a greater, fuller truth of the unity of being and knowing. The fullness of truth is in its subjective (personal, existential) embodiment. 'The being of truth', Anti-Climacus explains, 'is the redoubling of truth within yourself . . . that your life . . . expresses the truth approximately in the striving for it' (PIC 205). This is especially so when one considers Christianity. Anti-Climacus later states that, 'Christianly understood, truth is obviously not to know the truth but to be the truth' (PIC 205). And again, 'in original Christianity all the expressions were formed according to the view that truth is being' (PIC 206). From the Christian point of view, full truth is not a set of definitions but truth in being; it is a life (PIC 206).

For Kierkegaard, the full, complete and unique manifestation of this truth in existence is found in the person and life of Jesus Christ. Thus, for Kierkegaard, to speak of truth in existence is to refer to Christ. Thus, Kierkegaard writes of: 'Jesus Christ, to name the supreme example, truth itself' (PoV 125). 'His life', Kierkegaard writes, 'is the essential truth' (CD 122) – Christ is 'the Truth and the Life' (PIC 78) – 'the truth was in Christ a life, for he was the truth' (PIC 205). In his journals, Kierkegaard writes that, 'all Christianity is subjectivity. Christianity is no doctrine; it is a doctrine existentially realized in one single man, in the God-man' (JP 4553). Again, as Anti-Climacus writes: 'Christ is the truth in the sense that to be the truth is the only true explanation of what truth is. . . . Truth in the sense in which Christ is the truth is not a sum of statements, not a definition etc., but a life. . . . The truth was in Christ a life, for he was the truth' (PIC 205). In this manner Kierkegaard seeks to understand Jesus' claim in John 14.6: 'I am the way and the truth and the life' – that is Christ, 'being the truth is a life' (PIC 207).

Kierkegaard observes that with Christ the words of his teaching found full existential embodiment in the work of his life. In *Judge for Yourself!*, Christ is seen to be truth in existence in that, 'what He said, He was' (JFY 170). Thus Christ, 'not only spoke the truth but was the truth, he who was the Word in such a way that he was what he said' (JFY 159). Again, 'His teaching was really his life, his existence' (JFY 191). As Anti-Climacus writes: 'he himself is his word; he is what he says – in this sense, too, he is the Word' (PIC 14). He 'made the truth true, or he made it true that he is the truth'.[9] Christ was not merely one who strived admirably to live in accordance with the absolute requirements of Scripture; 'He was the Scriptures given life' (JP 342).

As Truth in Existence, Christ's existence, in Kierkegaard's reckoning, provides the supreme example of proper human existence. It is in this vein that Kierkegaard describes Christ as 'the way', as the 'one Way' (CD 20) – through this life (the way to live) beyond this life (the way through which we ascend to our eternal hope) – for 'his debasement [his earthly life] is the Way, but he was also the Way when he ascended into heaven' (WL 248). 'There is', Kierkegaard writes, 'only one who is "the Way and the Life," only one guidance that in truth leads a person through life to life' (UDVS 217) – 'one guidance' for 'believers' as 'pilgrims, strangers, and aliens in the world' (UDVS 218). Kierkegaard considered the truth to be a life or a way of living, and this truth/life/way is identified uniquely and finally with Christ (PIC 207). As Kierkegaard writes in his journals, 'He is himself the way – this is so that no fraud may be perpetrated about there being many ways. There were not many ways, of which Christ took one – no, Christ is the way' (JP 361). A common way that Christ's ultimate human existence, Christ's being 'the way', is presented in Kierkegaard's works (certainly in his later works) is in terms of Christ's perfect obedience to the will of the Father (CD 85).[10] 'Surely,' he writes, 'his will from eternity was in harmony

---

9 Kierkegaard writes: 'the highest a person is capable of is to make [*gjøre*] an eternal truth true, to make it true that it is true – by doing [*gjøre*] it, by being oneself the demonstration, by a life that perhaps will also be able to convince others. Did Christ ever get involved in demonstrating one or another truth, or in demonstrating the truth? No, but he made the truth true, or he made it true that he is the truth' (CD 98).

10 '"No one can serve two masters." These are his words, and he was the Word: he served only one master' (JFY 179).

with the Father's; his free decision was the Father's will' (UDVS 253).[11]

This way, this supreme existence, that is expressed in Christ's life is a narrow one that consists not of external conformity but of certain qualities (FSE 57). In *Judge For Yourself!*, Kierkegaard describes Christ as 'the only sober one' (JFY 113). For Kierkegaard, to become 'sober' is, 'to come to oneself in self-knowledge and before God as nothing before him, yet infinitely, unconditionally engaged' (JFY 104). He later defines sobriety as, 'to come so close to oneself in one's understanding, in one's knowing, that all one's understanding becomes action' (JFY 115). Christ, here as the only human that is as humanity was intended to be – the only one not disengaged from life, deluded, distorted and corrupted ('intoxicated' (JFY 116)) – displays this unconditional engagement with and unconditional fulfilment of the unconditioned requirements of the Unconditioned One (JFY 159). He is 'transparent' before God in that what God desires is perfectly replicated in Christ's existence (JFY 107). He is the unity of thought and existence.[12]

As living the ultimate, unconditioned, sober, transparent existence Christ then constitutes 'the true criterion' for human existence (JFY 199). 'Christ's life upon earth, every moment of this life, was truth' (PIC 203), and 'when we walk side by side with the man who is the Truth, when the Truth is the criterion, we are still like children alongside a giant' (CD 278). For, as Anti-Climacus observed, Christ's life is, 'the very judgement by which we shall be judged' (PIC 181). His life is the objective moral standard; he is 'eternity's examination' (JP 1937). Thus is the incarnation not just some metaphysical event but rather 'the earnestness of existence' (SUD 130).[13]

---

11 Perhaps even presenting an orthodox two-wills Christology (in which the human will submits perfectly to the divine will), Kierkegaard writes: 'Obedience is so closely related to the eternal truth that the one who is Truth learns obedience' (UDVS 255). 'What he learned from sufferings was human obedience. . . . The obedience belongs to his abasement' (UDVS 263).

12 Thus, Christ is, 'an exposition of which it holds true that the exposition is that which is expounded' (JFY 119). Kierkegaard observes that in relation to this, 'we are all hypocrites' (JFY 119). We never are what we say.

13 Kierkegaard writes: 'when the prototype says it, then it is earnestness, because his life is the truth thereof' (JFY 179).

In his exposition, Kierkegaard pays special attention to the suffering that Christ underwent as a result of his being Truth in Existence. Because of the human world's habitual opposition to the truth there is an inversion – such that truth and goodness are persecuted, such that it is 'essentially a part of "the truth" to suffer in this world' and suffering is 'the negative form of the highest' (PIC 198, 154; BoA 162).[14] Thus, Christ's life, as Truth in Existence, is characterized by suffering. Christ was necessarily misunderstood by the world whose values stand in opposition to the truth that he revealed. As Kierkegaard writes in a late journal entry: 'In this world of temporality and sensuousness and, as Christianity teaches, in this world of sin, the idea can actually be only in suffering. Only once has the idea been unconditional, in Christ; his life was therefore unconditional, absolute suffering' (JP 365). Christ's 'loftiness' is thus perceived to be 'abasement' (PIC 259). For Kierkegaard, Christ was a man of sorrows who 'entered into the world in order to suffer', whose 'entire life was the heaviest suffering' (CUP 597; UDVS 255).[15]

Christ's suffering – which, for Kierkegaard, is the fate of truth in the world – is due to the dissonance between his life and the human social world to which he came. He was misunderstood 'in everything' – appeared 'as lunatic as wanting to set up, in the midst of this world, a kingdom that is not of this world' (PIC 170; JFY 175). He was a stranger – 'unconditionally a stranger in the world, without the slightest alliance with anything or with anyone at all in the world, where everything is actually a matter of alliance' (JFY 170). 'The God-man' was isolated, rejected – 'the most forsaken and hated and wretched'[16] – 'betrayed, mocked, abandoned by all, all, all' (MLW 316). In this rejection, Christ also suffers as the Sign of Offence – suffers in his love for those who reject him and so reject their own good, and harming themselves – 'his greatest

---

14 'Truth must be essentially regarded as struggling in this world' (WL 366).

15 Perhaps one can see the depiction of 'the unhappiest one' in *Either/Or* as a parody of Christ (EO 220–1).

16 Kierkegaard writes in his journals: 'Christ . . . gives absolute expression to that which naturally no human being achieves: absolutely holding to God in all things. Consequently his life must with unqualified necessity collide absolutely with the world, with men, and he become the most forsaken and hated and wretched of all. . . . For there is strife between man and God, and one must choose sides' (JP 1859).

sorrow was when the suffering one would not let himself be helped' (UDVS 231).[17]

Christ's suffering love for humanity – his being the truth that is rejected and suffers at the hands of the world – is seen supremely for Kierkegaard in the crucifixion. The life of God incarnate 'was retrogression instead of progression' through which 'he ascends rung by rung through all the marks of abasement, until finally he is crucified' (CD 277). 'That God's son, when he was revealed in human form, was crucified, rejected by temporality', by the world, was not accidental (UDVS 89–90); it was, for Kierkegaard, the necessary outcome of the one who was Truth confronting the untrue world. As he writes: 'The crowd is untruth. Therefore Christ was crucified' (PoV 109). In the cross, we see Christ as rejected, as isolated, as excluded – outside the city. There the truth, the true way, suffered – suffered as love does in and for the world. On the cross, 'it was love that suffered' (MLW 165) – 'He was crucified precisely because he was love . . . because he refused to be self-loving' and so 'expressly manifested that love is hated, truth is persecuted' (TERE 59; PIC 198). This, 'Christ's innocent death', Kierkegaard writes, is 'the most severe judgment passed upon the world' – that 'love was not loved' (TwDCF 171–2).[18]

The crucifixion of Christ then, for Kierkegaard, is a judgement upon the world. In 'the Holy One crucified [one sees] the evil and corruption of the whole world disclosed' (UDVS 337–8). It is in the very act of atonement that 'the guilt of the race . . . becomes manifest' (TERE 65). Christ, as Kierkegaard observes in his journals, 'was the truth, absolute truth; therefore he could not simply defend himself, but he had to permit men to become guilty of his death – that is, to reveal the truth [of God's goodness and the world's corruption] in a radical way' (JP 316). Perfect love could not spare the world its rejection of truth on the cross. 'It is this love', Kierkegaard writes, 'which in its eternal, divine perfection was in him who, as the Truth, had to express absolutely that he was the Truth and therefore let the ungodly world become guilty in this way' (TERE 88). In this way, the cross is 'the unity of truth and love' (TERE 88).

---

17 'What heavy suffering: to have to be the stumbling stone in order to be the Savior of the world!' (UDVS 254).

18 Kierkegaard writes of Christ that 'by being love that was not loved you were a judgment upon the world' (TwDCF 169).

Truth in existence, then, who was the judge and the criterion, who was the way of love, who was true life, was hated, 'mocked and spat upon', rejected by the untrue crowd, judged, condemned and put to death (MLW 21).

Christ as the Mediator of Truth in Existence

For Kierkegaard, Christ is not only Truth in Existence; he is also the Mediator of Truth in Existence. The 'Truth' that Christ is is also communicated to, mediated to the human subject – and is thus concerned with remaking the subject (CUP 130). Christ, while being the truth, plays a role – in fact, several fundamental roles – in the individual's coming likewise to be 'existing in what is true' (CUP 249). The truth that Christ is is what we are to become – and Christ not only is the Way, but is the way into this true life (TwDCF 188).

The general portrait of Christ as Mediator of Truth in Existence manifests itself in two distinct, more specific portraits. First, Christ is an active agent – the giver of Truth. As such, he is depicted as the Teacher, the Gift or the Saviour. This portrait of Christ as the active Mediator of Truth in Existence stresses divine activity in relation to the individual. Second, Christ is seen as a passive agent – as the model of Truth. As such, he is depicted as the Prototype, the Pattern, or the Exemplar. This portrait of Christ as the passive Mediator of Truth in Existence stresses the individual's activity in relation to Christ.

These two portraits also show how the individual's response to Christ is both passive, insomuch as we receive and accept the gift of Christ, and active, insomuch as we respond to and imitate Christ. In this passage from *Upbuilding Discourses in Various Spirits*, Kierkegaard stresses both the active and passive elements of Christ's mediation of truth to the individual on life's journey:

> You who yourself once walked the earth and left footprints that we should *follow* [passive]; you who from heaven still look down on every pilgrim, *strengthen* the weary, *hearten* the disheartened, *lead back* the straying, *give solace* to the struggling [active]; you who will come again at the end of time to judge each one individually, whether he followed you – our God and our *Savior* [active], let your *prototype* [passive] stand very clearly before the

eyes of the soul in order to dispel the mists, *strengthen* [active] in order *to keep* this [passive example] alone unaltered before our eyes so that by resembling you and by following you we may find the right way surely to the judgment, since every human being ought to be brought before the judgment – oh, but may we also be brought by you to the eternal happiness with you in the life to come. Amen. (UDVS 217; italics mine)

In his journals, Kierkegaard writes explicitly of this dialectical duality regarding Christ's work for us:

> Yet it must be firmly maintained that Christ has not come to the world only to set an example for us. In that case we would have law and works-righteousness again. He comes to save us and to present the example. This example should humble us, teach us how infinitely far we are from resembling the ideal. When we humble ourselves, then Christ is pure compassion. And in our striving to approach the prototype, the prototype itself is again our very help. It alternates; when we are striving, then he is the prototype; and when we stumble, lose courage, etc., then he is the love which helps us up, and then he is the prototype again. (JP 334)

Christ as active agent or the giver of truth: teacher, gift, saviour

Christ, for Kierkegaard, 'is' love (EUD 67; WL 99; CD 280; TwDCF 181). In him love itself is revealed to us (WL 3–4). As love, as acting out of pure love for us as our 'friend', Christ condescends to help us (CD 258). It is this loving friend who 'walked the infinitely long way from being God to becoming man; he walked that way in order to seek sinners!' (PIC 20). Out of love, Christ then is portrayed in Kierkegaard's work as actively taking the initiative to give or to impart his Truth to the individual.

In *Philosophical Fragments*, in particular, this active giving is seen in that, in the moment, Christ gives the condition for saving faith to the individual. Climacus writes that the believer, 'knows the god by having received the condition from the god himself' (PF 66; see also PF 69). Here the potential believer is made aware by the present Christ ('the god') of one's sin or 'untruth' (PF 14–15). This consciousness of sin is the condition that Christ presents to the potential believer as the necessary condition for one's entry into the Christian way of truth (PF 51, 93, 111). The active imparting of the condition for one's being in truth occurs in 'the moment' and, as such, in the situation of contemporaneity with Christ. This contemporaneity as the occasion 'to become a follower' requires 'the report of the contemporaries' (PF 100). Yet, beyond mere historical reconstruction (contemporaneity 'then') the actual presence of Christ (contemporaneity 'now') is necessary for the imparting of the condition and hence to mediating of Truth in Existence to the individual.[19] As Climacus writes, 'the god's presence is not incidental to his teaching [his providing the individual with the Truth] but is essential. The presence of the god in human form . . . is precisely the teaching, and the god himself must provide the condition' (PF 55–6). This condition for the reception of Truth in Existence can only be given to the individual first hand,[20] and hence Christ ('the god in human form') must be present or contemporary with the individual (PF 104). The living presence of Christ that is encountered in this kind of contemporaneity is possible in that Christ is 'an eternally present one for he is true God' (JP 318), and, as Anti-Climacus writes, 'in relation to the absolute, there is only one time, the present' (PIC 63).

Kierkegaard – or, more properly, Climacus – also presents Christ as 'the teacher'. Here Christ is seen as the divine–human teacher who – and who alone – can mediate essential truth to the individual 'learner'. The teacher is the one who gives both the condition as the occasion for acceptance or rejection (allowing for human freedom) and the truth (showing divine grace) (PF 14). But, as Climacus continues, this 'teacher' is not just a teacher insomuch as he does not just teach but 'transforms' the 'learner' by imparting truth-in-existence (PF 14). And so can only the Incarnate Christ be this teacher in that only 'the god himself' can transform another (PF 15).

Perhaps the best way to make sense of Climacus's speaking of Christ's essential activity as being that of a teacher is to see it as a

---

19 'The report of the contemporaries becomes the occasion for everyone coming later to become a follower – by receiving the condition, please note, from the god himself' (PF 100).

20 One 'cannot receive it at second hand' (PF 69).

metaphor for the economy of faith that depicts salvation as a 'truth'
to be given by a 'teacher' and received by a 'learner'.[21] Climacus
goes on to write that given the rather peculiar capacities of this
teacher, other more accurate designations might be given him:

> What then should we call such a teacher ... ? Let us call him a
> savior, for he does indeed save the learner from unfreedom, saves
> him from himself. Let us call him a deliverer, for he does indeed
> deliver the person who has imprisoned himself. . . . And yet, even
> this does not say enough, for by his unfreedom he has indeed
> become guilty of something, and if that teacher gives him the
> condition and the truth, then he is, of course, a reconciler who
> takes away the wrath that lay over the incurred guilt. (PF 17)

Stretching again the metaphor of a teacher or a communicator,
Kierkegaard contends that, with Christ, the teacher is greater than
the teaching (PIC 123). Indeed, in *Christian Discourses*, he writes:
'The Gospel itself is certainly the actual teacher, he the Teacher
– and the Way and the Truth and the Life' (CD 9). Here Christ, as
the Truth that is to be communicated, communicates himself as 'the
Gospel' – he is at once the teacher and the good news.

In his journals, Kierkegaard speaks of Christ's functioning in the
capacity of the Mediator of Truth in Existence in the broad terms of
'the gift'. This general depiction of Christ as gift is usually set over
and against the depiction of Christ as prototype (JP 1908). Christ
is the undeserved and gracious gift that 'came down from heaven
to bring blessing to the fallen human race' (CD 296). Again, Christ
is at once the gift that came to us and the giver that gives himself,
communicates to us the truth that he is.

Christ is also presented as the divine–human healer or physician
(PIC 61–2). Christ is the 'helper' who aids us where we most need
it and cannot help ourselves (PIC 21–2). Such a helper gives healing, comfort and rest to the sick, the despairing, the weary. Indeed,
Christ, in Anti-Climacus's reckoning, says: 'Remain with me, I
am that rest, or to remain with me is that rest' (PIC 15). Again,
Christ is the helper, and yet 'the helper is the help' (PIC 15). As the

---

21 Another Climacan metaphor for the economy of faith is seen in his story of
the king/lover and the maiden/beloved (PF 26–30).

helper, Christ is on the way with you to help on the way . . . to him;
Kierkegaard writes: 'he who says "Come here" is with you on the
way; from him there is help and forgiveness on the way of conversion that leads to him, and with him is rest' (PIC 19).

Finally, Christ is portrayed in Kierkegaard's writing in the more
traditional terms for his functioning as the active Mediator of Truth
in Existence – in terms of being the Saviour, the Redeemer, the
Reconciler. He recognizes Christ as the 'saviour' (PF 17; CD 283)
– 'The Savior of the world' (JFY 191) – who came into the world
with the purpose of saving 'all' of 'mankind' (PIC 34–5, 238). Here,
Christ is, again, the gift and the giver – 'grace and the giver of grace'
(ThDCF 143). He is the one, indeed the only one, through whom
we are saved – the only name 'in heaven and on earth', the 'one
road', 'the only name in which there is blessedness' (UDVS 225;
CD 222–3).

Christ is God's gracious action on our behalf in his death as the
atonement for our sins (TERE 64). In his death, Christ 'out of love
sacrificed himself for the world' (CD 288; CA 104; UDVS 232).
Christ's death is a substitution in which he takes on himself and
carries our sin and suffers punishment in our place,[22] effecting an
infinite satisfaction (UD 159). His 'atoning death' on our behalf
'hides a multitude of sins' – covers and hides them 'with his *holy
body*' in his death on the cross (TwDCF 185–6). Christ's atonement
'bring[s] forth being' from the 'non-being' of sin by bringing about
the forgiveness of sins (CA 83, 117) – a paradoxical 'retroactive'
'annul[ling of] the past' that is, as Climacus writes, 'bound up with
God's having existed in time' (CUP 224).

In the crucifixion, Kierkegaard sees Christ's rejection, Christ's
isolation as our way to communion. On the cross, Christ is rejected,
hung outside the city, lonely and forsaken. Here Christ, the isolated
one, 'stands at the crossroad, there where temporal and earthly suffering placed its cross, and calls' to the 'fugitive' – to the 'solitary',
'wretched' and 'unhappy one' walking on 'the loneliest way' – calls

---

22 Kierkegaard writes: 'What is the Redeemer but a substitute who puts himself
completely in your place and in mine, and what is the comfort of Redemption but
this, that the substitute, atoning, puts himself completely in your place and in mine!'
(ThDCF 123). Christ 'chose to carry all the sin of the world and to suffer punishment' (CA 38). He is the 'one who is able to put himself completely in your place,
just as in every sufferer's place' (ThDCF 116).

to them, invites them to himself (PIC 16). Christ calls and does not humiliate the one who is guilty and isolated in sin: 'he will not identify you by contrast, by placing you apart from himself so that your sin becomes even more terrible; he will grant you a hiding place with himself, and hidden in him he will hide your sins' (PIC 20). From the cross, Christ as one lifted up draws all to himself, into communion. 'Homeless in the world' – rejected and exposed – he yet becomes a place of cover, of eternal safety, a hiding place, a home (TwDCF 181).[23] This is so in that, for Kierkegaard, the cross brings about reconciliation, bringing us into kinship with God in Christ, and so 'eternally reunites the separated ones' (JFY 209; WL 69; PIC 18).

Christ as passive agent or the model of truth: the prototype

In addition to the portrait of Christ as the active giver or Mediator of Truth in Existence, Kierkegaard provides us with a portrait of Christ as the Mediator of Truth in Existence as a more passive model of this Truth – as the Prototype – into whose likeness Christ as the Gift/Teacher/Saviour intends to help the individual believer to be transformed (JP 1863). Christ is both the Saviour and the Prototype (PoV 131; JFY 147). Kierkegaard posits that, as the one who fulfils and existentially manifests the fullness of the ideal ethical require-ment, Christ is the prototype for human existence (PIC 107, 239; JFY 197). He writes that in everyone's soul there is 'a longing like that of erotic love . . . a longing, a wish, that craves . . . a guide and teacher in life . . . [an] example . . . [and] the most diverse proto-types appear and disappoint and reappear' (TDIO 58–9).[24] Christ, however, *is* the prototype – 'the holy prototype for the human race and for every individual' (JFY 147; UDVS 197) – the 'paradigm' (PIC 108) – whose earthly life 'set the task' of human life (CD 76–7; UD 158). For Kierkegaard, the central 'teaching' of Christ, his 'truth' is 'really his life, his existence'; his life is an expression of the truth (JFY 191, 179; CD 54; PIC 34–5). As the prototype, Christ's

---

23 'You have life only by remaining in him – in this way he is also the hiding place. Only by remaining in him, only by living yourself into him are you under cover' (TwDCF 188).
24 This passage is likely the earliest usage of 'prototype' in Kierkegaard's pub-lished authorship.

life is the way, the 'one road' (UDVS 225); Christ is he 'who is the way' (WL 175).[25] The way of Christ is the 'one guidance that in truth leads a person through life to life', and believers in Christ are to be 'pilgrims' on this way (UDVS 217–18). Indeed, Kierkegaard depicts the prototype as coming in order to 'leave footprints' so that we might learn from him, follow him, imitate him (CD 76–7; PIC 238; JFY 147).

For Kierkegaard, Christ's life as the model or pattern of Truth in Existence is also the standard by which the human race is judged (PIC 34; TERE 64). Christ is, as Anti-Climacus writes, 'the criterion' (SUD 114). Christ as 'the prototype . . . unconditionally places everyone under obligation' (MLW 292). In Christ we see the fulfilling of what Kierkegaard describes as, 'the unconditioned requirement' (JFY 159). Christ is the only one of whom it can be said that 'he serves only one master' (JFY 175). While Kierkegaard agrees that Christ's being the one who fulfils the law makes him the redeemer from the law, he also states that this fulfilling the law makes Christ the prototype. He observes, appropriately in *Works of Love*, that it is in Christ's perfect love that the law is fulfilled, in that, 'in love the law is completely defined' (WL 101). Indeed, Christ 'was love, and his love was the fulfilling of the Law' and thus revealed what it is to truly love (WL 99, 3–4; UDVS 232).

In focusing on Christ as the Prototype, Kierkegaard sought, in part, to provide a corrective to the popular Christianity of his day with an emphasis on action, passion and strenuousness that he perceived as being decidedly lacking (JP 1873). Using his particular flair for wordplay, he declares that, 'alas, it can be said that imitation [*Efterfølgelsen*] usually "follows behind" [*følge efter*] in a very peculiar sense – so far behind that it is almost not following at all' (JP 1890).[26]

---

25 As Kierkegaard writes in his journals, 'the Holy Scriptures are the highway signs: Christ is the way' (JP 208).

26 The tone of Kierkegaard's advocacy on the need for the prototype as a corrective can be readily perceived in the following selection from his journals (JP 1866):

It is easy to see that a person has to be utterly broken before he takes refuge with the one crucified. Nowadays we say: He suffered and died simply to save me. Fine, but it is equally true that the fact that his whole life was suffering was to leave me footprints in which to walk.

It really does not do to wheel away from the crucified one into a dance hall, to let him be crucified in order that I shall live to the tune of: Enjoy life – and even

The relation between Christ as saviour and Christ as prototype

Having examined Kierkegaard's portraits of Christ as Mediator of Truth in Existence – both the active giver of Truth in Existence (Saviour, Teacher, Gift) and the passive model for Truth in Existence (Prototype) – we now turn to examining how these two aspects of Christ as Mediator of Truth in Existence (active and passive) relate to each other. Considering the issue of sequence, of which activity is prior, Kierkegaard, in some passages, posits that Christ is first the giver of grace and then the prototype. He writes: 'Imitation or discipleship does not come first, but "grace"; then imitation follows as a fruit of gratitude, as well as one is able. . . . It begins with joy over being loved – and then comes a striving to please, which is continually encouraged by the fact that even if he does not, he is still loved' (JP 1886).[27] Yet in still other passages, he suggests that imitation comes first – that it is the strenuousness of the prototype, of the requirement, that drives one to see one's need for grace.[28] Eventually, it seems that Kierkegaard came to see a kind of continual alternation between the two aspects of Christ as Mediator of Truth in Existence in the life of the believer. This final mediating position of sorts is seen in *Judge For Yourself!* (his final book), where he writes:

> When the striving one droops under the *prototype*, crushed, almost despairing, the *redeemer* raises him up again; but at the same moment you [Christ] are again the *prototype* so that he may be kept in the striving. . . . Yet you left your footprints, you, the holy *prototype* for the human race and for every individual, so that by your *Atonement* the saved might at every moment find confidence and boldness to want to strive to *follow* you. (JFY 147; italics mine)

---

more – enjoy life unabashedly, for there is One who has let himself be crucified for you.

27 Kierkegaard writes: 'Does there not come a moment when a man says: There really is grace; and imitation, as Luther says so superbly, ought not plunge a man into despair or into blasphemy. If that moment comes, then in spite of all its pain, imitation is a matter of love and as such is blessed' (JP 1903).

28 See JP 1853 and JP 273.

This position of alternating between active and passive portraits of Christ corresponding to and calling forth alternating passive acceptance and active response on the part of the believing individual is also seen in this late journal entry in which the first movement in the dialectic is different in his two consecutive descriptions (JP 1908):[29]

> Luther rightly orders it this way. Christ is the gift – to which faith corresponds. Then he is the prototype – to which imitation corresponds.
>
> Still more accurately one may say: (1) imitation in the direction of decisive action whereby the situation for becoming a Christian comes into existence; (2) Christ as gift [the response to which is] faith; (3) imitation as the fruit of faith.

Part of the work of Christ as Saviour is the way in which he enables our following of Christ as the Prototype by at once expelling anxiety and fear and also inspiring confidence and boldness (UDVS 49; JFY 149, 209). More significant than this, for Kierkegaard, however, is Christ's calling us and drawing us to himself as a uniting of the portraits of Christ as both active helper and passive prototype. When Christ as 'the inviter' calls us or invites us to himself, this call is both a gracious, free invitation – to accept the gift of Christ – and a call to live differently – to follow Christ as the Prototype (CD 265). As such, the call is a call to participate in Christ as both a being graced and a task. The call of Christ ('Come to me') comes less as a demand but as an offer of help, a free invitation. As Anti-Climacus writes: 'But he, the only one who in truth can help and in

---

29 Kierkegaard writes in his journals:

As the prototype Christ still belongs to the proclamation of the law; Christ's own life as the prototype was the very fulfilling of the law.
And precisely by fulfilling the law he ransomed us from the law to grace.
But then imitation comes again, not as the law but after grace and by grace. (JP 1884)

And again (JP 1919):

Christ is the Atoner. This is continually in relation to the past. But at the same moment he is the Atoner for the past he is 'the prototype' for the future.
Here, alas, is the difficulty. Measured by the criterion 'imitation,' the first step in my future will again make me in need of the Atoner – indeed, I cannot even make a beginning because I am stifled by anxiety.

truth can help all, consequently the only one who in truth can invite all, he makes no condition whatsoever' (PIC 13). Christ 'makes no difficulty; he does only one thing: he opens his arms' (PIC 19). And again, in the call Christ takes the first step toward us – 'the inviter did not dare to wait until those who labour and are burdened come to him – he himself lovingly calls them. All his willingness to help perhaps would still not help if he did not say these words and thereby take the first step, for in the calling out of these words ("Come here to me") he does indeed come to them' (PIC 21). However, the invitation also 'stands at the crossroad' and calls us to change our path – to turn around and to follow Christ into his truth, his true way (PIC 18–19). In drawing people to himself Christ is calling them to a conversion; as Anti-Climacus prays, 'draw them to yourself from the way of perdition to the way of truth' (PIC 261–2).

Christ, as drawing to himself as 'something higher', asks us to make a choice (PIC 151–2). The invitation, the drawing is a paradoxical one: the self is drawn to Christ as something extrinsic and yet drawn to become itself – called and invited and drawn to truth, to the truth in existence that is manifest in Christ. Christ is the extrinsic truth of our intrinsic being.[30] In this, Christ lovingly encourages others to love him as their own good and for their own good – a self-giving that is a self-receiving.[31]

Finally, there is a uniting of Saviour and Prototype in Kierkegaard's understanding of Christ as the Way. The follower of Christ follows him from death to life – follows him on the way of resurrection (FSE 56).[32] With an eye to the text on the ascension in Acts 1,

---

30 Anti-Climacus writes: 'When that which is to be drawn is in itself a self, then truly to draw to itself means first to help it truly to become itself in order then to draw it to itself, or it means in and through drawing it to itself to help it become itself. . . . [T]he self is a redoubling, is freedom; therefore in this relation truly to draw to itself means to posit a choice . . . [A] self can truly draw another self to itself only through a choice – thus truly to draw to itself is a composite' (PIC 159). 'Christ also first and foremost wants to help every human being to become a self, requires this of him first and foremost, requires that he, by repenting, become a self, in order then to draw him to himself. . . . [H]e wants to draw him only as a free being to himself, that is, through a choice' (PIC 160).

31 'No, mercifully, or lovingly, or in love, you are love of such a kind that you yourself love forth the love that loves you, encourages it to love you much' (ThDCF 137).

32 Kierkegaard writes: You 'bowed your head in that degrading death – but you lifted it again. . . . Would that we might follow you' (FSE 56).

Kierkegaard presents Christ as the way that leads to heaven (FSE 64–6). As he writes: 'Between heaven and earth there is only one road: to follow Christ' (UDVS 229).[33] As such, Christ is the way of life that leads to life beyond death – a way of temporal life ordered to eternity. Christ's is the high and secure road, the way, to 'final blessed joy', to 'eternal happiness' (UDVS 227).

The second Christological dynamic

Having examined Kierkegaard's portraits of Christ as Truth in Existence and of Christ as both the Giver and Model of Truth in Existence, we will now turn to see how these portraits interact with one another to form a single Christological dynamic. The portraits of Christ as Saviour (Teacher or Gift) and as Prototype are different modes by which the portrait of Christ as Truth in Existence comes into contact with the existence of the individual. We begin by seeing Truth in Existence as that which is lacking in the individual. Because of sin, humans do not live in conformity with the truth; they lack truth in existence – they are 'untruth' (PF 14; CUP 208). Christ's embodying of Truth in Existence interacts with the existence of the individual in two different ways: as the active mediator (giver, teacher, gift) and as the passive mediator (model, pattern, prototype). As Kierkegaard writes in *For Self-Examination*: 'Christianity's requirement is this: your life should express works as strenuously as possible; then one thing more is required – that you humble yourself and confess: But my being saved is nevertheless grace' (FSE 17).

Whereas the first dynamic primarily functions to bring the individual to an awareness of the transcendent distance from God in Christ, the second dynamic primarily functions to close the distance in actuality between Christ and the individual by both Christ's approaching the individual and the individual's approaching Christ. Kierkegaard's second Christological dynamic can thus be described as a 'nearing' dynamic – in which there is a 'nearing' of the object to the subject and the subject to the object (as opposed to a 'distancing' in the first dynamic). It should also be noted that whereas

---

33 'There is only one eternal hope on this earth: to follow Christ into heaven' (UDVS 229).

the first dynamic emphasizes God/Christ's holiness, mystery and unknowableness, the second dynamic emphasizes God/Christ's grace, condescension and self-revelation.

The second dynamic functions to emphasize both the transcendence and immanence of God/Christ to the end of transforming the individual. This comes about through making one distant in one's awareness of one's relation (one's untruth) so that one may truly begin to come nearer (truer). One must first recognize one's untruth (by comparing oneself to the prototype) before one can, through grace and striving, seek to become truth. To put it another way, in one's putting oneself under the prophetic prototype that judges our lives as distinct and distant – infinitely and qualitatively – from the divine way-of-life, one is in the proper position to accept the grace of God through Christ and because of that grace strive again to adore Christ by way of imitation.

Whereas Kierkegaard's first Christological dynamic posited an either/or choice between the more proximal and existentially defining portraits[34] (Object of Faith/Sign of Offence) that reflects two different ways of relating to the initial (more distal) portrait (Absolute Paradox), his second Christological dynamic – while similarly presenting two existentially defining portraits (Giver of Truth/Model of Truth) that reflect two different ways of relating to the initial portrait (Truth in Existence) – presents these two ways of relating not as mutually exclusive alternatives that one must choose between but as two very different, alternating ways that Christians must relate to Christ as Truth in Existence if they are to approach him at all. Whereas the first dynamic is either/or, the second dynamic is both/and.

This both/and relation evidently occupied Kierkegaard's mind late in his life, as one can see manifest in the numerous journal entries dedicated to it.[35] In his later journals, he writes that, 'with regard to the Atonement, to put on Christ means, for one thing, to appropriate his merit . . . , and for another, to seek to be like

---

34 The portraits of Christ that define one's existence in one's relation to them.

35 Even in an early entry, Kierkegaard observes that, 'the profundity of Christianity is that Christ is both our redeemer and our judge, not that one is our redeemer and another is our judge, for then we certainly come under judgment, but that the redeemer and the judge are the same' (JP 287).

him, because he is the prototype and the example' (JP 1858).[36]
Again, he writes that, 'inasmuch as there is to be striving, he is the
prototype whom one ought to resemble, but the prototype is also
the Saviour and Redeemer who helps the Christian to be like the
prototype' (JP 1863).[37] Kierkegaard more explicitly brings out the
paradoxical nature of this both/and relation in his observing that,
'"the prototype" slays all, as it were, for no one achieves it. "The
Redeemer" wants to save all. Yet Christ is both' (JP 1934).[38] Christ,
for Kierkegaard, is at once the gracious Saviour who comes to us
and helps us in our time of need and the perfect Pattern for human
existence who judges our existence and challenges us to follow him.
In thanksgiving for our salvation we strive to imitate the example
of our Saviour; in humility and brokenness we seek the grace of our
Prototype who breaks us.

Having looked at both the similarities and differences between
Kierkegaard's two Christological dynamics, we propose that the
most helpful way to see the relationship between these two dynamics is in seeing the first teleologically suspended in the second. The
first dynamic is both suspended (relativized) and preserved (still
operative) in the second dynamic. The first is lifted up into the
second. This teleological suspension is seen specifically in that the
portrait of Christ as the Giver of Truth in the second Christological
dynamic overlaps with or substantially repeats the portrait of
Christ as the Object of Faith in the first Christological dynamic.
Both of these portraits essentially entail the humble acceptance of
both one's own lacking and Christ's gift of grace. One sees in this
coincidence of functions both continuity between the two dynamics
and development beyond the first dynamic in the second, in that

---

36 Around this same time Kierkegaard writes (JP 1857):

The prototype must be the prototype, that is, there ought to be striving toward
likeness, and yet at the same time the prototype is that which by its infinite
distance crushes the imitator, as it were, or thrusts him back into an engulfing
distance – and yet again the prototype is himself the compassionate one who
helps the person to become like him. The doctrine of the prototype, rightly
understood, encompasses everything.

37 See also JP 334 quoted above and JFY 209.

38 Along similar lines, Kierkegaard writes in his journals (JP 1917):

The Prototype–Grace
   This is the redoubling established at the same time by God; the one seems to
contradict the other, but they complement each other.

the passive acceptance of Christ in faith that is the end goal of the first dynamic is the starting point that one must move beyond in the second. The first dynamic can be seen as initiatory, describing the process of entering into the Christian dialectic of grace/works that constitutes the second dynamic. This can be seen in that the choice of faith in Christ as Absolute Paradox that one makes in the first dynamic establishes Christ's authority as the Prototype for said individual. In brief, faith (as the goal of first dynamic) establishes the authority that is necessary for imitation (as the goal of the second dynamic). So faith as humble acceptance is affirmed in the higher context of full faith as acceptance and imitation. It is to this fuller faith – this fuller understanding of the Christian way of life – that we must now turn.

7

The Christian Way

For Kierkegaard, the true way of life is the Christian way. The Christian way is a life lived in light of and in accord with (a life true to) the way things are – in light of Kierkegaard's theological understanding of the world, humanity, God and Christ as presented in Chapters 5 and 6. This final chapter is a sketch of this way that is the truth.

A Second Ethics

As ethics is based in the first philosophy of metaphysics, so does theology or dogmatics as the 'second philosophy' – the 'secunda philosophia . . . that totality of science whose essence is transcendence or repetition' – become the basis for a 'second ethics' – a different way of living based on Christian truth (CA 21). Kierkegaard's theological vision of the world replaces (or suspends) metaphysics as the basis for this different ethics. As Vigilius Haufniensis writes: 'The first ethics presupposes metaphysics; the second ethics presupposes dogmatics but completes it also in such a way that here, as everywhere, the presupposition is brought out' (CA 24). This 'bringing out' of the 'presupposition' – in which the metaphysical or dogmatic 'thesis' becomes a 'task' – is the work of appropriation. It is the second movement of a double-movement, a simplicity after reflection (PoV 6–9), an 'existing in' one's 'thinking' (CUP 73–4).[1] It is in such an appropriation where one is properly, Christianly concerned for oneself, for one's life and oriented toward the upbuilding – and so toward 'the validity of life'[2] – 'the relation to life, to the

---

1 As having its fullness, its fulfilment in this second movement, Christianity entails a 'teleological truth' (PoV 34).

2 Frater Taciturnus writes, 'that the single individual has infinite significance and that this is the validity of life' (SLW 492–3).

actuality of the personality' (SUD 5–6). Thus, Climacus writes that 'if Christianity is essentially subjectivity, it is a mistake if the observer is objective' (CUP 53); it is not Christian 'to be rich in truths and poor in virtues' (EUD 350). For Kierkegaard, '*the issue* κατ' ἐξοχήν [in the eminent sense] of the whole authorship' is simply '*becoming a Christian*' (PoV 8, 63), and so he is concerned 'to make clear what in truth Christianity's requirement is' (PoV 16) – 'to audit the definition: Christian' (MLW 341, 343). For the Christian's 'life is essentially action' (FSE 11); it is to 'strive', 'to do it' (MLW 37; JFY 116) – their life's task is 'to be transformed' (MLW 302). Christianity, then – which so 'aims at a person's total transformation' (MLW 248) – is a matter of requirement and 'ideality' (PIC 7, 190; PoV 16; MLW 47, 119).

The Way, Imitation, Repetition, Virtues

Kierkegaard presents the Christian life as a journey – as a way, a road – and the Christian as a traveller, as a pilgrim moving and progressing through time toward a sought end (CD 33–4; LFBA 10). This 'road to perfection' – 'the hard but also the good way' – is a narrow and difficult road (CA 117; MLW 271; UDVS 187; FSE 65). Progressing along this way one moves, continually striving, forward and upward (CD 20; UDVS 49; MLW 212) – all along the way discerning, turning, correcting at the crossroads of life (CD 20; UDVS 13).

The Christian life is not merely a set of 'objective' rules; it is a living. Nor is it a purely 'subjective' sentiment, a whatever-one-makes-of-it-as-long-as-one-is-passionate; it is a living in relation to reality. The way is a between – as a being before the eternal in the midst of perpetual change and difference of time, as a way revealed and enabled by the eternal one in time in Christ. The way is a living ethical constancy – a repetition in relation to God in Christ. The Christian virtues are at the core, the existential heart, of Kierkegaard's *theologia viatorum* – for they do not merely say what is, but guide, show the way in light of what is (such light as is available to one still on the way). The Christian virtues are the ways of the one Way, more determinate articulations of the Way, answers to the question: how do I live the Way? 'The road is',

Kierkegaard writes, 'how it is walked' (UDVS 291) – but it is not just any 'how'.

This way is revealed to us in Scripture and supremely in Christ. Scripture, for Kierkegaard, is a gift given to us to help us to understand how we as individuals are to live (FSE 13, 35ff.). We should thus listen to this privileged divine perspective on human life – we should take it as a guide, as signs on the way (FSE 44ff.).[3] However, if 'the Holy Scriptures are the highway signs', Kierkegaard writes, 'Christ is the way' (JP 208) – 'He was the Scriptures given life' (JP 342).

The Christian way is living in Christ who is the way, the truth and the life. Christ not only reveals the way/truth/life to us, as if it were something extrinsic to himself, he reveals them in himself and gives them to us in himself. Kierkegaard writes:

> Since he is the Truth, you do not find out from him what truth is and now are left to yourself, but you remain in the Truth only by remaining in him; since he is the Way, you do not find out from him the way you are to go and now, left to yourself, must go your way, but only by remaining in him do you remain on the way; since he is the Life, you do not have life handed over by him and now must shift for yourself, but you have life only by remaining in him – in this way he is also the hiding place. Only by remaining in him, only by living yourself into him are you under cover. (TwDCF 188)

The way of Christ is 'the way of truth' – into, onto which Christ draws us 'from the way of perdition' (PIC 261–2). The truth of Christ is a life – 'the truth was in Christ a life, for he was the truth' (PIC 205). Anti-Climacus writes: 'Christ is the truth in the sense that to be the truth is the only true explanation of what truth is. . . . This means that truth in the sense in which Christ is the truth is not a sum of statements, not a definition etc., but a life' (PIC 205). We have true life, we are our highest selves, our true selves in Christ (SUD 113). In drawing us to himself, he draws us into being the truth, into freely appropriating and choosing to be what we are.[4]

---

3 See Kierkegaard on the 'royal coachman' (FSE 86; JFY 107ff.).

4 Anti-Climacus writes: 'when that which is to be drawn is in itself a self, then truly to draw to itself means first to help it truly to become itself in order then to

'The truth is the way', and 'being the truth is a life – and this is indeed how Christ speaks of himself: I am the Truth and the Way and the Life' (PIC 207). We 'live into him' as the narrow way that leads to life (Matt. 7.13–14). We 'live into him' as the good tree that manifests what it is (Matt. 7.15–20). In following, we 'live into him' as in a house founded on a rock (Matt. 7.24–7) – and are so 'under cover', secure.

For Kierkegaard, following in the way of Christ is often presented in terms of Christian existence as striving to imitate Christ as the Prototype. He writes in his journals: 'As soon as there is a prototype, there is the obligation to imitation. What does imitation mean? It means striving to conform my life to the prototype' (JP 1867).[5] Christians are thus, for Anti-Climacus, 'not adherents of a teaching but imitators of a life' (PIC 237). Imitation [*Efterfølgelse*] is to follow [*følge efter*] (FSE 67) – as a 'pilgrim' who would follow Christ in his 'footprints' (UDVS 217–19, 226–9; CD 76–7). As the Prototype, Christ's life is a 'summons' – calling 'follow me' – calling one to be a 'disciple', one who strives to 'resemble' Christ (CD 42–3; JFY 207).

Christ is the truth that we strive to become. Time for the Christian, then, is a progression – a way ordered to imitation – a repetition forging an increasing stability, an increasing identity of sorts in the midst of non-identity (of becoming). Being ordered to the truth of Christ who is our truth, we progress towards truth, towards being as we truly are as human beings, becoming true in following the way of Christ. A disciple, an imitator, is then one who seeks to be a non-identical repetition of Christ.[6]

This kind of a life of establishing an identity/unity that perseveres over time in relation to Christ, a life of repetition/imitation, this kind of a life is one of faithful continuity – a 'unity of state and movement' – a consistency over time (EUD 192; CA 135;

---

draw it to itself, or it means in and through drawing it to itself to help it become itself. . . . So it is when truth draws to itself, for truth is in itself, is in and for itself – and Christ is the truth. . . . [H]e wants to draw him only as a free being to himself, that is, through a choice' (PIC 159–60).

5 This aspect is also seen in a very early journal entry: 'Christ's whole life in all its aspects must supply the norm for life of the following Christian and thus of the life of the whole church' (JP 273).

6 'Repetition' in the first authorship is largely replaced (*aufgehoben*) by 'imitation' in the more explicitly Christian second authorship.

UDVS 7).[7] This way, this 'path of virtue', is something stable, a continuity along/upon which one moves (CUP 403; SUD 105–6).[8] This
acquired simplicity of a kind of 'second nature' is the 'increasingly
established continuity' of good habit – of a momentum in a good
direction (vs sin's 'increasingly established continuity') (LFBA 38;
EO 453; SUD 106).

The Christian life, life in Christ, the Christian 'how' is presented in Kierkegaard's works in terms of the Christian virtues – the
characteristic habits of a disciple/follower of Christ.[9] After getting
the (dogmatic/metaphysical) map (as presented in Chapters 5 and
6 above), these virtues are the directions for one's journey. Unable
to reduce the way of Christ to any one verb, the Christian virtues
provide a more determinate answer to how we are to live in accordance to the truth of who we are in relation to Christ.[10] While the
specific term 'virtue' is not a focal category in Kierkegaard's published works, I contend that it is nonetheless a powerful organizing
idea for presenting his understanding of the Christian life.

An Enabled Life

This active striving towards Christ's model, of imitation, repetition, of Christian virtue, leads one to a place of passive acceptance
of the divine gift – which then enables one's progress on the way.
As Kierkegaard writes in *For Self-Examination*, striving to do good
works functions, 'to cause the need for grace to be felt deeply in
genuine humble inwardness and, if possible, to prevent grace . . .
from being taken totally in vain' (FSE 24).[11] The Christian life for

---

7 'Fidelity is thinking and speaking uniformly about it while everything is changing' (UDVS 317–18).

8 Kierkegaard writes of 'virtue's narrow way' (JP 631).

9 Kierkegaard notes: 'Patience, faith, humility, etc., in short, all the Christian
virtues' (JP 941).

10 Kierkegaard writes: 'This Socratic thesis is of utmost importance for Christianity: Virtue cannot be taught; that is, it is not a doctrine, it is a being-able, an exercis-
ing, an existing [*Existeren*], an existential [*existentiel*] transformation, and therefore
it is so slow to learn, not at all as simple and easy as the rote-learning of one more
language or one more system' (JP 1060).

11 Indeed, Kierkegaard writes in *Judge for Yourself!* that the greatest 'lifting up'
I can experience is when 'I turn from my best deed as from something base and find
rest in grace' (JFY 154).

Kierkegaard, then, is not only one of activity, it is an oscillating, reciprocal interplay between receptivity and activity, receiving the gift and striving in Christian existence toward Christ.[12] God's help is enabling and participatory, not coercing. The Spirit's empowering and enabling is described as 'invisible', such that 'to be helped by it is to learn to walk alone', that its help is like instinct in a bird (JFY 95; EUD 398–9; UDVS 221). God's help co-operates with our own resolution, our own acting (EUD 192; TDIO 50). Christ to us alternates between the Prototype for our imitation and the Saviour who is our help. Kierkegaard reflects in his journals: '"The prototype" must be presented as the requirement, and then it crushes you. "The prototype", which is Christ, then changes into something else, to grace and compassion, and it is he himself who reaches out to support you' (JP 349).[13]

In this receptive moment, we are in communion with God, are given God's gracious presence in the Holy Spirit (EUD 139, 396). Kierkegaard writes that 'God gives not only the gifts but himself with them in a way beyond the capability of any human being' (EUD 99). On account of receiving God, we are enabled, helped in various ways. The presence of God helps one to come to understand oneself differently and so to conform oneself to, to manifest, to be 'transfigured' into the likeness to God (EUD 399–400; UDVS 220). In this changed, transformed life, one 'gains one's soul', is given new life, from God (EUD 174; FSE 73). Though, just as Christianity is not a 'quack doctor', the supernatural help of the Spirit entails a negative, sobering moment (FSE 80; JFY 98). 'The life-giving Spirit', Kierkegaard writes, 'is the very one who slays you' (FSE 76–7) – 'who teaches dying to' (JFY 98) – seeking 'to wound selfishness at the root' (FSE 79).

Finally, Kierkegaard, in *For Self-Examination*, presents the 'theological virtues' of faith, hope and love as gifts of the Spirit – as miraculously enabled on the far side of the death of the immediate

---

12 As Kierkegaard simply states: 'Do what you can for God, and God will do for you what you cannot do' (EUD 368–9).

13 Kierkegaard also writes in his journals, that 'imitation must be stressed again, at least dialectically, in order to teach standing in need of grace; it must be emphasized that imitation is demanded of everyone – then let him rely on grace' (JP 1905). Again, he writes: 'When the striving one droops under the prototype, crushed, almost despairing, the Redeemer raises him up again; but at the same moment you are again the prototype so that he may be kept in the striving' (JFY 147).

faith, hope and/or love of merely human effort. 'Such', Kierkegaard writes, 'are the gifts the life-giving Spirit brought' to the apostles on Pentecost (FSE 85). 'It is', he writes, 'when all confidence in your-self or in human support, and also in God in an immediate way, is extinct, when every probability is extinct, when it is dark as on a dark night – it is indeed death as we are describing – then comes the life-giving Spirit and brings faith' (FSE 82). When we see there is no hope according to natural hope, 'the Spirit promptly agrees and says, "Quite right, there is no hope, and it is very important to me that this be asserted, since precisely from this, I, the Spirit, show that there is hope: the hope that is against hope"' (FSE 83). Finally, showing us that 'what we extol under the name of love is self-love', the Spirit gives us a love willing 'to suffer, to endure all things, to be sacrificed in order to save this unloving world. And this is love' (FSE 83–5).

The *Passio Essendi*: Silence and Patience

Kierkegaard sees a certain receptivity as a precondition for the theological virtues of faith, hope and love. Wonder, as an imme-diate positive 'passion', is presented as such a precondition, as a beginning, a first thought (CA 146; TDIO 18; UDVS 191); as he writes: 'If there is anything we in these times have forgotten, it is to wonder, and therefore also to believe and to hope and to love' (CD 107). Likewise does Kierkegaard point out the 'doing nothing' of silence, of stillness in solitude that is the proper beginning – the being before God in reverence, as nothing, in the fear of the Lord that is the beginning of wisdom (LFBA 10–11; SLW 18, 378–9).[14] Often, he describes this initial moment of Christian religiousness as negative – as a kind of purgation, a 'dying to' (FSE 76),[15] a shaking ('shuddering', 'trembling', 'throes'), a breaking down (TA 92; BoA 112–13; PIC 135). This negative moment is a certain 'giving up', a resignation,[16] a renunciation of relative ends and finite comforts

---

14 Kierkegaard writes: 'in a certain sense is it nothing I shall do? Yes, quite true, in a certain sense it is nothing. In the deepest sense you shall make yourself nothing, become nothing before God, learn to be silent. In this silence is the beginning, which is to seek first God's kingdom' (LFBA 10–11).

15 '"Life begins in death", says the lowly Christian' (CD 46).

16 Kierkegaard writes: 'Die to the world. And when you are the one who is dead,

(SLW 396; CUP 429, 432; CD 178) – a preparatory despair (SUD 59, 67, 116; EO 511).

One of Kierkegaard's most suggestive ways of understanding this initial receptive condition is in terms of patience. Paradoxically stated, in patience one 'gains one's soul'.[17] In patience, one comes to 'understand that he does not possess himself' and that we receive who we are (EUD 169, 163). We receive us – we receive that which receives – we become in receiving. 'To gain one's soul in patience' – the words contain a 'redoubling repetition' – 'the words in their entirety are a kind of picture of the whole process of gaining, that it takes place much as the words proceed with their communication – that is, it is all repetition' (EUD 169–70). Christian repetition is not merely our repeating, our making, our forging over time; for our repeating, the repeating that we are, our making is not merely our own making – we receive. This receptivity prior to our urgent striving – what William Desmond calls the *passio essendi* that enables our *conatus essendi* – is the matrix of our becoming. As Kierkegaard writes: 'it is patience itself in which the soul in patience inclosingly spins itself and thereby gains patience and itself' (EUD 171). Patience is indeed something we 'do' – a being in which we are not only, or even fundamentally, our own doing. It is a being toward ourselves that is in accord with, being true to, what we are.

Patience – 'just as active as it is passive and just as passive as it is active' (EUD 187) – is a gaining that is a preserving, a preserving that is a gaining. One gains one's soul by preserving it – what is in time, what is received, must be preserved, repeated, continually 'spun'. This spinning maintains oneself as a living, becoming unity in the flux of time.[18] 'To preserve one's soul in patience', Kierkegaard writes, is 'to keep the soul bound together in patience' in the midst of 'the long battle with an indefatigable enemy, time, and with a multifarious enemy, the world' (EUD 192). The enemy

---

you lose nothing by losing that which in the understanding of the living is everything' (CD 146). This is resonant with William Desmond's concept of posthumous mind.

17 How can one gain something 'which signifies precisely the condition for being able to gain the same possession'? (EUD 163).

18 One gains the soul, Kierkegaard writes, 'in no other way than by preserving it' (EUD 187).

is dispersal into mere plurality, mere sequence. One should 'take care to associate circumspectly with temporality' (CD 100); it must be dwelt in properly, for in time the given is not to be taken for granted but to be maintained. Apparently passive patience is an active perseverance or endurance because human life, or any life at all, does not simply 'stay' in time, it must actively 'stay' in the midst of the passing – patiently repeating that itself not pass (SLW 143). Patient repetition makes and receives a unity (from plurality) that persists through time (EUD 460–1).

This paradoxical way of being is related, in Kierkegaard's work, to the theological virtues. Patience as a maintaining of oneself in relation to God – as ordered to God in a 'covenant' (EUD 192) – is expressed or manifested in the theological virtues of faith, hope and love.[19] Indeed, this active and passive making and persisting manner of repetition in patience is characteristic of Christian virtue as a way of being in time in relation to the eternal as revealed in time in Christ. Faith, hope and love enact patience, bring it about, repeat it (EUD 198).[20] Patience's preserving of the soul happens in faith, hope and love. This is captured in the image of the patient watchfulness (moment after moment) of one who faithfully 'keeps the lamp lit . . . expectantly waiting' for the beloved (UDVS 238). As Kierkegaard writes: 'Patience wants to preserve only the soul; it has the courage to give up everything else; and when the soul does not believingly aspire to the eternal, does not hopefully hurry toward the future, is not lovingly in understanding with God and human beings, then the soul is lost' (EUD 193).

The theological virtues also transform patience. The Danish terms that Kierkegaard uses for patience (*Taalmod*) and meekness (*Sagtmod*) are built upon the root word for courage (*Mod*).[21]

---

19 Patience is manifest 'in faith's covenant with the eternal, in hope's covenant with the future, and love's covenant with God and human beings' in which human beings 'believingly aspire to the eternal', 'hopefully tranquil about the future', and are 'lovingly in peace and unity with God and human beings' (EUD 192).

20 'Only the true expectancy, which requires patience, also teaches patience' (EUD 221).

21 Kierkegaard writes: 'There is in the language a marvelous word that also fits readily in many a connection but never intensely in any connection except with the good. It is the word courage [*Mod*]; wherever there is good, courage is also present there; whatever happens to the good, courage is always on the side of the good. The good is always courageous . . . never turns its back on danger but always faces it. . . .

Patience, *Taalmod*, is a courage that suffers or bears-with (*taale*: to bear, to suffer, to tolerate). Meekness or gentleness, *Sagtmod*, is a soft or gentle (*sagte*) courage that is joyous even in the midst of suffering. My proposal is that, in Kierkegaard's work, the transition from patience to meekness occurs through the theological virtues of faith, hope and love. Faith, hope and love – by orienting life to/by God's love in Christ with the help of the Spirit – are the way to move from a persevering or bearing-with oneself[22] to resting transparently in what one is, quietly, softly – to peaceful being as one is as an established continuity that is in accord with reality – from patient silence to joy.

The path of the Christian theological virtues is the way to this joy in the midst of suffering. Though the burdens of self-denial and of the world's opposition make the journey hard, Christ's burden is light. For in Christ we are shown the difficult way of truth, and yet we are also shown the persistent and eternal love of God. Then, Kierkegaard writes, 'the road, even if it is the most difficult, and the condition, even if it is the most bitter, are unconditionally joyful' (UDVS 282).

Faith

The Christian life is one of participation with God. While patience, as being receptive, is our doing, God is the one who initiates or re-initiates our relationship with him in giving us the enabling condition which we then appropriate. Christian faith – the faith that is 'stronger than the world' – is a gift of the Holy Spirit (EUD 36; FSE 81–2). In this, one receives the condition first hand – 'from the god himself' (PF 69). This gift, as a grace in the midst of our faithlessness, is one of a miraculous re-creation (CD 286; EUD 36; CUP 576). Faith, on our part, is our appropriation of the gift in an act of decision or resolution – an affirmation that is a new immediacy, a 'primitivity in appropriation' that does not come of a matter

---

There is courage [*Mod*], which bravely defies dangers; there is high-mindedness [*Høimod*], which proudly lifts itself above grievances; there is patience [*Taalmod*], which patiently bears sufferings; but the gentle courage [*sagte Mod*] that carries the heavy burden lightly' (UDVS 239–40).

22 'Patience [*Taalmod*] is silent, but meekness [*Sagtmod*] carries the heavy weight lightly' (UDVS 240).

of course (SLW 258, 399; TDIO 26; SUD 58). Reading together *Fragments* and *Stages*, the given grace of the condition is like the first immediacy of falling in love – which happens to us despite us – while the active resolution of faith is like the vows of marriage (SLW 152, 156).[23]

Christian faith – while gathering together and teleologically suspending the attributes of ordinary, ethical and religious 'faith' (see Chapter 2) – focuses on the person of Jesus Christ (CD 284). Christian faith in Christ takes a historical phenomenon as something 'outside the individual' as the 'point of departure' for one's 'eternal consciousness' or 'eternal happiness' such that one is 'infinitely interested in the actuality of another . . . another person', 'that the god has existed as an individual human being' (PF 87, 109; CUP 324–6).[24] 'Faith in the eminent sense', for Climacus, believes in the paradox of the incarnation (PF 87; CUP 227–8; see also SUD 99). The incarnation, for Kierkegaard, as both eternal/divine and historical/human, can only be grasped in a manner like unto its nature with God giving the condition and the historical report giving the occasion – with the historical actuality of another person (which can only ever be an 'approximation') being the basis for one's eternal happiness – with a decision in time having eternal consequences. Faith, then, 'expresses the paradoxical relation to the paradox' (CUP 323).

The seemingly mad venture of faith[25] is a new beginning, a breakthrough into a new life taking a new fundamental starting place with the incarnation (PIC 96, 120). Faith's new beginning is a break with the past in its receiving of the forgiveness of sin.[26] The gift of

---

23 Kierkegaard writes: 'reflection is discharged into faith, which is precisely the anticipation of the ideal infinite of resolution. Thus through the purely ideally exhausted reflection the resolution has gained a new immediacy that corresponds exactly to the immediacy of falling in love' (SLW 162).

24 Climacus writes: 'No philosophy (for it is only for thought), no mythology (for it is only for the imagination), no historical knowledge (which is for memory) has ever had this idea – of which in this connection one can say with all multiple meanings that it did not arise in any human heart' (PF 109). Also: 'The paradox is that this apparently esthetic relationship . . . nevertheless is to be the absolute relationship with God' (CUP 561). So Kierkegaard comments that 'the historical is precisely its essential aspect' (PF 182 sup).

25 'It is always lunacy to venture' (CUP 426).

26 'Christianity that by means of the Atonement wants to eliminate sin as completely as if it were drowned in the sea' (SUD 100).

forgiveness, of mercy, is something we need ('as the primary necessity'), but can only receive as a gift in faith (TDIO 13)[27] – 'the sign of God's greatness in showing mercy is only for faith. . . . God's greatness in showing mercy is a mystery, which must be believed' (CD 291). The work of grace, for Kierkegaard, is not merely something extrinsic to the individual, but is something that effects a change in the real mis-relation, the sickness, of the self toward a righted relation, the cure for the sickness; this is 'the Christian's blessedness' (SUD 15). 'From forgiveness', Kierkegaard writes, 'a new life will spring in the believer' (UDVS 247); one becomes another person (SLW 483).

Faith is a new orientation, a new 'second nature' in opposition to sin's 'second nature' (SUD 82) – 'disarm[ing]' the 'sophistry of sin', extricating the self from sin's entangling (CA 117) – turning from sin's 'endless detour' (EO 390). As in sin, the self experiences time as a process of degradation toward perdition (a sickness unto death – a dying, a disintegration, a descent) – in faith, the self experiences time as a process of healing, of unifying, of sanctification toward eternal happiness. Against the past habit or continuity of sin, faith is a new habit, a new second nature that binds the self together and mediates the stability of the eternal to the human person as 'the divine joint' that holds together the human individual 'ship' (PF 96; UDVS 269). Faith as a virtue is a process of repetition, a 'chain of resolution' whose 'constant renewal' forges a unity, a continuity over time, integrating and making one's soul 'sound and happy' (EUD 27–8, 352). Such a 'fidelity' to the eternal 'is thinking and speaking uniformly about it while everything is changing' (UDVS 317–18).

Christian faith, for Kierkegaard, also orients one toward the future. Faith is expectant, hopeful (EUD 22; CD 75; UDVS 238). The anticipation of faith is a conviction, a certitude of something not present of which 'uncertainty is the sign' (CUP 455; CA 156–8), a founding that cannot be presently substantiated because it looks to a larger founding order – that bases its expectancy in God, not in the world (EUD 24–7). As in the order of reality – with God creating the world, and the world as dependent upon, suspended from God – so in the order of our relation to reality – with faith in

---

27 'With regard to gaining the forgiveness of sins, or before God, a person is capable of nothing at all' (UD 158).

God founding our relation to the world (EUD 24). Faith empowers
one, giving the confidence and courage of one 'press[ing] forward
victoriously' in 'the battle of faith' (CUP 225; EUD 19; CD 75;
CA 117; WL 151-2).[28] 'There is', Kierkegaard writes, 'no fortress
as secure as' the 'fortress of faith' which 'is a world to itself, and
. . . has life within its ramparts' – where 'the more you cut faith off
from all supplies from the surrounding world . . . the more secure
is the fortress' (CD 86-7).

Faith, in the present, rests transparently in God, trusting in God's
creation, rule and providence in which one is who one is (CA 161;
UDVS 259).[29] In faith, anxiety is overcome inasmuch as it is teleologically suspended (not annihilated, but 'rightly used' in 'another
role' (CA 53)), given the chastening role of stripping away anything upon which one might rest save that which is not passing
– helping one to see in time the fragile foundation of all that is not
the rock. Thus, Haufniensis writes: 'With the help of faith, anxiety
brings up the individuality to rest in providence' (CA 161). Faith
walks 'without care', secure on the basis of one's relationship to
God (CA 20-1; CD 21; WL 77).[30] Yet the faith that brings rest is
'a restless thing', its quieting 'always disquieting at first' (FSE 17;
TwDCF 176-7). In faith, seeing one's rest in the eternal (in the
invisible) makes one (visibly) active in the midst of the time. 'Faith',
Kierkegaard writes, 'expressly signifies the deep, strong, blessed
restlessness that drives the believer so that he cannot settle down at
rest in this world' (UDVS 218). Faith's founding upon something
transcendent, something elsewhere, is transforming, manifesting
itself and making itself 'recognizable in his life' (FSE 19). The rest
of faith is in the midst of the journey, of the struggle.

---

28 Continuing with such masculine metaphors, Climacus sees here 'the ample
firmness of faith' as evident – as 'when the ship has sprung a leak, then enthusiasti-
cally to keep the ship afloat by pumping and not to seek the harbor.' Here 'faith
works vigorously in the depths – joyful and victorious' (CUP 225).

29 Faith 'in relating itself to itself and in willing to be itself, the self rests transparently in the power that established it' (SUD 49) . . . 'rests transparently in God' (SUD
30). 'Faith is: that the self in being itself and in willing to be itself rests transparently
in God' (SUD 82). In faith one can 'rest in the thought that God is to rule in everything' (UDVS 259).

30 Kierkegaard writes: 'Only faith's freedom from care [is, divinely speaking,
the soaring] whose beautiful but imperfect symbol is the bird's easy flight' (UDVS
194).

Faith, for Kierkegaard, is a 'being with', as present, the divine. 'To believe is man's relation to the divine' (SUD 95) – a being with 'the good' and 'grasping' and 'holding fast' 'the eternal' (UDVS 101). Christian faith in particular is a being with Christ, a 'contemporary with Christ's presence' such that 'his presence here on earth never becomes a thing of the past' (PIC 9). Being with that which is other, faith affirms the otherness and difference of the divine and is 'on good terms' with it; its relation to the divine other is not offence but wonder and worship. 'To worship' is 'the expression of faith', expressing the infinite, chasmic, qualitative abyss between' oneself and God (SUD 129); faith is 'to wonder blessedly' (UDVS 233).[31] In the midst of such an affirmative being with otherness, 'the joy of faith' – the joy 'saved' by faith (CD 75) – is not a 'fleeting emotion' dependent upon one's finite circumstances (FT 34; CD 75; EUD 25).

For Kierkegaard, the Christian theological virtues of faith, hope and love are different modes of being joyful in the midst of suffering. Faith, for Kierkegaard, suffers in the world. The eternal is recognized in the temporal by being rejected (UDVS 89). The Christian, in faith, relates to the eternal in time . . . in time – relating in the midst of time to Christ as the eternal in time. As such, the believer, in their believing, becomes a site of the conflict between the world and the eternal, and the world's rejection of the eternal and of Christ; the believer becomes, indeed, a site of faith's victory over the world and so becomes a witness for the truth (EUD 330; FSE 18).

Seeing suffering in terms of carrying burdens, of bearing the difficulty of life, Kierkegaard presents faith as lightening one's burden, as enabling the burden to be borne lightly (UDVS 232, 235, 247). In faith, one loses the heavy burden of the consciousness of sin – the burden of oneself – and takes on the paradoxical 'light burden' of discipleship, of meekness (UDVS 232).[32] Faith is a way of meek-

---

31 Kierkegaard writes: 'the certainty with that happiest greeting of most blissful wonder: It is impossible! . . . Her wonder is the wonder of faith, and her continuing to wonder is faithfulness to the power that made the impossible possible' (UDVS 237).

32 Kierkegaard writes: 'The one who takes away the consciousness of sin and gives the consciousness of forgiveness instead – he indeed takes away the heavy burden and gives the light one in its place . . . The person who has faith believes that everything is forgotten but in such a way that he carries a light burden – because does he not carry the recollection that it is forgiven him!' (UDVS 246, 247).

ness that bears heavy burdens as light, that is joyous in the midst of suffering.[33]

Faith's suffering in the world, indeed, can be beneficial. The school of sufferings educates for eternity inasmuch as suffering, in the light of faith, can teach obedience (UDVS 250). 'Suffering', Kierkegaard writes, 'is a dangerous schooling', for obedience does not follow suffering 'directly'; there is the possibility of meaningless, despairing suffering in which one 'casts away faith, refuses to believe that the suffering will procure anything' (UDVS 255–6, 313). Yet, if you have faith, suffering 'turns a person inward' and acts as 'the guardian angel who keeps you from slipping out again into the world', reminding you that what you seek is not here (UDVS 256, 259). In the school of sufferings, the one who has faith learns obedience.[34] 'Faith and faith's obedience in sufferings', Kierkegaard writes, 'love forth the growth, because the object of all faith's works is to get rid of egotism and selfishness in order that God can actually come in and in order to let him rule in everything' (UDVS 259).[35] One learns 'dying to' (UDVS 257; FSE 76; JFY 131–2). As faith has to do with the relation between the temporal and the eternal, Kierkegaard writes, 'what other connection and harmony are possible between the temporal and the eternal than this – that God rules and to let God rule!' (UDVS 257).[36] Indeed, as Kierkegaard writes in *Upbuilding Discourses in Various Spirits*, there is an integral relation between suffering, obedience, faith and eternity:

> Only suffering educates for eternity, because eternity is in faith, but faith is in obedience, but obedience is in suffering. Obedience is not apart from suffering, faith is not apart from obedience, eternity is not apart from faith. In suffering obedience is obedience, in obedience faith is faith, in faith eternity is eternity. (UDVS 263)

---

33 'Meekness', Kierkegaard writes, 'pertains to having faith, to carrying the light burden of forgiveness, to bearing the joy of forgiveness . . . Forgiveness, reconciliation with God, is a light burden to carry, and yet it is exactly like the light burden of meekness' (UDVS 246).

34 'Only one thing is learned: obedience' (UDVS 257).

35 'The suffering', Kierkegaard writes, 'is the very guarantee that the attachment is not self-willfulness' (UDVS 257).

36 In the school of sufferings, one 'learns to let God be the master, to let God rule' (UDVS 257).

Faith, for Kierkegaard, does not stand over against obedience or works, but comes to fruition in faithful obedience.[37] 'There is no fortress as secure as faith's', Kierkegaard writes, and 'with faith in this fortress lives obedience' (CD 86, 87). Faith's obedience is a submitting or coming into line, into accord with God and God's will (BoA 34; MLW 272). 'By unconditional obedience', Kierkegaard writes, 'your will is one with God's will and therefore God's will is done by you on earth as it is in heaven' (LFBA 32). Obedience is then a kind of appropriation of the reality and authority of God – making what is true, true for you – 'in relation to God and the eternal the appropriation is obedience' (UDVS 259). Obedience is being passionately engaged with the reality of the object of faith (UDVS 62; BoA 34–5).

Finally, 'the proper praise, hymn, and canticle of praise', Kierkegaard writes, is to praise God 'by joyous and unconditional obedience' (CD 86). Faith's obedience is joyful for 'in obeying God's will – when his will [as loving and wise] is certainly my only true good ... it is simply and solely my own good that is advanced' (CD 86). It is a service that is not servile, but edifying, serving the self's true good. In this service, in faithful obedience, one makes one's life into a 'hymn of praise' – a song – an expression of joy before the Other one is with, before, in faith (CD 85–6).

Hope

Patience comes to expression in hope as a dwelling in the present in relation to the future – not fearfully or anxiously or uncertainly but with expectancy. Patience and expectancy 'correspond to each other' (EUD 220); 'the true expectancy' both 'requires patience' and 'teaches patience' (EUD 221).[38] The expectancy of hope says: Be patient, it will happen – expectancy is not 'maybe', but rather

---

37 'In every human being there is an inclination *either* to want to be meritorious when it comes to works *or*, when faith and grace are to be emphasized, also to want to be free from works as far as possible ... Christianity's requirement is this: your life should express works as strenuously as possible; then one thing more is required – that you humble yourself and confess: But my being saved is nevertheless grace' (FSE 16, 17).

38 Kierkegaard writes of 'the form of expectancy that is in patience' (EUD 208).

'It must happen' (EUD 217). This expectancy, this hope, as Kierkegaard writes, 'pertains to a person essentially and does not leave it up to his own power to bring about the fulfillment. Therefore every truly expectant person is in a relationship with God' (EUD 221). Hope is a theological virtue in that, to have true expectancy, to hope with certainty in something that one does not have control of in the midst of the flux of life, is to believe in God. Beyond this, hope, for Kierkegaard, is a gift of the Holy Spirit – a new hope when there is no hope according to 'the understanding'.[39]

Hope orients and, in so orienting, gives stability to the life of the Christian. It is a relation to eternity that gives 'unshakable' security in the midst of the uncertainty of life (EUD 330; CD 114). In hope, one's present existence in time is ordered by one's relation to the eternal, ordered to the end of an eternal happiness (CD 72) – immortality beyond death, 'the truly beatific union [that] is concluded only in heaven' (CUP 175; SUD 7–8; EUD 328–9). Hope '*help*[s] *a person to understand himself in temporality*' and gives him, in this ordering, rest and calm in the present (EUD 259, 263–4). This orientation – this 'absolute respect (*respicere* [to look to])' toward such an 'absolute' end – 'absolutely transform[s] existence' (CUP 406, 393). Hope's orientation guides one's journey, one's progression toward salvation, toward the object of one's 'infinite interest' (CD 214–21; CUP 16, 389) – as a gaze 'continually looking ahead', 'aim[ing] from a distance' (CD 21; UDVS 101, 229). The journey in hope is a living, a walking in the world ordered to an eternal end beyond the world – a hyperbolic life that does not make sense without this presently invisible end that is looked to in hope. Such an orientation shows petty things to be petty. It is a liberated rest, 'fresh air and a prospect' (WL 246).

Like faith, hope's rest is a (paradoxical) restless rest; its stability is not a stasis but a consistency; it is not stopping on the way but a peaceful way. Hope is a different relating to the future that changes

---

39 Kierkegaard writes: 'The hope of the life-giving Spirit is against the hope of the understanding ... The Spirit promptly agrees and says, "Quite right, there is no hope, and it is very important to me that this be asserted, since precisely from this, I, the Spirit, show that there is hope: the hope that is against hope"' (FSE 82–3). One can even infer from the following passage that he associates hope especially with the Holy Spirit – as love with the Father and faith with the Son: 'there certainly is no perfectly happy love except that with which a person loves God, and no perfectly blessed faithfulness except that with which a person clings to Christ' (CD 284).

one's involvement in the present,[40] for in hope one is engaged in life with an 'infinite passion of expectancy' (CUP 16). One's way of being is not 'light-minded' disinterest but an urgency motivated by 'the one thing needful' (EUD 258). As Climacus notes, for a person existing as a human being within the temporal 'process of becoming', in which the present is fleeting, all acting is 'related to the future', but to act *'sensu eminenti'* is to 'relate himself to the future with infinite passion' (CUP 306).

A consequence of hope of an eternal happiness, for Kierkegaard, is joy in the midst of 'this earthly, troubled life' (EUD 254). To deliberate (*overveie*) over one's present suffering in relation to the object of one's hope is to weigh (*veie*) regarding a 'relation between two magnitudes' (UDVS 306). In this deliberation, the eternal happiness of Christian hope outweighs temporal suffering (UDVS 308) – compared to eternal happiness, temporality's suffering is but 'a moment', even 'a mirage' (CD 97–102). On the balance of deliberation, 'the expectancy of the great weight of glory', 'an eternal salvation in the next world' is capable of making one's present hardship and affliction 'brief and light' (UDVS 315–16; EUD 264–5). Indeed, earthly suffering and eternal happiness 'actually cannot be weighed on the same scale' for in one's 'presentiment of this eternal happiness he . . . smashes the balance' inasmuch as 'the slightest part of the happiness of eternity weighs infinitely more than the longest earthly suffering' (UDVS 319).

Suffering, further, functions to awaken one, to sober one inasmuch as an awareness of the danger and fragility of life helps one to learn to find one's confidence in something other than the false contentment of finite securities (SLW 379).[41] Hardship 'preaches for awakening', makes us attentive to hope's voice; hardship 'helps repellingly' by 'ruthlessly' preventing us 'from obtaining any other help or relief whatever' (CD 109–10). Hope is born through suffering, 'extracted by means of the rack', the purgative shaking and

---

40 Kierkegaard writes: 'When, with the help of the eternal, a person lives absorbed in today, he turns his back to the next days. The more he is eternally absorbed in today, the more decisively he turns his back to the next day; then he does not see it at all. When he turns around, the eternal becomes confused before his eyes and becomes the next day' (CD 73).

41 Here one has, as Frater Taciturnus writes, 'heard the howling of the wolves and learned to know God' (SLW 380).

breaking of finite hopes 'in which' the hope against hope of eternal happiness 'becomes unshakable' (CD 112; EUD 330). Thus Kierkegaard contends that *only* the blessedness of eternity is adequate or capable to answer to the otherwise crushing suffering of life (EUD 339). The certain hope/expectancy of future blessedness communicates joy into the midst of our present suffering.

Finally, hope – in building one up, in giving one security and assurance in the present, in lightening one's present burdens – builds up love – liberates one, empowers one to love. Love, Kierkegaard writes, is 'built up and nourished by its hope of eternity and then in turn deals lovingly with others in this hope' (WL 248). The weight of the expectancy of eternal salvation gives one a changed perspective, a different centre of gravity, that enables one to resist the urge 'to partition and divide', to 'distinguish . . . between mine and thine' (EUD 265). 'The person who turns away from the temporal to the eternal and is concerned about his salvation is reconciled with himself and with everyone else' (EUD 267). In being oriented beyond the world, beyond the present, one is reconciled, brought to be at peace, with the world, in the world, in the present. The one that seeks the higher receives the lower as well.

Love

For Kierkegaard, the supreme mark of the Christian way, the true way, is love (WL 13–14). The essentially Christian is in living, in acting, and the ideal of Christian love is sheer action (WL 99). The activity, the life of love is what God requires of us (WL 4). This ideal is not actual in any human being save 'him who was love' – Jesus Christ as our Saviour and Prototype who loved solely for the other's benefit (WL 99–100).[42] The Christian way is the way of the one who is Truth in existence, the way of Christ – 'the explanation' (WL 101).

Christian love, for Kierkegaard, is first a love for God. God is the only proper object of love in the fullest sense – 'the sole true object of love' – the only 'perfectly happy' love (WL 108, 121, 130; CD 284). The heart that relates to God, if it is to be a 'pure heart', must

---

42 'No one lived with him who loved himself as deeply as Christ loved him' (WL 100).

be 'first and last a bound heart', bound to God 'without limit' (WL 147–8). Our love should be in accordance with reality, for God as the absolute is properly due an absolute regard, to be loved 'unconditionally' (WL 19, 108). For, 'it is impossible to relate oneself with eternal faithfulness to what in itself is not the eternal' (WL 313). This love is the 'most joyful of all' because one loves God as the good, as his good – in his love for God he 'abides with the good' (UDVS 101; CD 79).[43] For Kierkegaard, our love for God is based in our need for God. As he writes:

> The fundamental and primary basis for a person's love of God is completely to understand that one needs God, loves him simply because one needs him. The person who most profoundly recognizes his need of God loves him most truly. You are not to presume to love God for God's sake. (CD 188)

We do not benefit God in himself with our love; we do not give something to God that God lacks in himself. We fulfil ourselves and God's loving purpose for us in loving God. It is 'blasphemy' to 'presume' to love God unselfishly – with a love that is not based in self-love, that is not erotic – as if one did not need 'God's help at every moment and that without God he is nothing' (ThDCF 142; CD 63). Here, love is a work of patience, an activity of receptivity – of our *passio essendi*. Paradoxically, then, the highest expression of our self-love, of our good, is to love God more than ourselves – to love God, selfishly, more than we love ourselves. In loving God, we crave that which satisfies (CD 64) – never less than our deepest desire and need but always and necessarily greater – for we need to love God more than we love ourselves. Such a love for God is the proper ordering of the self to reality.

The fulfilling of this need, Kierkegaard maintains, is not merely the filling of an absence, a negating of a negative, but a good in excess of any lack, a blessing in excess of satisfaction; our end is the fullness of 'the eternal life' that is communion with God (CD 16). Love of God is love of 'the sole true object of love', the only one whom it is always happy to love (WL 108, 130). Human love of God is at once the end and the means to the end of human life. The

---

43 Kierkegaard writes: 'the Christian loves God and therefore is no self-tormentor' (CD 79).

desired end of life is loving communion with God – our loving the God who loves us, who is love – and our love of God draws us ever forward into this loving communion.

Our longing for God is a gift from God that calls us toward God as our good (a gift we may not accept in gratitude, a call we may decline) (CD 251, 254; UDVS 14). As something that God enables in us, it is both a gift and a task – something given to us by God to which we must hold fast (CD 251). Longing for God, for Kierkegaard, is a gift from the trinitarian God – given to us 'from God', 'through' Christ – 'it is the working of the Spirit in you' (CD 154).[44] Through the 'prompting of the Spirit' we are called upon to participate with, to follow the Spirit – through God, to follow God to God (CD 253). To love God is 'a suprahuman relationship' for 'it is God, the Creator, who must implant love in each human being, he who himself is Love' (WL 216). In this divine–human relation, we receive from God God's love which gives birth to our love for God (though not necessarily so) (EUD 45–6). This gift through which God 'loves forth love' is a 'call' – such that one 'can resist it; he can prevent its deeper generation within him', or one can 'accept it with gratitude as a gift of God' (TwDCF 176; CD 254).

Faith goes beyond any mere knowledge of God's love and actively engages in the relationship with God as other. As Kierkegaard writes (CD 194): 'A knowledge that God is love is still not a consciousness of it. Consciousness, personal consciousness, requires that in my knowledge I also have knowledge of myself and my relation to my knowledge. This is to believe, here to believe that God is love, and to believe that God is love is to love him.'[45] In faith, we relate to the invisible God (WL 5). But beyond believing in God, loving God unites us to God, making us like God. Love 'makes the lover one with what he loves' (CD 84). Again, 'only love', Kierkegaard writes, 'unites wholly, unites the dissimilar in love, here unites the human being wholly to God, who is love' (CD 84). Loving God makes us like God, and, like God, loving. 'Christianity's task', he

---

44 Such is Kierkegaard's prayer: 'help us so that we might love you much, increase our love, inflame it, purify it' (ThDCF 137).

45 This may be close to what Johannes de Silentio means when he writes that 'he who loves God without faith reflects on himself [does not really love God]; he who loves God in faith reflects upon God' (FT 37).

writes, is 'humanity's likeness to God. But God is Love, and there-fore we can be like God only in loving' (WL 62–3).

The love of God, for Kierkegaard, enables our love for other people. To love the people one sees one must begin with loving the unseen God to 'learn what it is to love'; the more one loves the unseen, the more one will love the people one sees (WL 159–60). In coming into conscious relationship with God as God has revealed himself, one learns that God is not envious [*misundelig*], but is merciful [*miskundelig*]. God is 'continually pointing away from himself', constantly diverting the rightfully primary vertical God-relationship into horizontal love for neighbour (WL 160). Before God, one sees 'the neighbor' in every human being (WL 80). It is by initially focusing on the Unseen and what the Unseen has revealed that one gains the sight to find actuality (the true worth and beauty of a person) with eyes closed which one had failed to find with eyes open (WL 163–4). In this, our love and devotion to God is redirected into love for others. God asks for everything but nothing for himself; for God 'is too exalted to receive a person's love directly', and 'does not have a share in existence in such a way that he asks for his share for himself' (WL 160–1).

For Kierkegaard, 'what we extol under the name of love', the love that poets celebrate, is secretly 'self-love' (FSE 83; WL 19), the preferential love (*Forkjerlighed*) 'or passionate preference [which] is actually another form of self-love' (WL 53). The God-relationship entails a negative moment – a middle term – in dealing with our own self-love in relation to other people. Genuine love for the other, neighbour love (*Kjerlighed*) originates from our love for God as 'the decisive factor' (WL 57); it is 'only by loving God above all else that can one love the neighbor in the other human being' (WL 58).[46] It is difficult to extricate oneself from a self-centred way of being; one needs divine help to forget oneself in love (EUD 75–6). To this end, loving God is purifying, purgative; Christianity intends 'to wrest self-love away' (while teaching a 'proper self-love'), to 'thrust erotic love and friendship from the throne, the love based on drives and inclination, preferential love, in order to place the spirit's love [*Kjerlighed*] in its stead' (WL 17–18, 44). One's relationship

---

46 'Christianity teaches that love is a relationship between: a person – God – a person, that is, that God is the middle term' (WL 107).

with God, one's being before God in love, humbles (but does not humiliate) one (PoV 44–5; WL 342), gives one a 'holy modesty' that is 'inseparable from all true love' and 'originates because there is a God, and in modesty one feels one's lowliness' (WL 341). 'Truly loving God', Kierkegaard writes, is 'to feel oneself blessed in the extreme of self-denial' (WL 365). When one is in relation to the God to Whom one cannot compare oneself, one is, relatively, 'nothing before God' (WL 365–6).

The natural human understanding, for Kierkegaard, does not grasp what love is. The nature of love, revealed as it is in the Christian faith, is not only unknown but is positively opposed by 'what the natural man most readily and naturally understands' (WL 336). What one knows by oneself regarding love 'is very superficial' such that one 'must come to know the deeper love from God' (WL 364). The remedy for the natural human being's ignorance of true love is the transformation of vision through God's revelation. In *Works of Love*, Kierkegaard sees God as revealing what true love is to humans (WL 3, 110). God is the source of the transformed vision. Because 'no human being is love', God, who is 'Love itself' must teach humans love (WL 244, 336, 264, 265; 190). The God-relationship is necessary for human knowledge of genuine love (WL 113, 140, 159–60). When it comes to love, God is 'the educator' (WL 377). For Kierkegaard, the particular *loci* of this revelation for the Christian are Christ and the Christian Scriptures. The person and life of Christ are spoken of as the supreme 'explanation' of love, its 'highest example'; his life is 'the prototype', 'the Way' (WL 101, 287, 288, 180; 99, 100, 174, 248, 264, 317–18).

To truly relate to God as absolute, as one's first priority, demands unconditional obedience (WL 108, 117, 149, 185). The foremost expression of this authoritative claim upon one in *Works of Love* is that of the love command: that you shall love your neighbour as yourself (IIA–IIC). In 'the commandment', one is addressed in the second person by the highest authority (WL 68, 97, 106). Here, love is made one's duty – what one 'shall' do (WL 35, 37, 78). This is an apparent contradiction; divine authority turns the natural conception upside-down inasmuch as a commanded love is an idea that 'did not arise in any human being's heart' (WL 24). This is so, for Kierkegaard, because, with the normal conception, love is an inconstant impulse, 'the play of feelings, drives, inclinations, and passions, in short, that play of the powers of immediacy', a matter of preference; so to make love a duty, regardless of preference, is understandably taken to be offensive to 'natural man' (WL 25).

Worldly love, merely human erotic love and friendship, engages in human relationships toward the end of filling certain emotional needs and are thus, as Kierkegaard writes, 'dependent upon their objects' (WL 66); our deepest needs are to be filled only with reference to what other people can do for us; our deepest fulfilment rests on the whims of others. Because of this, these relations have a constant undercurrent of anxiety that can mount to despair if the object of one's desire is withdrawn. Also, on the worldly level, human value is accounted for by means of comparison (WL 186). One's worth can fluctuate with the supply and demand of the 'market'. In both of these situations, one's fundamental emotional needs are functions of a corrupt relational economy, and one can only hope to achieve security by trying to manipulate – to take control of such relations.

On the basis of one's relationship with God, one can come to see that the provision for one's emotional needs – value, security and purpose – are not dependent upon others but are ultimately met by God. Kierkegaard does not ignore our need and desire, he simply sees that our deepest need is for God (WL 39, 333). Indeed, this need is 'the greatest riches' because it reveals God as one's true object of love and as the fulfilment of one's highest happiness (WL 11, 132, 130). The phenomenon of this need for God is a treasure because it is a sign that reveals from whence we must seek our deepest fulfilment. All else will never lead to the fulfilment that we truly desire. True satisfaction, true self-love and true, proper pride are only to be found in relation to God (WL 107, 271). Because of one's God-relationship, one can know and feel one's deep value. The God, who is 'Love' itself, has acted out of love for us to give us all things that we truly need (WL 3–4, 336, 103, 264). This is seen supremely in God's gift of salvation in Christ (WL 69, 112). Beyond this, it is God who is the hidden source of our life and our love, who continually sustains us like an eternal spring (WL 3, 8–10, 271, 301, 312, 340). God has created us in his own image with a 'dowry of good nature and of love' (WL 69, 264, 159). Thus, there lies within us the inner glory of God's highest creation, and because of this quality present in all people, all people are equally invaluable (WL 72, 86–8).

Before God, the ravenous lack that haunts our relationships can become the filled chest of satisfaction and fruition that frees us to love others without ulterior motives. Before God, one passes from emptiness, sickness and starvation to fullness, health and over-abundance. With this filling, one can love as from a deep reserve; one 'loves with all his love; it is totally present in every expression; he continually spends all of it, and yet he continually keeps all in his heart' (UDVS 30).

Our proper love for others, neighbour love (*Kjerlighed*) is to love the neighbour as oneself. This 'royal law', the golden rule also teaches one how to love oneself; as Kierkegaard writes: 'To love yourself in the right way and to love the neighbor correspond perfectly to one another. . . . You shall love yourself in the same way as you love your neighbor when you love him as yourself' (WL 22, 23). As we are to see the neighbour as having inherent value beyond the value we give them as useful or pleasurable for us, so we are to see ourselves as possessing such an inherent value. Likewise, neighbour love properly orders erotic love and friendship; it founds, tele-ologically suspends these lower loves, gives them a security beyond themselves; as Kierkegaard writes, one should 'love the beloved faithfully and tenderly, but let love for the neighbor be the sanctifying element' (WL 62).

Our love for God and God's love for us is the '*primus motor*', 'the deepest ground', the foundation of the Christian life – the source that builds up (FT 239 sup; WL 210–12, 215). So too, our love for others has its secret source, its mysterious origin, its 'hidden life [that] is in itself motion and has eternity within itself', in God's love (WL 8–10). 'Just', Kierkegaard writes, 'as the quiet lake originates deep down in hidden springs no eye has seen, so also does a person's love originate even more deeply in God's love' (WL 9). In loving others, then, one is a 'co-worker' with God, furthering God's loving work in the world through one's own life (EUD 62; WL 86, 279). Such a person receives perseverance and strength: 'he draws nourishment for his love from God, he is strengthened by God' (WL 244; 113, 125, 278, 280, 322). One has the 'fresh air' of possibility and hope of the eternal (WL 246–9, 258).

When one places oneself in relation to God and under God's authority, 'there is durability in existence, because God has a firm hold on it' (WL 118). Commanded love is secured against change,

and so 'casts out all anxiety' regarding the vagaries of worldly love
(WL 32–3). 'That alone is love', Kierkegaard writes, 'which never
becomes something else' (EUD 55). The God-relationship is the
'most intimate relationship' and one's 'eternal foundation' (WL
152, 141). In it one has comfort in God's abiding love and thereby
'find the stillness in which God dwells' (WL 300, 329, 369). When
one has so 'undergone the change of eternity' by explicitly relating
oneself to God, the stable reality of the eternal is communicated
to the temporal, one's love becomes consistent over time, repeated
in the midst of the changing and in relation to the unchanging (to
God and God's love command) (WL 32, 34, 39–40). The love that
has undergone this 'change of eternity' 'has gained enduring continuance' (WL 32). In this love, the eternal 'forms the heart' (WL
12).[47] It is thus that healthy love, as the unity of the universal and
the singular, has 'quite another idea of time and of the meaning of
repetition' (EO 428–9, 465). God as the good 'elicits a pledge', and
in true love (*Kjerlighed*), love that is to become a duty, entails 'resolution's solemn agreement with the good' – a resolution in freedom
(EUD 359; TDIO 43). Resolution does not (merely) destroy preferential love – friendship and erotic love; it is its 'rebirth' into the
'secure abode within the impregnable fortress of duty' (TDIO 55–
6). Resolution's love (*Kjerlighed*) 'conquers' lesser loves by recon-
textualizing, refounding them (through teleological suspension), by
becoming their 'abiding place', their 'fortress' (TDIO 62–3).[48]

Kierkegaard understands genuine love as a gift, an expenditure
without return. Rather than the suspicious 'gift' of love as a 'way to
acquire tangible power, the way to all kinds of temporal and worldly
advantage' in which 'you were willing to give and to assist someone
in need who had nothing to give in return, and yet you demanded
something from him: his respect, his admiration, his subservience
– his soul', genuine love is 'that which gives away everything and
for that reason demands nothing, that which demands nothing and
therefore has nothing to lose' (PoV 111; EUD 146, 56–7). This
love, for Kierkegaard, is like meekness – not repaid, 'unrewarding',
'unrecognizable' (UDVS 243–4). Love, instead, forgives – hides a

---

47 The true human greatness, Kierkegaard writes, is to so 'master oneself in love
[*Kjerlighed*]' (CD 291–2).

48 Kierkegaard writes: 'Spontaneous love . . . is not consciously grounded upon
the eternal and thus it can be changed' (WL 31).

multitude of sins, keeps no record of wrongs (EUD 58, 62). This kind of love is a wonder before which the understanding stands still (SLW 120–1). Such a reckless abandoning of the selfish 'why' of love for other human beings – a love not primarily concerned with one's own benefit when relating to other people – is offensive to worldly wisdom (PIC 57–62). This, for Kierkegaard, speaks to the revealed nature of the Christian religion – for such an idea would not arise in a human heart (WL 100, 113).

In Kierkegaard's understanding of Christian love, a person's religious relation to God enables their ethical relation to others. Ethical being with others is not something left behind for an isolated religious relationship with God – the ethical is 'a passageway – which one nevertheless does not pass through once and for all' (SLW 477). The kind of isolation brought about by one's God-relationship 'increases the inwardness of the earthly relationships' (EO 539). The God-relationship's strengthening of the individual is a precondition for genuine community (EUD 97).[49] Relation to God founds a community with 'the bond of perfection that knits its members together in equality before God' (EUD 141). Because of one's God-relationship, one's awareness of God's presence, one comes to see that all people (including oneself) are equal before God – that relative to the majesty of God no distinction places one above another in terms of value (WL 342). But the quality of this equality is not some cool, sterile legal status before the divine book-keeper; with this luminous vision one beholds the glorious being and inherent value that God has created in every human being (WL 69). There is a 'universal divine likeness of all people' inasmuch as human beings are revealed to have been placed so high as to have equal kinship before God in Christ, for God has created them in his image and, out of his supreme love, Christ has come to redeem them (WL 125, 69, 264). As is beautifully depicted in the parable of the confused actors in the play: 'In each individual there continually glimmers that essential other which is common to all, the eternal resemblance, the likeness' (WL 88). This 'eternal resemblance' shines through earthly distinctions to betray 'the inner glory' of every human being, 'the common watermark' that can

---

49 'The person who loved God and in this love learned to love people was strengthened in the inner being' (EUD 97).

only be seen by eternity's light (WL 87–8, 89). In the midst of the various gradations and hierarchies, superiorities and inferiorities (either natural or socially constructed), Christian love lets earthly distinctions hang loosely (WL 87). This wonderful seeing and not-seeing makes us blind to dissimilarities when we want to use them as excuses for not seeing the good worthy of love in every person, yet it remains aware of the dissimilarities as the manifold particular situations one must navigate differently to truly love (WL 68–73).

Such love is a radiating power that works to help, to serve, 'to build up' (WL 211–14). Love is a 'power to alter the circumstances for others' (EUD 66).[50] The love of God enables and sustains the love of others – our loving others and our therefore seeking their highest good in their being loving. Love builds up love (WL 215–17). For Kierkegaard, a significant part of our inherent created goodness is that we are given the capacity to truly love – that there is a 'ground', a created foundation of love implanted within us (WL 216, 219, 224). Seeing that to truly love is the crown of what a human can achieve, this created ground, this 'dowry of good nature and of love' is of immense value (WL 159, 215, 225). So, when our vision of the world and humanity is transformed we are obliged to assume, to presuppose, that love is present within any and every other person (WL 216, 217, 219). Every person has the potential to love, 'the possibility of the good' and can thereby achieve their fullest human potentiality (WL 253). The gift of love is circulated between God, oneself and others. To truly love one's neighbour (horizontal), one must first relate in devotion to God (vertical). But God's character is such that he continually points away from himself as the object of love (vertical) toward the neighbour as the object of love (horizontal). But then to properly love another (horizontal) is to help another to relate in devotion to God (vertical).

Finally, such Christian love of God and neighbour suffers because of its dissonance with the social world.[51] 'Love', Kierkegaard writes, 'is a revolution' (WL 265). Christianity's highest good is seen to

---

50 'Every life, love's life also, is as such hidden but is made manifest in something else' (WL 8).

51 Anti-Climacus brings up the counter case: 'This danger must necessarily disappear if all at the time I am living are true Christians, for then, of course, everything around me will be sheer encouragement and incitement for me also to become a true Christian' (PIC 222).

be an 'extremely dangerous good' (WL 198). Love is not loved by the world, rather 'love is hated' for 'sin hardens itself against love and wishes to be rid of it' (PoV 90; EUD 63–4). Addressing Jesus Christ, Kierkegaard writes, that 'by being love that was not loved you were a judgment upon the world . . . the judgment that "love was not loved"' (TwDCF 169–72) – that Christ was treated 'as an act of love is usually rewarded in the world' (PoV 10). Indeed, Kierkegaard presents Christ's death on the cross as the one supreme work of love that calls for imitation (MLW 165).[52] He writes: 'For that very reason he was put to death, because he sought nothing for himself. . . . He was crucified precisely because he was love . . . because he refused to be self-loving' (TERE 59).

Suffering and Joy

This leads to a consideration of suffering more generally. For Kierkegaard, the truth suffers in the world.[53] Christianity is 'the suffering truth' – opposed and 'hated', by the world (MLW 52, 321, 120). The Church, composed of 'strangers and aliens', still on the way in the midst of the world, struggles; its truth is 'the contending truth' (MLW 257; PIC 201, 211, 89). The Church on Earth is the 'Church militant' (CD 229; PIC 209) – 'in the midst of this world, a kingdom that is not of this world' (JFY 175) – the community of a 'militant piety' that is engaged with 'being Christian within an environment that is the opposite of being Christian' (PoV 130; PIC 212). The world opposes the Church militant (as the locus of Christian truth at present[54]) because its demand for absolute devotion and its de facto judgement upon the world (inasmuch as the good and true suffer the world's opposition) are an offence to it (LFBA 32; UDVS 97; PIC 117).[55]

For Kierkegaard, the world – the human social world – is ruled

---

52 'There is only one work, and, wonderously enough, you know at once whom it is about, about him, about Jesus Christ, about his atoning sin, which hides a multitude of sins' (TwDCF 186).

53 'Here in the world the truth walks in lowliness and abasement' (MLW 299).

54 As Kierkegaard writes: 'Only the Church militant is truth' (PIC 219, 232).

55 'Christianity and being a true Christian must to the highest degree be an offense to the natural man' (JFY 140).

by illusions and 'lies and baseness and injustice' (PoV 59, 63).[56]
The world is the domain of the authority of the crowd – driven by
desire for the approval (and fear of the disapproval) of the majority
– of the 'they', 'what "they" will say and judge' (CD 232).[57] The
crowd is related to Kierkegaard's understanding of the 'political' as
the immanent ordering of a 'kingdom of this world' that will recognize no authority beyond itself (MLW 14; BoA 5).[58] This kind of
worldly established order is idolatrous for, as Anti-Climacus writes,
it 'wants to be a totality that recognizes nothing above itself but
has every individual under it and judges every individual who sub-
ordinates himself to the established order' (PIC 91). 'The deification of the established order', he continues, 'is the secularization of
everything' (PIC 91) – for to make the immanent established order
divine (the highest authority) is to remove any transcendent divinity
(that could stand over against a given established order in judgement, as with the prophets) as such. Set against the Church militant
that suffers in the midst of the established order is Christendom,
the Church triumphant as a counterfeit double of Christianity, an
'illusion' of a Christianity that is triumphant in the world under the
terms of the established order (CD 229; MLW 74, 170, 212).[59]

For Kierkegaard, the Church militant suffers in the world because
it is the Church on the way, the Church of Christ, the Way and
the Truth that suffers in the world. The imitation [*Efterfølgelse*] of
Christ, to follow [*følge efter*] him as a disciple in the midst of the
world, is to open oneself to the kind of persecution [*Forfølgelse*]
that he suffered (FSE 67) – it is to deny yourself, take up your cross
and follow him (UDVS 221; MLW 165; ThDCF 118). As opposed
to 'common human sufferings', 'authentic Christian suffering' is 'to

---

56 Kierkegaard writes: 'I have tried to express that the world, if it is not evil, is
mediocre, that "the demand of the times" is always foolishness and fatuousness, that
in the eyes of the world the truth is a ludicrous exaggeration or an eccentric super-
fluity, that the good must suffer' (PoV 88).

57 Kierkegaard also describes the crowd as 'the numerical, of wanting to make
the numerical the authority for what truth is' (PoV 126).

58 Kierkegaard writes: 'In these times everything is politics. The viewpoints of
the religious is worlds . . . apart from this, just as the starting point and ultimate goal
are also worlds . . . apart, since the political begins on earth in order to remain on
earth, while the religious, taking its beginning from above, wants to transfigure and
then to lift the earthly to heaven' (PoV 103).

59 It should be noted that Kierkegaard believed in the true Church triumphant,
the true Christendom, but likely only eschatologically (CD 228–9).

suffer in a way akin to Christ's sufferings' – to suffer voluntarily at the hands of others for endeavouring 'to do the good' (PIC 107–8, 173; FSE 67; MLW 135; JFY 169). Being the rejected truth, his crucifixion is a judgement upon the world – in which 'the guilt of the race that becomes manifest' (TERE 65) – and a saving of the world (at least potentially) – which 'is the Atonement for the whole race' (TERE 64, 88; TwDCF 169–71). To follow, to serve, to witness to the truth that is in Christ is to be willing to suffer even to the point of death, like the martyrs for Christ, the 'glorious ones' (TERE 67; PoV 68, 97, 109; MLW 324–5).

Yet, the heart of the Christian way, certainly for Kierkegaard, is one of paradox. Its way is gift and task, self-denial and self-fulfilment, dying and living, passivity and activity, the easy yoke and the cross, suffering and joy. This way is paradoxical, in part, because it is a word from the higher to the lower.[60] The higher, the truer, dwells in the lower, the less true, with dissonance, seeming to be absurd (CD 227). Those that the lower sees as unhappy may be truly happy because they are in a right relation to reality. It is thus that the Christian can 'find joy in the bitterness of suffering' (UDVS 232) – because the way of joy, the true way to her true good, is in the midst of (and, indeed, is the same as) her present way of suffering.

Kierkegaard describes the distinctive Christian 'how' as 'meekness' – itself a supremely paradoxical 'how' (UDVS 246). The burden, the suffering, the yoke that the Christian bears is born as light, carried joyfully. 'Meekness makes the burden light and carries it lightly' (UDVS 243) – it is 'to carry the heavy burden lightly' (UDVS 239). It is the wonder of Sisyphus bearing the heavy rock lightly, joyfully. Meekness (*Sagtmodighed*) is a gentle courage that bears heavy burdens lightly because of one's relationship with God. Through the theological virtues of faith, hope and love, one develops a deeper and more consonant attunement to God (in Christ through the Holy Spirit) on life's way. 'Gentle courage', Kierkegaard writes, 'is good at doing things little by little' – through the consistency of repetition. The meek Christian is 'boldly confident' for 'in his faith he breathes soundly and freely, and yet his courage is so meek that what he has to bear looks like a mere trifle' (UDVS 243). Hopeful,

---

60 Think here of the Beatitudes in the Sermon on the Mount.

the one who has 'gentle courage is not worried even about tomorrow', for meekness carries lightly 'the burden of time, the burden of the future' (UDVS 242). Meekness is a life ordered beyond the world expecting 'no reward on earth' (UDVS 245). Finally, meekness is generous agapeic fullness that does not need to be repaid or rewarded but can give and is 'solicitous to forgive' (UDVS 243–5).

For Kierkegaard, joy in the midst of suffering is evidence in the present temporal world of something other than this world (BoA 186). Such joy does not make sense within a finite frame – it is ordered beyond it. This joy is paradoxical – 'the Christian is poor, yet not poor but rich' and '"Life begins in death", says the lowly Christian' (CD 22, 46). It is a higher joy that seems absurd to the lower because 'God's thoughts are eternally higher than the thoughts of a human being, and therefore every human conception of happiness and unhappiness, of what is joyful and what is sorrowful, is faulty thinking' (UDVS 284). It is to be 'happy', to be 'joyful' 'out on 70,000 fathoms of water' – where suffering 'is the 70,000 fathoms of water' (SLW 470, 477; CUP 140, 288).[61] It is to be suspended over nothing, suspended from the higher.

There is joy in the Christian life that comes from one's being with God, from one's relationship with God. For Kierkegaard, different qualities of joy can be discerned relative to the central characteristics of God – relative to God as eternal, as the good, and as loving.[62] The Christian has the joy of resting in God's changelessness. To him, the changelessness of God is 'sheer joy and gladness' (MLW 269). Here, one enjoys God's eternity as the ground of one's own existential security. To rest in God's changelessness as an 'eternally safeguarded' and 'happy home' (MLW 279) as a beloved spring's 'faithful coolness' that 'is not subject to change' is to find security in God's availability; God for the Christian is 'everywhere to be found', 'always to be found and always to be found unchanged' (MLW 280–1). The Christian also has the joy of relating to God as the good end that they desire as their 'happiness', or 'blessedness' (both translations of *Salighed*) (CD 222) – the blessing that is 'the good in itself; it is the one thing needful, is infinitely more glorious and blessed than all success' (CD 297). Finally, the Christian

---

61 This last bit is Climacus in the *Postscript* reading Frater Taciturnus in *Stages*.
62 See Chapter 5.

has joy in God's love for them. 'The thought that God is love', Kierkegaard writes, 'contains all joy in itself' (UDVS 282). Our 'unconditional joy' is 'worshipfully to dare to believe "that God cares for you"' (LFBA 43). God's love to us is joy as light from the one sun radiating.

Communion

The way of Christian virtue is a being-with, a being in loving community with God and others. The true way, for Kierkegaard, is toward communion. The Christian way, for Kierkegaard, is a dwelling in time such that one is 'present', 'contemporary with oneself', for being in relation to God, the eternal as other to time, enables one to be present with an 'acquired originality' in the rush of time – not to be outside time, but to be truly present in it 'today' (CD 74–5; LFBA 38).[63] 'Before God', the believer 'is himself', is 'contented with being himself' – is true to what one is (CD 40; SUD 5). It is as if faith, hope and love put one in right relation with God who is the centre and foundation of reality and thus allow one to *be* more fully, to acquire an identity in relation to the reality.[64] Kierkegaard describes this state as a 'soberness', a self-knowledge acquired by being before God as the unconditioned (JFY 104–6).

In this being 'present to oneself', the Christian is aware 'that a human being absolutely needs God at every moment' (BoA 106; CD 91). This absolute need for God is 'the fundamental and primary basis' of one's love for God; one loves God 'simply because one needs him', and 'the person who most profoundly recognizes his need of God loves him most truly' (CD 188). In this love for God, we are 'united to' God; love 'makes the lover one with what

---

63 Kierkegaard writes: 'Ordinarily most people are apocalyptically, in theatrical illusions, hundreds of thousands of miles ahead of themselves, or several generations ahead of themselves in feelings, in delusions, in intentions, in resolutions, in wishes, in longings. But the believer (the one present) is in the highest sense contemporary with himself' (CD 74).

64 Kierkegaard writes: 'There is only one who completely knows himself, who in himself knows what he himself is – that is God. And he also knows what each human being is in himself, because he is that only by being before God. The person who is not before God is not himself either, which one can be only by being in the one who is in himself' (CD 40).

he loves' and so 'unites the human being wholly to God, who is love' (CD 84). Then, to be so 'united to' God in love is to be united to one's 'absolute need' and 'highest good'; it is 'a life that, so to speak, overflows with a blissful sense of life' (CD 200).

In Kierkegaard's work, this 'uniting to' God is depicted as a mutual indwelling – both our being 'in' God and God's being 'in' us. As a Christian, we 'remain in God' and in Christ as our rest and security (PIC 15) – an 'inclosure [that] signifies the greatest expansion' (CA 134). A person remains one, is maintained as an identity over time, as she rests in the changeless one (MLW 268). Kierkegaard writes:

> Christianly you *remain* in God. If you remain in God, then whether you live or die, whether life treats you well or badly, whether you die today or not for seventy years, whether you find your death at the bottom of the ocean where it is deepest or you are blown to fragments in the air – you still will not find yourself outside God, you *remain*. Hence you are present to yourself in God. (LFBA 44)

Classically, Anti-Climacus describes the believer as 'resting transparently in God' and so having 'his life in the consistency of the good' – transparent in accepting the reality of one's self as established by God (SUD 14, 30, 82, 107). In this transparent resting in God, the believer has 'his self over against the eternal power, whose fire has permeated it without consuming it' (EO 529). As transparent as the ocean that reflects the height of heaven – 'reflects in its pure depth the heavenly sublimity of the good' – one is 'transfigured in God' and 'illuminat[ed]' 'so that he resembles God' (EUD 400; UDVS 121). God's light becomes our light – transparent to the sublimity, the glory of God.

Furthermore, our being, for Kierkegaard, is communicative, is social. We have both a deeply rooted need for and a 'dowry of' love (WL 155, 159). A person 'is himself communicating' such that 'in the giving of oneself the self is gained' (EUD 45; SUD 50). In loving God, one is truly happy – 'it is simply and solely my own good that is advanced' (CD 86; ThDCF 142). 'Truly loving God' is 'to feel oneself blessed in the extreme of self-denial' (WL 365). One is joyous because the God one loves is loving and wise and to do his will is to do oneself good. There is a mutuality inherent in our love of God, for we love God as our own good (WL 108, 130). Our long-ing for communion with God is a gift from God in which we are called upon to participate with, to follow the Spirit in holding fast to this longing – through God's help, to follow God to God (CD 251–4). Kierkegaard describes this longing for God as 'the working of the Spirit' within us given to us 'from God' and 'through' Christ (CD 254). We are drawn by God into the divine life of the Trinity as the fulfilment of our very being.

Additionally, in the Christian way, the God-relation enables a different kind of human community. As Kierkegaard writes, 'only by loving God above all else can one love the neighbor in the other human being' (WL 58). By loving the unseen God who is the 'sources of all love' one 'learn[s] what it is to love'; God, who is 'continually pointing away from himself', asks for everything but nothing for himself (WL 3, 160). This opens the possibility of a religious com-munity, a politics 'viewed with the passion of the infinite' within 'the circle of my loved ones with whom I have the faith in common' (SLW 410; CD 243). This communal love is actively enabled and supported by God as it is 'implanted' in us by God through 'a supra-human relationship' so as 'to infinitize what is in the human' (WL 216, 244, 333–6, 384).

Such an enabled community is one of reciprocity and mutuality in which loving one's neighbour is in harmony with proper self-love.[65] An understanding of Christian community permeates the dissimi-larities that exist between people with 'the sanctifying thought of Christian equality', so overcoming the temptations of dissimilarity, the temptations of pride or envy (WL 73, 70). For eternity's light enables us to see 'the common watermark', the inner glory of our equality, that 'in each individual there continually glimmers that essential other which is common to all, the eternal resemblance, the likeness', the image of God (WL 87–9). Thus Kierkegaard writes 'that the religious is the transfigured rendition of what a politician . . . has thought in his most blissful moment' (PoV 103). For 'ulti-mately only the essentially religious can with the help of eternity

---

65 See again the passage mentioned above: 'To love yourself in the right way and to love the neighbor correspond perfectly to one another; fundamentally they are one and the same thing. . . . You shall love yourself in the same way as you love your neighbor when you love him as yourself' (WL 22, 23).

effect human equality [*Mennske-Lighed*], the godly, the essential, the not-worldly, the true, the only possible human equality; and this is also why – be it said to its glorification – the essentially religious is the true humanity [*Menneskelighed*]' (PoV 104).

The theological virtues, 'the goods of the spirit', function for the good of others. They are, as Kierkegaard writes, 'in themselves essentially communication; their acquirement, their possession, in itself a benefaction to all' (CD 117). This is so insofar as one becomes an indirect communication of these virtues – when 'the others see themselves in him' as one in a play (CD 117). One's way of being in life can function to fund the possible way of being of those who observe this way of life.

The Christian way is not in isolation but is a *Meddelelse*: a sharing, a participation, a being-between, a communicating. The way of the Christian virtues, 'the true way, the way of perfection, to make others truly rich, must be: to communicate the goods of the spirit, in other respects to be oneself solely occupied with acquiring and possessing these goods' (CD 120). The nature of 'the true riches' is 'communication', for 'when he, instructing, admonishing, encouraging, comforting, communicates these goods, he does indeed very directly make others rich' (CD 120). The essential 'good of the spirit', common to the theological virtues, is 'communication', is being in relation. It is 'impossible to possess the goods of the spirit for oneself in the selfish sense', and 'this is not due to the possessor but is due to the goods themselves, which are communication' (CD 118). As we communicate these virtues to others we communicate communication, furthering, continuing, repeating, the exchange of community.[66]

This 'communication' can be seen in the way in which love 'presupposes' love in the other. Loving another means seeing the potential for the best in them and so presupposing love to be present within them. In this way love 'draws out the good', 'loves forth love' by presupposing 'that it is present in the ground' (WL 217). This is to see the gift of God within the other (for 'no human being is capable of laying the ground of love in the other person' (WL 219)) and their potential for good. Love gives the gift by seeing the

---

66 Kierkegaard writes of 'communicating the goods of the spirit, by communicating what in itself is communication' (CD 122).

other as already in possession of it; 'Love does not seek its own; it rather gives in such a way that the gift looks as if it were the recipient's property.' This help that does not wish to be seen as a help is 'the greatest beneficence' (WL 274). Love does not seek to influence, to build up, through power or coercion, but through an indirect communication that helps the other to see the resource for their good in their communion with God. Such a free community grounded in Christian virtue and God's enabling is at once joyous and secure (SLW 84; EUD 100; TDIO 55–7).

Finally, the life of God as love is made manifest in our loving communion with him and in our midst (WL 8). As God is eternal, our good end and our loving creator, we can be most like God in our being loving; as Kierkegaard writes, 'when you love the neighbor, then you are like God' (WL 62–3). In loving community, we are God's co-workers, participants in his work of love (EUD 86; UDVS 199; WL 279; MLW 294).[67] Thus, Christianity 'wants to breathe the eternal life, the divine, into the human race' (WL 135). The life of the Christian virtues, for Kierkegaard, is based on God's love; this life rests patiently in the love that abides, 'that sustains all existence' and 'never wastes away' (WL 301, 311–13).[68] As he writes in his early journal overlooking Sæding of 'divine fatherly love, the one single unshakable thing in life, the true the Archimedean point',[69] so he writes in his last journal entry of God's love and grace and humanity's blessed end: 'to praise, adore, worship, and thank him – the business of angels' (MLW 610–11 sup).

The singular Christian way, for Kierkegaard, is the way of truth, of being true to the way things are, of living truly. His *theologia viatorum* seeks to be a guide on this way, a guiding vision for the pilgrim on life's way. As a Christian way, this life is that of a follower, a disciple, an imitator of Christ. As such, this true human being in Christ is a progression from untruth to truth, from fragmentation to wholeness, from isolation to community with God, with others, and with oneself.

---

67 God, for Kierkegaard, seeks our free participation with him in love: 'Compel you, no, the God of love will not do that at any price' (MLW 294; UDVS 62).

68 'The tasks of faith and hope and love and patience and humility and obedience – in short, all the human tasks, are based on the eternal certainty in which they have a place of resort and support, the certainty that God is love' (UDVS 277).

69 He writes this in 1840 before beginning his authorship (JP 5468).

The Christian Way

The truth is the way; the truth to which we are called is a way of living, a way of life that is true to reality, that is pioneered, enabled and revealed in the one truth and the one way, that is Jesus Christ – our way, our truth, our life – the one who from on high, and yet in our midst, with authority, yet humbly, shows and calls us to follow him and so to seek first the higher and to find the lower will be added to it.

Index of Names and Subjects

Index of Names and Subjects

Index of Names and Subjects